Southern China

By concentrating on one of the key locations of global manufacturing, this volume offers a contribution to contemporary industry studies. The rates of growth that have characterized the southern Guangdong province in the last three decades are unique, even with respect to the more general and often cited Chinese experience. But what role have governments played in these decades of growth? What are the aims and tools of industrial policies promoted in this core location of contemporary manufacturing? And what are the implications of the Guangdong experience of growth for the international debate on contemporary industry?

Referencing the international debate on industrial development, specialized Chinese academic literature, official government documents, statistics and in-depth fieldwork, this book offers a unique view on the complex set of long-term national and local government plans and policies that have gone hand in hand with the last three decades of impressive change in this highly industrialized region. In this framework, local industrial development policy, innovation policy and migration policy are carefully analyzed as three of the main strategic interventions selected by government authorities to promote the desired gradual structural change and technological upgrading in industry.

This book will be of interest to students and scholars of Chinese studies, economics and business, development policy and industrial policy. Furthermore, the volume presents stimulating material for both policy makers and entrepreneurs.

Marco R. Di Tommaso is Full Professor of Applied Economic Studies, University of Ferrara, Italy; Honorary Guest Professor, South China University of Technology, China; Director of the China and Italy School of Policy and Director of c.MET05 Interuniversity Centre for Applied Economic Studies (universities of Firenze, Ferrara, Marche, Napoli l'Orientale).

Lauretta Rubini is lecturer of Business and Organization at the Faculty of Engineering; researcher at Teknehub, University of Ferrara, Italy; PhD in Business at the University of Birmingham, UK; Visiting researcher at South China University of Technology, China; Project Manager of the China and Italy School of Policy Project.

Elisa Barbieri is researcher and lecturer of Applied Economics at the University of Ferrara, Italy; PhD in Economics at the University of Ferrara, Italy; MSc in Development Economics at the University of Manchester, UK; Visiting researcher at South China University of Technology, China; Project Manager of the China and Italy School of Policy Project.

Routledge Contemporary China Series

1 **Nationalism, Democracy and National Integration in China**
Leong Liew and Wang Shaoguang

2 **Hong Kong's Tortuous Democratization**
A comparative analysis
Ming Sing

3 **China's Business Reforms**
Institutional challenges in a globalised economy
Edited by Russell Smyth, On Kit Tam, Malcolm Warner and Cherrie Zhu

4 **Challenges for China's Development**
An enterprise perspective
Edited by David H. Brown and Alasdair MacBean

5 **New Crime in China**
Public order and human rights
Ron Keith and Zhiqiu Lin

6 **Non-Governmental Organizations in Contemporary China**
Paving the way to civil society?
Qiusha Ma

7 **Globalization and the Chinese City**
Fulong Wu

8 **The Politics of China's Accession to the World Trade Organization**
The dragon goes global
Hui Feng

9 **Narrating China**
Jia Pingwa and his fictional world
Yiyan Wang

10 **Sex, Science and Morality in China**
Joanne McMillan

11 **Politics in China Since 1949**
Legitimizing authoritarian rule
Robert Weatherley

12 **International Human Resource Management in Chinese Multinationals**
Jie Shen and Vincent Edwards

13 **Unemployment in China**
Economy, human resources and labour markets
Edited by Grace Lee and Malcolm Warner

14 **China and Africa**
Engagement and compromise
Ian Taylor

15 **Gender and Education in China**
Gender discourses and women's schooling in the early twentieth century
Paul J. Bailey

16 **SARS**
Reception and interpretation in three Chinese cities
Edited by Deborah Davis and Helen Siu

17 **Human Security and the Chinese State**
Historical transformations and the modern quest for sovereignty
Robert E. Bedeski

18 **Gender and Work in Urban China**
Women workers of the unlucky generation
Liu Jieyu

19 **China's State Enterprise Reform**
From Marx to the market
John Hassard, Jackie Sheehan, Meixiang Zhou, Jane Terpstra-Tong and Jonathan Morris

20 **Cultural Heritage Management in China**
Preserving the cities of the Pearl River Delta
Edited by Hilary du Cros and Yok-shiu F. Lee

21 **Paying for Progress**
Public finance, human welfare and inequality in China
Edited by Vivienne Shue and Christine Wong

22 **China's Foreign Trade Policy**
The new constituencies
Edited by Ka Zeng

23 **Hong Kong, China**
Learning to belong to a nation
Gordon Mathews, Tai-lok Lui, and Eric Kit-wai Ma

24 **China Turns to Multilateralism**
Foreign policy and regional security
Edited by Guoguang Wu and Helen Lansdowne

25 **Tourism and Tibetan Culture in Transition**
A place called Shangrila
Åshild Kolås

26 **China's Emerging Cities**
The making of new urbanism
Edited by Fulong Wu

27 **China–US Relations Transformed**
Perceptions and strategic interactions
Edited by Suisheng Zhao

28 **The Chinese Party-State in the 21st Century**
Adaptation and the reinvention of legitimacy
Edited by André Laliberté and Marc Lanteigne

29 **Political Change in Macao**
Sonny Shiu-Hing Lo

30 **China's Energy Geopolitics**
The Shanghai Cooperation Organization and Central Asia
Thrassy N. Marketos

31 **Regime Legitimacy in Contemporary China**
Institutional change and stability
Edited by Thomas Heberer and Gunter Schubert

32 **U.S.–China Relations**
China policy on Capitol Hill
Tao Xie

33 **Chinese Kinship**
Contemporary anthropological perspectives
Edited by Susanne Brandtstädter and Gonçalo D. Santos

34 **Politics and Government in Hong Kong**
Crisis under Chinese sovereignty
Edited by Ming Sing

35 **Rethinking Chinese Popular Culture**
Cannibalizations of the canon
Edited by Carlos Rojas and Eileen Cheng-yin Chow

36 **Institutional Balancing in the Asia Pacific**
Economic interdependence and China's rise
Kai He

37 **Rent Seeking in China**
Edited by Tak-Wing Ngo and Yongping Wu

38 **China, Xinjiang and Central Asia**
History, transition and crossborder interaction into the 21st century
Edited by Colin Mackerras and Michael Clarke

39 **Intellectual Property Rights in China**
Politics of piracy, trade and protection
Gordon Cheung

40 **Developing China**
Land, politics and social conditions
George C.S. Lin

41 **State and Society Responses to Social Welfare Needs in China**
Serving the people
Edited by Jonathan Schwartz and Shawn Shieh

42 **Gay and Lesbian Subculture in Urban China**
Loretta Wing Wah Ho

43 **The Politics of Heritage Tourism in China**
A view from Lijiang
Xiaobo Su and Peggy Teo

44 **Suicide and Justice**
A Chinese perspective
Wu Fei

45 **Management Training and Development in China**
Educating managers in a globalized economy
Edited by Malcolm Warner and Keith Goodall

46 **Patron–Client Politics and Elections in Hong Kong**
Bruce Kam-kwan Kwong

47 **Chinese Family Business and the Equal Inheritance System**
Unravelling the myth
Victor Zheng

48 **Reconciling State, Market and Civil Society in China**
The long march towards prosperity
Paolo Urio

49 **Innovation in China**
The Chinese software industry
Shang-Ling Jui

50 **Mobility, Migration and the Chinese Scientific Research System**
Koen Jonkers

51 **Chinese Film Stars**
Edited by Mary Farquhar and Yingjin Zhang

52 **Chinese Male Homosexualities**
Memba, *Tongzhi* and Golden Boy
Travis S.K. Kong

53 **Industrialisation and Rural Livelihoods in China**
Agricultural processing in Sichuan
Susanne Lingohr-Wolf

54 **Law, Policy and Practice on China's Periphery**
Selective adaptation and institutional capacity
Pitman B. Potter

55 **China-Africa Development Relations**
Edited by Christopher M. Dent

56 **Neoliberalism and Culture in China and Hong Kong**
The countdown of time
Hai Ren

57 **China's Higher Education Reform and Internationalisation**
Edited by Janette Ryan

58 **Law, Wealth and Power in China**
Commercial law reforms in context
Edited by John Garrick

59 **Religion in Contemporary China**
Revitalization and innovation
Edited by Adam Yuet Chau

60 **Consumer-Citizens of China**
The role of foreign brands in the imagined future china
Kelly Tian and Lily Dong

61 **The Chinese Communist Party and China's Capitalist Revolution**
The political impact of the market
Lance L.P. Gore

62 **China's Homeless Generation**
Voices from the veterans of the Chinese civil war, 1940s–1990s
Joshua Fan

63 **In Search of China's Development Model**
Beyond the Beijing consensus
Edited by S. Philip Hsu, Suisheng Zhao and Yu-Shan Wu

64 **Xinjiang and China's Rise in Central Asia, 1949–2009**
A history
Michael E. Clarke

65 **Trade Unions in China**
The challenge of labour unrest
Tim Pringle

66 **China's Changing Workplace**
Dynamism, diversity and disparity
Edited by Peter Sheldon, Sunghoon Kim, Yiqiong Li and Malcolm Warner

67 **Leisure and Power in Urban China**
Everyday life in a medium-sized Chinese city
Unn Målfrid H. Rolandsen

68 **China, Oil and Global Politics**
Philip Andrews-Speed and Roland Dannreuther

69 **Education Reform in China**
Edited by Janette Ryan

70 **Social Policy and Migration in China**
Lida Fan

71 **China's One Child Policy and Multiple Caregiving**
Raising little suns in Xiamen
Esther C.L. Goh

72 **Politics and Markets in Rural China**
Edited by Björn Alpermann

73 **China's New Underclass**
Paid domestic labour
Xinying Hu

74 **Poverty and Development in China**
Alternative approaches to poverty assessment
Lu Caizhen

75 **International Governance and Regimes**
A Chinese perspective
Peter Kien-Hong Yu

76 **HIV/AIDS in China – The Economic and Social Determinants**
Dylan Sutherland and Jennifer Y.J. Hsu

77 **Looking for Work in Post-Socialist China**
Governance, active job seekers and the new Chinese labor market
Feng Xu

78 **Sino–Latin American Relations**
Edited by K.C. Fung and Alicia Garcia-Herrero

79 **Mao's China and the Sino–Soviet Split**
Ideological dilemma
Mingjiang Li

80 **Law and Policy for China's Market Socialism**
Edited by John Garrick

81 **China–Taiwan Relations in a Global Context**
Taiwan's foreign policy and relations
Edited by C.X. George Wei

82 **The Chinese Transformation of Corporate Culture**
Colin S.C. Hawes

83 **Mapping Media in China**
Region, province and locality
Edited by Wanning Sun and Jenny Chio

84 **China, the West and the Myth of New Public Management**
Neoliberalism and its discontents
Paolo Urio

85 **The Lahu Minority in Southwest China**
A response to Ethnic Marginalization on the Frontier
Jianxiong Ma

86 **Social Capital and Institutional Constraints**
A comparative analysis of China, Taiwan and the US
Joonmo Son

87 **Southern China**
Industry, development and industrial policy
Marco R. Di Tommaso, Lauretta Rubini and Elisa Barbieri

88 **State–Market Interactions in China's Reform Era**
Local state competition and global market building in the tobacco industry
Junmin Wang

89 **The Reception and Rendition of Freud in China**
China's Freudian slip
Edited by Tao Jiang and Philip J. Ivanhoe

Southern China

Industry, development and industrial policy

Marco R. Di Tommaso
Lauretta Rubini and
Elisa Barbieri

Routledge
Taylor & Francis Group
LONDON AND NEW YORK

First published 2013
by Routledge
2 Park Square, Milton Park, Abingdon, Oxon OX14 4RN

Simultaneously published in the USA and Canada
by Routledge
711 Third Avenue, New York, NY 10017

First issued in paperback 2017

Routledge is an imprint of the Taylor & Francis Group, an informa business

British Library Cataloguing in Publication Data
A catalogue record for this book is available from the British Library

Library of Congress Cataloging in Publication Data
A catalog record has been requested for this book

ISBN 13: 978-1-138-11576-7 (pbk)
ISBN 13: 978-0-415-68454-5 (hbk)

Typeset in Times New Roman
by Book Now Ltd, London

Contents

Tables

Figures

Acknowledgements

There are many people we would like to thank, who have offered important contributions to our research projects on China and thus to the writing of this book. Before thanking them, we wish to underline that the ideas and opinions expressed in this publication are entirely those of the authors and do not necessarily reflect the views of the people who have worked with us in China or elsewhere.

We first wish to thank S.E. Ambassador Federico Failla of the Italian Ministry of Foreign Affairs, recently nominated Ambassador of Italy in Indonesia. He served for many years as Consul General of Italy in Guangzhou (China) and then at the Ministry of Foreign Affairs in Rome as Head of the Italy and China Coordination Table. His vision, his sophisticated analysis, his constant intellectual and institutional support to our research and teaching activity in China have been of enormous value.

We are very grateful to the General Consulate of Italy in Guangzhou (China) that has played a pivotal role in supporting and encouraging our relationships with academic and government partners. In particular, we are greatly indebted to Paolo Miraglia del Giudice who served for 5 years (2006–2011) as Consul General of Italy in Guangzhou (China). We are immensely grateful for his constant institutional support and his bright intellectual contributions. We are also thankful to the other Italian diplomats whom we have met over the course of our work in China: Mr Fabrizio Arpea (former Consul General of Italy in Guangzhou), Mr Edoardo Napoli (Consul of Italy in Guangzhou) and Mr Benedetto Lettieri (Consul General of Italy in Guangzhou). We finally wish to acknowledge the important contribution offered by Mr Giovanni Floris (General Italian Consulate of Italy in Guangzhou) in many meetings with Chinese government officials.

Our particular thanks go to Prof. Patrizio Bianchi, leading Italian economist and former Chancellor of the University of Ferrara, for supporting us during these years of research with his unique intellectual backing and stimuli. We would like to sincerely thank all the friends, colleagues and students we have met in this decade of unique partnership with the South China University of Technology (Guangzhou). In particular, we would like to express our gratitude to leading Chinese economist Prof. Hailin Lan, for having shared with us his knowledge on business studies, China and Guangdong province. Our heartfelt thanks go to Prof. Manli Huang of the South China University of Technology for being a reliable and highly prepared research partner and for her genuine friendship. Our further special thanks go to Prof. Zhenquan Sha for having genuinely supported the strong relationship between the South China University of Technology and the University of Ferrara.

We would also like to thank our colleagues at Sun Yat-sen University (Guangzhou) and Shantou University for the meetings, workshops and conferences jointly organized and held over the years, that have provided us with thoughtful insights and stimulating perspectives.

Our acknowledgements also go to Prof. Stuart Schweitzer (University of California, Los Angeles), Prof. Pietro Masina (c.MET05 and L'Orientale University in Naples) and Prof. Donato Iacobucci (c.MET05 and Politechnic University of Marche) for having always provided our research group with useful and provocative ideas. Our particular thanks go to our colleague and friend Prof. Stefano Bonnini of the University of Ferrara for having accompanied us along some of the steps of our research path. We are also indebted to the two anonymous referees for their useful and inspiring comments.

We would also like to thank all the participants of the five editions of our *China and Italy School of Policy* (www.cisp-project.it) for policy makers and of the two editions for managers and entrepreneurs: Bi Lumin, Cai Guanghong, Chen Hanfan, Chen Hanmei, FengHuohuan, Guan Chunhua Huang Ruohe, Huang Xiaoai, Huang Zhong, Li Huifei, Li Ke, Li Qiaojin, Li Ronghua, Li Xiongxin, Lin Jun, Lin Ping, Lin Yugui, Liu Shoulian, Lun Liwen, Shen Yinglai, Tang Nanshan, Tang Weiguo, Wan Shuping, Wang Zhenghua, Wu Tao, Xiao Peng, Yan Zhankang, Yang Xinzhong, Yu Hantian, Zhou Peishan, Zhong Ziran, Su Lina, Qiu Zhouqiang, Su Wei, Wei Lin, Huang Wei, Zhong Daguo, Hu Deliang, Jia Xuan, Wang Jieyi, Shi Lixiang, Chen Jian, Deng Yihai, Huang Huiying, Lu Haiqing, Tang Yujuan, Que Miaoli, Zheng Wubiao, Cao Qiong, Qiu Anping, Huang Qi Feng, Yuan Hai Tao, Yi Tong Tong, Su Lina, Zhang Zhi Qiang, Zhang Mo Qin, Zhuang Si Cong, Huang Hai Bin, Wang Yue Jun, Pan Wen Long, Yin Yu Peng, Li Yuan Zhi, Guan Yi Kang, Wang Yue, Xiao Qi Mei, Zheng Jia Rong, Huang Jian, Nie Jin Ming, Hu Chang Jiang, Deng Jian Sheng, He Qimou, Yang Yingmian, Lin Jinsong, Wei Wenzhong, Liu Minqing, Wei Dingli, Yu Jixiao, Wan Shuping, Li Ronghua, Kang Yingzhao, Xu Jiankui, Wen Shaojun, Zhang Yongfa, Chen Zhuo, Zhang Huisheng, Liu Wei, Jiang Zhongyu, Kang, Nianfu, Lu Ye, Xuan Yang, Zhou Zhitong, Lin Shaojun, He Chenghong, Ning Kang, Xiao Xingxian, Chen Lihao, Chen Jianhong, Chen Jiasheng, Chen Lie, Hou Bihong, Ji Suju, Li Luwei, Li Baoxin, Li Chuanfang, Li Ming, Li Lu, Liang Chunqiu, Liang Xiaohong, Liu Yaping, Liu Yuhua, Ma Jianqiang, Qiu Yi, Qu Zheng, Wen Yongyu, Wu Xiaolin, Wu Dongwen, Wu Tangsheng, Xie Weisheng, Yang Zhaohui, Zhang Xin, Zhang Hai, Zheng Dongfeng, Liu Xiaodong, Li Jundong, Zhang Hanxi, Chen Xiaoqun, Fang Mingzhi, Huang Linghuan, Huang Manling, Xiong Lingyao, Li Ying, Xiong Aiwu, Li Chunping, Xie Hui, Zhang Feng, Liu Ruizhong, Tang Weixin, Sha Zhenquan, He Xiaohui, Huang Xiaoli, Jiang Jinliang, Li Feng, Li Shijian,

Liu Shuang, Wen Siya, Xiang Zhonghong, Xiao Jinghui, Zheng Dayong, Zhou Qin and Ye Jinfeng.

Among these, in particular, we would like to acknowledge Mr He Qimou and Mr Zhong Ziran of the Department of Science and Technology of Guangdong province, who over the years have become important partners in the development of our research activities with the Guangdong government.

Our work has greatly benefited from the collaboration and steady interaction with the Department of Science and Technology and the Department of Human Resources of Guangdong province, which have provided us with valuable information on the functions and actions of the Guangdong government. We strongly appreciate the collaboration and help provided during our fieldwork in China by the Italian community in Guangzhou, in particular, from Dr Marco Bettin of the Italian Chamber of Commerce in China, Dr Paolo Lemma and Dr Luigina Cirone of the ICE-Italian Trade Commission.

We also thank the Emilia Romagna Regional Government (Italy) for the support granted to some of our activities in China, and in particular, we thank the former Regional Councillor for Productive Activities Duccio Campagnoli, the current Regional Councillor for Productive Activities Giancarlo Muzzarelli, Dr Ruben Sacerdoti and Dr Gianluca Baldoni.

We are also indebted to Cristina Iordan for her great commitment to our research project and for the professionalism she always demonstrates when supporting our China and Italy School of Policy. Her skills and working attitude have been of the utmost importance in facilitating the interactions with all parties involved in our research activity.

In addition, our gratitude goes to all the students and PhD students who have been working with us in Ferrara during these years: Annalisa Baradel, Lucia Bazzucchi, Agnese Gardenghi, Enrico Gavazzoni, Gianluca Farini, Valentina Mini, Luca Motta, Monica Occhi, Silvia Podetti, Giacomo Rossi, Angela Sarcina, Mattia Tassinari, Marta Tommasino and Elisabetta Zerlotin. We also thank Alessandro Ansaloni and Desi Scappini for their technical support in data presentations and map design. Finally, our thanks go to Blanca Rocio Cendejas for her valuable language revision.

We all owe so much to our parents, brothers and sisters, and they know why: the Di Tommasos (Amalia, Angelo, Maria Cristina, Filena Marianeve, Agostino Ghigo), the Rubinis (Flavia, Beppe, Nicola) and the Barbieris (Ornella, Bruno, Riccardo). We dedicate this book to our beloved: Antonella, Chiara Alessandra, Francesca Amalia, Alessandro, Anna and Pedro.

Although this book is the result of extensive research jointly carried out by the three authors, a possible attribution by chapter is as follows: Marco Di Tommaso has primarily contributed to Chapters 1 and 9, Elisa Barbieri to Chapters 7 and 8 and Lauretta Rubini to Chapters 3, 4 and 5. The authors have equally contributed to the final version of Chapter 6.

Abbreviations

ADS	above designated size
BDS	below designated size
CEPA	Closer Economic Partnership Agreement
CJV	contractual joint venture
DSTGG	Department of Science and Technology of Guangdong Government
ECB	European Central Bank
EJV	equity joint venture
EPO	European Patent Office
EPZ	export processing zone
ETDD	economic and technological development district
ETDZ	economic and technological development zone
EU	European Union
FDI	foreign direct investment
FTZ	free trade zone
GDP	gross domestic product
GPRD	Greater Pearl River Delta
GSY	Guangdong Statistical Yearbook
HIDZ	High-Tech Industrial Development Zone
IMF	International Monetary Fund
IP	industrial policy
IS	import substitution
IT	information technology
JV	joint venture
NBS	National Bureau of Statistics
NPC	National People's Congress
ODI	outward directed investment
PCT	Patent Cooperation Treaty
PLC	prefecture-level city
PRC	People's Republic of China
PRD	Pearl River Delta
PRD-EZ	Pearl River Delta Economic Zone
R&D	Research and Development
SAR	special administrative region

SBGP	Statistical Bureau of Guangdong Province
SEZ	special economic zone
SME	small and medium enterprise
SOE	state-owned enterprise
ST	specialized town
TVE	township and village enterprise
UA	urban area
USPO	US Patent Office
WB	World Bank
WFOE	wholly foreign-owned enterprise
WTO	World Trade Organization
YRD	Yangtze River Delta

1 Introduction

1.1 Industry, policy and planning

1.1.1 The 'invisible pendulum': three decades of debate

It is well known that the issue of *why*, *how* and *if* government should intervene in industrial development has always been a very controversial topic. Looking at the last three decades, we have witnessed a periodic oscillation of dominant opinions and attitudes both in academic and policy-maker circuits. As if guided by an invisible pendulum, routinely, years of consensus have been followed by years of blame, while years of rethinking and support have been replaced by years of attacks and severe criticisms.

In the post-boom 1970s, the idea that governments might play an important role in promoting industrialization was quite common. The biggest European countries, struggling with oil shocks, high rates of unemployment and rapid deindustrialization processes, adopted industrial policy (IP) measures mainly to consolidate their post-Second World War production base, to encourage strategic structural adjustments and to relax the labour–capital conflict (Geroski, 1989; Kassim and Menon, 1996; Bianchi *et al.*, 1994; Soete, 2007). In the same years, IP became a popular issue in the United States (Reich, 1982; Norton, 1986; Bingham, 1998; Ketels, 2007) because of the economic and social crisis and because of the Japanese challenge, its influential interventionist model and the 'myth' of the Ministry of International Trade and Industry (MITI) (Sakoh, 1984; Johnson, 1982; Okimoto, 1990; Di Tommaso and Schweitzer, 2012). In the other half of the industrialized world, the Soviet Union and its satellite countries controlled industry with even stronger tools, such as national planning (Lavigne, 1974; Amann *et al.*, 1977; Nove, 1992). Finally, looking at the periphery of the industrialized world, post-colonial developing countries either adopted a Soviet-style industry planning or experienced import substitution (IS) strategies, suggesting the need for interventionist governments to be able to guide industrial development (Kirkpatrick *et al.*, 1984; Wade, 1990; Colman and Nixon, 1994).

Then, at the beginning of the 1980s, the years of American Reaganomics and British Thatcherism rapidly arrived and the dominant policy message became 'no government intervention' and thus 'no-industrial-development-policy'.

These were the years that prepared for the consolidation of the Washington Consensus propelled by the dramatic fall of the Berlin Wall and the final debacle of almost all of the planned economies (with China – that passed through that 'heavy storm' without collapsing – as one of the most visible exceptions). For a long list of industrialized countries this debacle meant the end of industry planning, but the new dominant atmosphere also brought along very strong attacks against IP and more generally against any kind of government intervention. It was the triumph of the 'getting-prices-right' paradigm that was considered the best recipe for the so-called developed, developing and transition economies (Amsden, 1989; Stiglitz, 2002; Chang, 2001; Bianchi and Labory, 2006). Even the interpretation of the industrial growth of some Asian countries – ungenerously defined as a 'miracle' – was utilized in this perspective. In the view of many Western scholars and international institutions, in those years the most successful East Asian countries had experienced an incredible growth, thanks to a firm liberalization, the opening up of their economies to foreign capital and the withdrawal of governments from selective policy interventions (World Bank, 1993; Amsden, 1989; Colman and Nixon, 1994). The policy prescriptions for any industrialized, industrializing and transition country were clear: deregulation, privatization, liberalization and more generally the need to obtain the withdrawal of government from industries and markets. In a few years, the 'pendulum' completed its oscillation. It was a political turn supported by a vast academic consensus that had gradually shifted from traditional *market failure* arguments to more extreme *government failure* positions (Chang, 1996; Krueger, 1990). A new framework that, with well-defined simple pillars, could not tolerate industry planning and IP.

After at least two decades of generalized consensus, the 'pendulum' started to move back again. We began the first few years of this century with the 11 September 2001 shock and the initial reactions of Western countries that were blindly going in the direction of the forthcoming 2008 international crisis. These were years of confusion for 'the West' and years of growth and massive changes for some 'emerging' giants (China, Brazil, India, Russia) and other dynamic 'emerged' countries (South Korea, Taiwan) that progressively gained the status of international industrial powers following Western-consensus-independent planning and policy recipes (Chang, 1996, 2002, 2006, 2007). In 2008, the Lehman Brother failure was only the first signal of what was going to happen. The entire global economy entered the tunnel of the ongoing 'big crisis'. These are years that have induced many governments in Western countries to give strong and immediate policy answers, years of a new rethinking of national development strategies characterized by the resurgence of a debate on IP (Aghion *et al.*, 2011; Birdsall and Fukuyama, 2011; Lin, 2012; Wade, 2012).

1.1.2 The Chinese 'long flight': 1978–2008

In the same three decades, while the 'pendulum' was following its oscillations, the People's Republic of China had progressively experienced its planned 'long flight'. Even if (as we are going to argue) proof of correlation and causality are still difficult to demonstrate rigorously, there are two unchangeable facts. First, the 'flight' has been characterized by unique, unprecedented successful growth and industrial development performances. Second, these exceptional performances have been accompanied by an impressive battery of national and regional policies rooted in a complex set of long-term government plans, with the explicit aim of promoting growth, industrialization and gradual and continuous structural change.

The 'flight' initiated at the very end of the 1970s. While Western countries were entering the Thatcher–Reagan age, China began its first economic (and social) policy experiments. Experiments that were carefully controlled by the government, limited in extension (in terms of people, sectors and localities involved) but very innovative in terms of what was tested (Lardy, 1992; Krugman and Obstfeld, 1991; Wei, 1995; Napoleoni, 2011). It was the prudent take-off of 'the long flight', it was the beginning of Deng's era of reforms. An era characterized by attraction of overseas capital and foreign direct investments (FDIs), export-promotion policies, establishment of some selected special economic zones where the opening up could be gradually experimented and carefully controlled: 'closed islands' allowing for what was not possible in the rest of the country, offering unique attractive characteristics (non-unionized and skilled labour; land, building and business facilities; logistic and transport infrastructure) and preferential policies (tax rebates and other financial incentives), all aimed at encouraging investment, technology import and export-oriented production (Yang, 1997; Ma, 1999; Wang and Hu, 1999; Démurger, 2000; Démurger *et al.*, 2002).

Then, during the Western Washington Consensus era, step by step the Chinese government authorities further implemented their long-term plans of industrial development with the target of managing and controlling the gradual change of the Chinese economy. Fine-tuning (speed and time) the change was the main challenge, given that the process of opening up and reform implied enormous risk of social and political collapse. Thus, these were again times of gradual economic experimentation that started to involve a growing and carefully selected number of people, actors, sectors and territories (see Chapters 4 and 5), a complex process of radical and controlled change that people and regions experienced with different speeds, thanks to a set of orchestrated plans and policies at the national and local levels (Chapter 6). These were the years of the first stages of accelerated growth for China founded on the exploitation of its immense pool of migrant labour (Chapter 5) and the progressive opening up of its economy, with the aim of acquiring capital and new technology from abroad (Chapters 4 and 7; Nolan, 2001; Naughton, 2007; Napoleoni, 2011). Thus – exactly in the years when the Washington Consensus was at the top of its influence in the industrialized, developing and transition economies – the Chinese government made its biggest effort in encouraging and controlling the entire reorganization of its industry following its long-term outward-oriented strategy of change and development (US-China Economic and Security Review Commission, 2009; Nolan, 2001; Liu, 2005; ul Haque, 2007; Chang, 2002).

Following what was defined as being in the interest of the nation, the Chinese government selected a set of goals declared strategic (growth acceleration, technology upgrading, competitiveness improvements, structural adjustments in industry, territorial re-equilibrium, etc.). These were officially launched at the national level through the five-year plans. They were then adopted by the local authorities and supported by *ad hoc* industrial plans and policy interventions. Structural change targets and interventions were made in order to promote a gradual shift towards those activities considered strategic for the industrial development of the country. These were selective policies in favour of what were defined as the 'pillar industries' (Lan, 2008). 'Sunrise policies' were promoted in those industries that were defined strategic for the future of the country. IP programmes were implemented to protect and to encourage the development of infant industries or support national champions and interventions targeted to support selected incumbents or to encourage new entrants operating in strategic industries (Nee, 2000; Garnaut and Song, 2004; Rodrik, 2004; Chang, 2002).

The private sector – once labelled as the 'tail of capitalism' – was also encouraged and progressively legitimized by the government. Specific policies for the small- and medium-sized enterprises (SMEs) and for local development were implemented (Tsai, 2007; Zheng and Yang, 2009; Dai, 2005; Fang *et al.*, 1999). The state-owned sector was not hurriedly privatized as was happening in those years, for example, in Eastern Europe following the Washington Consensus paradigm. On the contrary, state-owned enterprises (SOEs) were first forced to become champions of efficiency to be able to lead the country's outward-oriented strategy (Abrami and Zheng, 2008). SOEs were not sold to foreign capital, and the Chinese government allowed overseas companies to enter China under some specific conditions [joint ventures (JVs) and other kinds of similar partnerships] considered useful for the future independent growth of the Chinese economy.

Finally, after a period of continued growth, the 2008 international crisis arrived. The dramatic fall of international demand had a clear effect on the sustainability of the model. The two-digit continuous growth had so far been the key factor that had made the transition and the opening up process sustainable in economic, social and thus political terms. The Chinese authorities officially declared that 8 per cent growth was the limit under which it was not possible to guarantee social stability (Chapter 4). Thus, the national authorities quite soon announced the need for adjusting the outward-oriented strategy, launching parallel *go-domestic policies* to meet internal demand. This was a new unexplored change that was announced as soon as the first few symptoms of the international crisis were perceived by national and local government authorities (Chapter 4). The announcement was immediate even if no genuine analysis could really assume that the new inward-looking strategy would really be implemented with the same speed. There is no doubt in fact that decades of outward-oriented development have made the entire industrial (and economic and social) system quite rigid and unprepared for the need to consider the domestic market as a possible engine of growth as well.

The social risks associated with the growth deceleration, the strong dependency on international demand and the rigidity of the outward-oriented model made immediately clear why China is also highly vulnerable to the international crisis arriving from 'the West'. Moreover, after three decades of continuous changes, the demand of the leading segments of Chinese society has gone beyond the constancy of two-digit growth. There is an issue related to the 'quality of growth' that makes the entire process of development weaker than it was in the recent past. The new emerging middle class, the one that has led and driven the last decades of growth, today has great expectations in terms of quality of life and more sophisticated benefits associated with their growing income. Local and central authorities seem well aware of such a change, to the extent that the recent slogan referring to the creation of a 'harmonious society' while 'making people happy' can be read as signals of a political will to move forward in this direction (see Chapter 4) – signals that are explicitly sent by governments to the rest of the society.

1.2 Government and industry: 2012

At the end of these last three decades of debate and change, do we know more about what the optimal model of government involvement in contemporary processes of industrialization, growth and development would be? What about the role of industrial planning and IP in contemporary capitalism?

Observing China, the scenario is as follows: sustained growth, continuity in the way government intervenes with long-term planning and industrial policies. Looking at what 'the West' has become today, the picture can be drawn as follows: persistent slow rates of growth and a quite diffused reappearance of IP arguments and interventions (Di Tommaso and Schweitzer, 2012; Bianchi and Labory, 2011).

In other words, studying contemporary industry, it seems that today governments do play a role. This role undoubtedly varies across countries, but government involvement is one of the features of contemporary capitalism. This is true not only in the case of capitalism 'with Chinese characteristics' (Chung *et al.*, 2001) but also in the case of many other industrialized countries.

It is important to underline that the 'Chinese characteristics' – including the role that governments (at local and national level) are playing in promoting industry – will continue to influence global capitalism and industry. We can no longer consider China to be a marginal 'special case'. China *is* contemporary manufacturing. China *is* a relevant part of contemporary industry, China *is* a crucial part of the contemporary global economy. Thus, given that contemporary industrial powers have to play the game in the same global markets, China is implicitly forcing other countries to redefine their strategies and their institutions, to rethink the role governments play.

1.2.1 Western countries: 2012

Since 2008, in all Western countries growth has been very weak. After four years, the general situation is still extremely uncertain and all projections continue to confirm feeble rates of growth. At the same time, the possibilities for Western countries' governments to continue to achieve wider development goals seem particularly low because of a general consensus on the need to cut expenditures in fields like education, transportation and health. In this context, if planning, as a means of governing the industrialization process, has definitively gone out of the picture, with regards to IP the scenario is more controversial. The first reactions to the 2008 crisis in Western countries were bail-outing, stimulus interventions and some surprising discussions about what would be the best government policy in favour of recovery and growth. After the first shock, in America and Europe we have witnessed a progressive resurgence of national IP positions serving as tools by which to offer national strategies to guide countries out of the crisis. However, these attempts continue to appear generally weak. There are two main groups of reasons. First, government failures are not just theoretical assumptions of the neoclassical schools. On the contrary, they are real-world phenomenon associated with government policy practices (Chang, 1996; Krueger, 1990). As market mechanism failures are vividly present in contemporary people's ordinary life, so are government failures. Rent-seeking mechanisms, public bodies' inefficiencies and corruption are diffused characteristics associated with government interventions that are rapidly communicated and stressed to citizens by contemporary aggressive media. If then IP is perceived as *giving money and privileges to a few companies*, government intervention in industry dynamics automatically becomes a source of concern. However, IP is not simply about giving money to firms and it is also reasonable to argue that in many circumstances government agencies have shown records of efficiency and effectiveness. Yet, in a simplistic and polarized media-led debate, IP often ends up being described as a waste of public money and a further burden to the government budget. In this environment it is clear that both in Europe and in the United States there is a lack of consensus which makes policy interventions weak even in the preliminary phases of definition and discussion. Moreover, because of the relationship with politics, policies risk being inadequate for current needs. Both in Europe and in the United States, policies fail to address long-term issues because every intervention is constrained by the need to manage the short-term demand of politics. In other words, we have what we could define as 'poll-based industrial policy' tailored to the short-term narrow political consensus; this policy is not suited to respond to complex social and economic long-term dynamics. Another factor that makes IP weak in Europe and in other Western countries is connected to the incapacity of national governments to manage transnational issues. In the majority of relevant problems related to contemporary industry, growth and development, the national governmental sphere of legitimation is too small. Clear examples are the management of transnational public goods such as knowledge or economic and financial stability.

1.2.2 China: 2012

Since the second half of 2008, China has also experienced a deceleration of its growth rate. However, although in 2012 most countries, including China, will experience a further slowdown, forecasting seems to support the idea that in 2013 the recovery will already be visible in China [Organization for Economic Co-operation and Development (OECD), 2011].

In other words, the Chinese process of industrial development, upgrading and structural change has continued; a process of change that is still ongoing, which follows Chinese government long-term planning rationales that are accompanied by a variety of IP interventions implemented at national and local levels. These are industrial policies promoted in coherence with the long-term planning thought of the late 1970s but also include industrial policies designed to rapidly respond to the contingent needs imposed by the crisis. The 'long flight' – that process of planned change accompanied by a wide range of specific government policies we described in the previous pages – at the moment has not been interrupted by the international crisis.

The persistent presence of national and local governments in the management of national industrial development clearly goes beyond the need to answer to market failures. On the contrary, planning and industrial policies have respectively continued to offer the country a strategic vision and specific tools to achieve national goals.

IP plays a crucial role because of the centrality that industrial development, upgrading and structural change have in the Chinese model. The capacity to guarantee those growth performances that are crucial to the general sustainability of the whole system is in fact based on the success of these processes. With this perspective in mind, since 2008, the planned outward-oriented industrial strategy has clearly shown its vulnerability to international demand. The dependency on foreign demand – given the centrality that growth has in the Chinese system – cannot be considered desirable. Of course, here the issue probably goes beyond the Chinese case. Contemporary global economies are all strongly interconnected and this set of complex interdependencies makes all national governments, whatever their traditional involvement, very weak because they are strongly subject to uncontrollable external events and practices (Haddad and Shepherd, 2011). However, as became clear at the end of 2008 when millions of migrant workers returned to their hometowns without any sure perspective on the possibilities of maintaining their jobs, this dependency on international demand is clearly very risky for China. An internal consensus based on an outward-oriented growth is fragile and has a clear impact on the whole internal economic and social equilibrium.

Having said this, it is also true that China may exploit the potential advantages offered by its unique domestic market. The possibility of stimulating the internal markets and the demands of huge segments of new Chinese actors (i.e. consumers and companies, towns and regions, generations, social groups) are the challenges that may offer new opportunities for growth to the extremely outward-oriented Chinese system. 'Go-domestic' industrial policies that are able to encourage the penetration of the internal, unexplored markets are going to become a crucial line of government intervention (see Chapter 4). Here, the challenges for industrial policies are many. Encouraging companies that have an established habit of operating in faraway international markets to explore the potentialities of other Chinese provinces means first lowering the existing entry barriers into non-local Chinese markets. These can be as follows: logistical barriers caused by the lack of adequate inland infrastructure that makes shipping goods abroad easier than transporting them within China; administrative barriers that in the outward-oriented model did not represent a problem, and that on the contrary played a positive effect by offering incentives to the successful go-global producers; barriers to knowledge companies may face due to the lack of information on local demand; finally, strategic barriers built by the dominant local incumbents during these decades of outward-oriented growth. These kinds of considerations may imply new investments in internal tangible and intangible infrastructures but also a more complex rethinking of Chinese industry. This general rethinking, probably, cannot avoid considering the antitrust perspective and arguments. Since it is clear that the extent of the market goes beyond national borders and that such recognition has justified the growth of many national champions, the dominant positions of these regional giants may also constitute a constraint for national development.

In other words, we may argue that today's IP in China has to open a second front, without abandoning the first one: effective go-domestic policies without losing the advantages accumulated in the last decades of successful go-global policies.

The success of the go-domestic industrial policies will be crucial for the general sustainability of the Chinese model of development. It will widen the base of consensus because an increasing number of people will have access to the benefits associated with growth. At the same time, it will make China less vulnerable to and less dependent on the unpredictability of international demand.

All of these considerations support the idea that the limitations of the Chinese model of development and change, based on the capacity to guarantee the planning-and-policy-guided growth, are connected to internal social stability. Growth has been the key factor that has so far allowed for the necessary consensus on change. Today, as government authorities know, growth cannot decelerate too much and it has to involve progressively wider segments of the population and territories. Looking at the last decades, Chinese and foreign observers have to be optimist: so far the benefits associated with the striking industrial development, and more generally with the impressive decades of continued growth, have progressively involved an increasing number of people.

However, if it is also true that these benefits continue to exclude broad segments of the population and territories, the capacity of transforming successful growth into an achievement of more complex development goals appears quite weak. The model vulnerability is strongly connected to this aspect. On one side, policies have to continue to promote growth. On the other side, it is also clear that growth is not enough anymore and that growth is conditioned by the capacity to guarantee a wider set of development goals for a growing number of people and territories. If the capacity to maintain impressive growth rates is still a crucial issue, the great challenge is about *development*. The new frontiers are clearly connected to the capacity to guarantee access to a more complex basket of tangible and intangible private and public goods. Access to health, education, culture, leisure, housing, transportation, a better environment and a better urban and metropolitan quality are just the main challenges of a longer list of people's demands. The capacity to meet this emerging demand of *Development* is the critical condition needed to maintain the current rate of growth and, more generally, to ensure the sustainability of the whole socio-economic system.

1.3 Studying industry and government in China

In the previous paragraph, we have underlined both for Western countries and China, what today appear to be the main challenges and we have highlighted a different role for government in industrial development. These differences appear to us to raise important issues on the desirability and necessity of government intervention in contemporary industry. In this scenario, given the weight China has on the international economy today, what can we learn from its industrial development policy experience?

When looking at China, 'Western observers' have little rigorous evidence about the relationship between government policy, growth and industrial development. Of course, if the question was 'which is the most successful country in terms of industrial growth?', the answer would be quite easy: it is China. In recent history, no other country has experienced such two-digit growth for such a long time. In the last three decades, the new 'Industrial Revolution' has occurred: the country has dramatically grown and industry has radically changed. Moreover, as we mentioned, there is evidence about how this 'long flight' was planned and how it has been implemented by national and local governments that have followed short-, medium- and very long-term objectives. In other words, there is no doubt about how growth has been successful and about the fact that industry planning, IP and government have been part of this picture.

Of course, as 'Western observers', we have to assume that planning and policies have also produced undesirable costs, because China cannot be considered to be immune from traditional government failures. Internal public organization inefficiencies, asymmetries of information, rent-seeking negative mechanisms and corruption are not distinctive characteristics of Western countries' governments.

Nevertheless, at least from the perspective of non-Chinese literature, it is still unclear how government intervention and successful industrial growth have really been interconnected in China.

In principle, there are at least two possible scenarios:

1 Industrial growth has occurred, thanks to IP. Here, we have a positive relation of causality.
2 Industrial growth has occurred despite IP. Here, we have a negative relation of causality or a null effect of the policy on industrial growth.

Alternatively, one might even say that this is not the relevant relationship to be studied. It would be too narrow. IP has to be viewed as part of a more general intervention promoted by Chinese governments that can be justified not in terms of growth, but in terms of other, wider objectives such as the sustainability of the transition process from a political and economic point of view.

This reading of the Chinese experience brings us, however, constantly back to the ancient ideological debate of state versus markets. 'Western scholars' have not yet produced sufficient evidence to quantify and demonstrate the existence of causal relationships (whatever their sign and magnitude) between policy and performance in contemporary China. There seem to be two main reasons:

1 First, they might be too influenced by traditional Western categories like state and markets, public and private, individual and collective and so on. It is not easy to apply these categories to the Chinese case, and not only because of high linguistic barriers. To raise some simple examples, one could refer to the difficulties Western scholars have in recognizing the boundaries between government and companies, public and private organizations, targets, policies and strategies. And then what about the third actor, the Party? How does it overlap, control, contrast, supervise, support, guide... industry and governments? Moreover, even when the debate is focussed on the specific issue of IP, there is a tendency to define it as 'money for firms' (Aghion *et al.*, 2011), whereas we argue, throughout our analysis, that in China industrial planning and policy are about defining short- and long-term industrial strategies.
2 Second, it seems to us that Chinese scholars and policy makers do not demonstrate a propensity to share data. In addition, at the moment, while Chinese scholars have increasingly had access to international business, economic and public policy literatures, this is still a one-way process of entry: the huge domestic Chinese language debate appears quite closed and it is still hardly accessible to Western scholars. As Western scholars, we are partly responsible because of our low propensity to invest in studying the Chinese language and culture, which could perhaps overcome this asymmetry. However, having recognized this, it is also true that acceptance of this asymmetry also offers interesting advantages to our Chinese academic and political counterparts.

In this context, searching for one final elegant and rigorous answer to the question of the optimal role of governments might be misleading. Especially if this answer – again – pretends to be valid in absolute terms, generalized for different contexts and referring to already accepted dichotomist categories (market vs. state, planning vs. markets, private vs. public, etc.). From this perspective, the risk is to exploit this real-world experience of development as happened at the time of the 'Asian Miracle', when different scholars believed they had found in the same Far-East history of development the scientific proofs for diametrically different economic theses.

Thus, in the absence of data and counterfactuals, the mere consistency of growth and policies cannot be considered enough. On the contrary, it can be read as having no rigorous evidence of planning and policy effectiveness.

Given the two incontestable facts (growth and a government interventionist role) it can still be questioned whether or not plans and policies have really played a positive role in promoting growth and industrial development. In fact, as was argued in describing other past experiences of growth, one may still ask if China's growth and progressive structural change have occurred 'despite of' or 'thanks to' government intervention (Chapter 8). Or, as it has been suggested by some (Sachs and Woo, 1997), has growth occurred thanks to the gradualism of economic reforms or despite such gradualism (in areas characterized by radical reforms)?

A possible counterargument might be that the question that can be posed is the opposite one: given how government intervention has been so pervasive and continuous over time, are we able to demonstrate that this intervention has been largely ineffective? Why should the presumption of policy effectiveness be demonstrated before (and over and above) the presumption of policy ineffectiveness? (Amsden, 1989).

However, insisting in this direction would mean accepting ideologically based arguments and perspectives. On the contrary, we would like to go beyond these traditional counter-positions.

1.4 China, 'Chinas' and Guangdong province

Our methodological answer to the questions posed in the previous paragraph is the reason we decided to publish this book and why we believe our work could offer a contribution to the international debate. One of the provocative messages we wish to send is that if we want to better understand the role of governments in China, and in contemporary industry, we should stop focussing on China as a whole.

Our methodological choice has been to limit the object of analysis in order to avoid what could become simplistic, ideologically based considerations. We have limited it by selecting the experience of development of one specific region of China: Guangdong province. We have limited the object of analysis by focussing on industrial and local development policy. We have gone through the details of the specific industrial programmes and policies. The aim is to provide a rigorous descriptive analysis of policy interventions, their stated objectives, their evolution over time and the extent to which gradualism was a planned feature of the reforms. And only on the basis of this thorough analysis can we propose some first considerations on the role of governments in contemporary industry and suggest some further research lines on policy effectiveness.

These choices are first supported by the recognition that China is a country of persistent diversities. Since the late 1970s when the process of opening up started, different people and different territories have participated in this process of change to variable degrees. Going further, we may say that the coexistence of territorial and social differences is one of the main characteristics of the Chinese experience of industrialization, growth and development. The planned and carefully monitored plurality of dichotomies between social and territorial segments is one of the most astonishing features of the 'long flight': urban versus rural; towns versus metropolis; coastal areas versus inland territories; industry versus agriculture; Chinese versus foreigners; inland Chinese versus overseas Chinese; temporary migrants and permanent workers; government managers and private entrepreneurs; local versus global. These are just some of the most evident 'controlled differences' that national and local governments have managed in these years of impressive growth and change. The capacity to guarantee the sustainability of the process of change has been based on the ability Chinese decision makers have shown in managing what has been deliberately thought of as a 'multi-speediness' process of development.

Thus, if the national government has planned and promoted the last three decades of impressive change from Beijing, it is also true that it has purposely promoted and allowed different local experiences of development, where local governments have assumed different roles, showing diverse degrees of intervention that range from promotion of SOEs in strategic sectors, to widespread attraction of FDI or promotion of local SMEs and private entrepreneurship.

In this framework, different local governments have clearly expressed unique degrees of autonomy in following central government policy prescriptions and in some selected cases they have been able to negotiate distinctive models of development and change.

In this context, the Guangdong experience cannot be considered just one of the possible regional case studies. On the contrary, the Guangdong province story of industrialization, growth and development is at the centre of the Chinese 'long flight'.

There are two main reasons for this centrality: the great economic weight of what has become today one of the most industrialized regions of the world (Chapters 2 and 3) and the role of 'laboratory' (Chapters 4–8) that this province has played. This makes Guangdong province one of the most interesting economically, socially and politically planned experiments of our contemporary history.

2 The southern China engine: Guangdong province

2.1 Main economic indicators

The last 40 years of Chinese history have radically changed the global economic scenario. Similar to any other great transition, China's economic rise has also not been possible without disequilibria: Chinese policy makers have in fact tested the effects of a process of opening up to the market economy only in some selected areas. Guangdong, together with Fujian, has been the first chosen and therefore, as we will see in more detail in Chapter 4, the most exposed to the experimentation phase.

Guangdong province is located in the south-eastern part of China, close to Hong Kong and Macao, the two special administrative regions (SARs), respectively controlled by the United Kingdom (up until 1997) and by Portugal (up until 1999). It borders Guangxi province to the west, Hunan, Jiangxi and Fujian provinces to the east and the South Sea of China to the south. Up until 1988, Hainan was also part of Guangdong province, then becoming an independent province.[1]

As we will see in more detail in Chapter 4, the peculiar geographic location of Guangdong has represented one of the main reasons driving the central government's decision to choose the province as one of the first locations in which to experiment with the market economy (Figure 2.1). The proximity to Hong Kong and Macao, which represented two ramparts of Western capitalism, has over the years favoured the diffusion of a widespread entrepreneurial spirit and of know-how coming from 'the West' throughout the whole province.

With a total area of 177,901 square kilometres, Guangdong province represents 1.87 per cent of the entire People's Republic of China (PRC), and 60 per cent of its territory is mountainous (Huikang, 2002; Liang *et al.*, 2008). The province is divided into 21 prefectures (Figure 2.2); the most developed part of Guangdong is the central area, the so-called Pearl River Delta (PRD) that will be analysed in detail in Section 2.5.

In 2010, the permanent population of the province amounted to 104.3 million people (about 7.8 per cent of the whole national population) plus nearly 84 million people with residence registration (Statistical Bureau of Guangdong Province (SBGP), 2011).[2] Guangdong ranked first among Chinese provinces according to population and seventh (excluding Hong Kong, Macao and the temporary residents) for population density, which in 20 years grew noticeably,

Figure 2.1 The Guangdong province in China.

Source: Authors' elaboration.

passing from 351 inhabitants per square kilometres in 1990 to 536 in 2010 (Table 2.1). Guangzhou, the capital of the province, in 2009 had more than 10 million permanent residents and 7.9 million temporary residents (for more information on the distinction between permanent population and temporary population, see Chapter 5).

Guangdong has one of the highest gross domestic product (GDP) growth rates of the whole nation, with an annual average of 15.2 per cent between 1980 and 2010 (SBGP, 2011). Figure 2.3 shows that, since 1980, the growth of the Guangdong GDP has always been higher than that of China in general. Furthermore, in the considered years, both China's and Guangdong's GDP growth has always been higher than that of the so-called G7 countries (Table 2.2). In 2009, Guangdong had the highest GDP of all provinces and municipalities (3,948 billion RMB, about 555 billion US$),[3] as well as the highest per capita GDP after Shanghai, Beijing, Tianjin, Zhejiang and Jiangsu, which is equal to 40,965 RMB (about 5,720 US$) compared to the 25,575 RMB (about 3,595 US$) of the whole country (SBGP, 2010; NBS, 2010).

Figure 2.2 The 21 Guangdong prefectures.

Source: Authors' elaboration.

Table 2.1 Guangdong permanent population (1990–2010) (thousands)

Year	*Total population*	*Non-agricultural population*	*Agricultural population*	*Density (inhabitants per km²)*
1990	63,472	15,782	47,690	351
1995	73,875	26,341	47,534	382
2000	86,500	34,897	51,603	422
2005	91,940	54,017	37,923	430
2009	96,380	56,480	39,900	536
2010	104,305	–	–	536

Source: Authors' elaboration on SBGP data, GSY, various years.

Note: Numbers refer to the total population with a residence certificate at year end.

In 2010, Guangdong's GDP was generated as follows: 50 per cent by the secondary sector, 45 per cent by services and 5 per cent by agriculture (SBGP, 2011). Industry therefore accounts for the main portion not only of the Chinese GDP, but also that of Guangdong's economy, even if in recent years there has

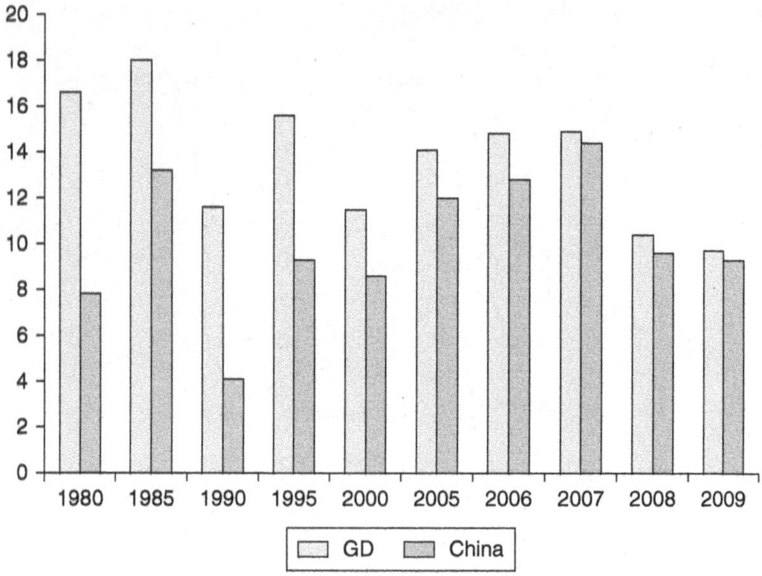

Figure 2.3 Guangdong and China's GDP growth rates (constant prices, %).

Source: Authors' elaboration on NBS (2010) and SBGP (2010).

Table 2.2 GDP growth rates in G7 countries, various years

	1980	*1990*	*2000*	*2005*	*2006*	*2007*	*2008*	*2009*	*2010*
Canada	2.2	0.2	5.2	3	2.8	2.2	0.7	−2.8	3.2
France	1.6	2.6	3.7	1.8	2.5	2.3	−0.1	−2.7	1.5
Germany	1.4	5.3	3.1	0.7	3.7	3.3	1.1	−5.1	3.7
Italy	3.4	2.1	3.7	0.7	2.0	1.5	−1.3	−5.2	1.3
Japan	2.8	5.2	2.9	1.9	2.0	2.4	−1.2	−6.3	4.0
United Kingdom	−2.1	0.8	3.9	2.2	2.8	2.7	−0.1	−4.9	1.4
United States	−0.2	1.9	4.2	3.1	2.7	1.9	0	−3.5	3.0

Source: World Bank indicators.

been a relevant development of the tertiary sector (increasing from 25.7 per cent of Guangdong's GDP in 1980 to 35.8 per cent in 1990 and to 45 per cent in 2010) (Figure 2.4). The weight of the service sector is still quite far from the percentages of more advanced countries (in 2011, it accounted for 71 per cent of the total GDP in Germany, 73 per cent in Italy, 77 per cent in the United Kingdom and 79 per cent in the United States), but the gap is decreasing over time.

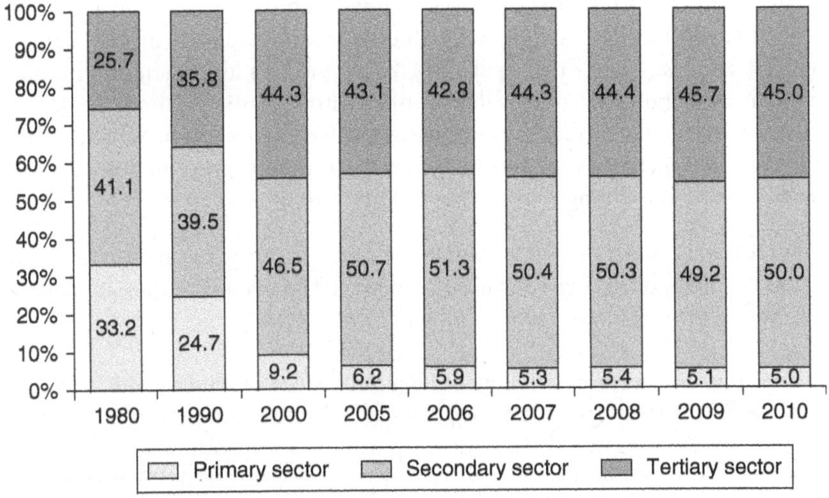

Figure 2.4 GDP composition in Guangdong by sector (%).

Source: Authors' elaboration on SBGP (2011).

2.2 Industry specialization in Guangdong

2.2.1 Some preliminary specifications on data

Before analyzing the industrial specialization in Guangdong, we have to introduce two distinctions used in the official statistics on industry:

1 Firms are divided according to their size into two categories: (a) below designated size (BDS) and (b) above designated size (ADS). According to the National Bureau of Statistics (NBS):

> Industrial enterprises above designated size refer to legal person industrial enterprises with annual principal business revenue of over 5 million yuan. In 2006 and prior to it, it referred to all state-owned industrial enterprises and [to] non-state-owned industrial enterprises with annual principal business revenue of over 5 million yuan. In 2007 and since then, it does not include state-owned industrial enterprises with principal business revenue less than 5 million yuan.[4]
>
> (NBS, 2010)

Given the limited availability of data, a detailed analysis of the industrial system of Guangdong province has to be mainly confined to ADS firms.

Before doing so, however, we must add a clarification. It seems logical to associate ADS with large firms and BDS with small ones. This is only partially true. While there are undoubtedly values that are noticeably higher or smaller than the 5 million RMB threshold, there is, however, a wide intermediate area in which these categories can overlap. Using sales as a classification criteria does not catch the value-added differences of the various industrial sectors: large firms operating in low value-added sectors with high sales volumes, but low unit value could overlap with medium high-tech firms with low sales volumes, but high unit value. Just to have an idea of the weight of ADS at the provincial level, in 2010, they represented on average 92 per cent of Guangdong's industrial output (SBGP, 2011).

2 The official statistics of the National Bureau classify the industrial sector into two categories: light and heavy industry. The two categories are defined as follows:

Light industry refers to the industry that produces consumer goods and hand tools. It consists of two categories, depending on the materials used:

1 Industries using farm products as raw materials: These are branches of light industry, which directly or indirectly use farm products as basic raw materials, including the manufacture of food and beverages, tobacco processing, textile, clothing, fur and leather manufacturing, paper making, printing and so on.
2 Industries using non-farm products as raw materials: These are branches of light industry, which use manufactured goods as raw materials, including the manufacture of cultural, educational and sports articles, chemicals, synthetic fibre, chemical products for daily use, glass products for daily use, metal products for daily use, hand tools, medical apparatus and instruments and the manufacture of cultural and clerical machinery.

Heavy industry refers to the industry which produces capital goods and provides various sectors of the national economy with necessary material and technical basis. It consists of the following three branches according to the purpose of production or the use of products:

1 Mining, quarrying and logging industry refers to the industry that extracts natural resources, including extraction of petroleum, coal, metal and non-metal ores and logging.
2 Raw materials industry refers to the industry that provides various sectors of the national economy with raw materials, fuels and power. It includes smelting and processing of metals, coking and coke chemistry, chemical materials and building materials such as cement, plywood and power, petroleum refining and coal dressing.
3 Manufacturing industry refers to the industry that processes raw materials. It includes machine-building industry which equips sectors of the national economy, industries of metal structure and cement products, industries producing means of agricultural production, such as chemical fertilizers and pesticides.

Table 2.3 Output value by industry: a China–Guangdong comparison (100 million RMB, 2008) – ADS firms

Industrial sector	*China*	*Guangdong*	*%*
Communication equipment, computers and other electronic devices	44,562.6	15,373.8	35.02
Measuring instruments and machinery for cultural activity and office work	5,083.3	1,351.6	26.59
Furniture	3,431.1	831.2	24.22
Plastics	10,969.4	2,423.1	22.09
Printing, reproduction of recording media	2,972.9	652.6	21.95
Electrical machinery and equipment	33,758.0	7,145.2	21.17
Metal products	16,085.0	3,095.3	19.25
Leather, fur, feather and related products	6,425.6	1,174.4	18.28
Textile wearing apparel, footwear and caps	10,444.8	1,725.3	16.52
Raw chemical materials and chemical products	36,908.6	3,123.9	8.46
Textiles	22,381.4	1,746.8	7.81

Source: Authors' elaboration on NBS (2009) and SBGP (2009).

> According to the above principle of classification, repairing trades engaged primarily in repairing products of heavy industry are classified into heavy industry, while those engaged in repairing products of light industry are classified into light industry.
>
> (SBGP, 2011: 362)

To maximize the quantity of available data and to attain a reasonable level of reliability of the gathered info, the data utilized in this book mainly comes from official statistics. Most are derived from the SBGP, with particular reference to the Guangdong Statistical Yearbook (GSY). The Yearbook represents the main data source at the provincial level, including information on the provincial accounts, population, industry, foreign economy and so on. Its main problem is a limited range of indicators at the prefectural level, and an even more limited range at the county level. In particular, at the county level there is much information available on the primary sector, but very little data on industrial production. Furthermore, at the county level the GSY usually provides aggregate data, merging the districts within the same prefecture so as to clearly differentiate the main urban centre (which usually corresponds to the sum of the districts) from the non-urban areas of the province.

In Shenzhen, Zhuhai and Foshan, where the prefecture is exclusively made up of districts, the GSY therefore does not allow for highlighting any difference between the prefecture and the county level. For Dongguan and Zhongshan, which do not have any territorial division at the county level, we have also utilized official sources at the prefecture level.

2.2.2 An overview of the industrial sector in Guangdong province

Having clarified some of the concepts used in official Chinese statistics and briefly introducing the data-gathering methodology, we can now move on to the analysis of the industrial sector in Guangdong province.

The average growth rate of industrial output in the 1980s and in the 1990s was 24 per cent, but it has slightly diminished in more recent years (2000–2009) to 17.6 per cent, mainly because of the sudden fall registered in 2009 due to the global crisis. In fact, if we exclude 2009, the average growth rate for the period 2000–2008 has been equal to 19.3 per cent, while in 2009 the increase has been only 6.4 per cent. In 2010, the provincial industrial system already seemed to be out of the crisis, with the industrial output boosting by an impressive 23.2 per cent (SBGP, GSYs, various years).

Guangdong can be considered the 'manufacturing centre' of the PRC, with a particular vocation for the production of electronic devices. The province, in fact, in this sector in 2008 accounted for more than 35 per cent of the whole nation (Table 2.3).

Furthermore, also particularly high are the percentages of measuring instruments (26.59 per cent), plastic products (22 per cent) and electrical devices (21 per cent) manufactured by firms located in the province.

As regards the evolution over time of the sectoral composition of the Guangdong manufacturing sector, in 2000, the light industry prevailed, since it represented more than half the total industrial production of the province (52.94 per cent of the gross output value of ADS firms; SBGP, 2001). A relevant role for the development of the province, however, was also played by heavy industry, including metal processing, tool machinery manufacturing, ship building and mineral extraction. In recent years, Guangdong has instead been concentrating its efforts in shifting towards higher value-added productions, characterized by a greater technology content. As we will see in more detail in Chapter 7, the promotion of high-tech sectors is among the current priorities of the provincial government. Data seem to show signs of effectiveness in reaching the identified targets. In particular, in 2010, light industries accounted for 38.3 per cent of the total value of ADS industrial production, while heavy industries (also including the high-tech sectors) had reached a remarkable 61.7 per cent (SBGP, 2011).

Moving then to consider specific sectors, in 2010, the manufacturing of communication equipment, computer and electronic devices alone represented 22.4 per cent of the total value of industrial output and 18.7 per cent of value added, followed by the production of electrical machinery and equipment (10.9 per cent of the output and 10.4 per cent of ADS firms value added). Among traditional industries, textiles and garment production represented 5.8 per cent of the total, the production of transport equipment accounted for 6 per cent and metal products for 4.8 per cent of the total value of industrial production of ADS firms (SBGP, 2011).

More information on the sectoral specialization of the province and on the effects of the 2008 international economic crisis on the industrial structure of the

Table 2.4 Variations in industrial output, 2007–2009

	% Variance (2007–2008)	*% Variance (2008–2009)*
Guangdong industrial output	18.6	2
Top 50 industrial output	13.2	2.3
Output of Guangdong electronic sector	14.9	2.2
Output of top 50 electronic firms	12.2	19.7
Output of remaining top 50 firms	13.7	−6.35

Source: Authors' elaboration on SBGP data, various years.

Table 2.5 Variations in industrial output of Guangdong top 50 firms according to the nationality of funding capital, 2007–2009

	% Variance (2007–2008)	*% Variance (2008–2009)*
Chinese-owned top 50 firms	13.3	2.1
Foreign-owned top 50 firms	12.8	2.8
Top 50 Chinese-owned electronic firms	4.4	45.6
Top 50 foreign-owned electronic firms	21.7	−7.5

Source: Authors' elaboration on SBGP data, various years.

province can come from the analysis of data on the top 50 industrial enterprises of Guangdong.

Even if they only represent 0.009 per cent of Guangdong firms, they account for about 24 per cent of the provincial industrial output (2009 data). About 50 per cent of them operate in the Information Technology (IT) and electronics sector and almost 60 per cent are funded with Chinese capital.

The analysis of their output variations in the period 2007–2009 emphasizes some interesting trends. According to the data shown in Table 2.4, the total industrial output of the province grew by only 2 per cent in 2009 (against an increase of more than 18 per cent in the previous year). Very similar variations can be highlighted for the top 50 firms, which overall show a slower growth in 2008 (13.2 per cent) and a similar reaction to the crisis (+2.3 per cent in 2009).

Breaking down the 2.3 per cent increase in the output of the top 50 firms according to sectors, it is possible to note that, while those top 50 firms operating in the electronic field have registered a 19.7 per cent rise in their output in 2009, the remaining leading firms have instead faced a cutback of 6.35 per cent.

Other interesting information can be derived by deepening the analysis of the top 50 firms' output variations according to the nationality of the funding (Table 2.5).

Apparently, the Chinese top 50 firms have registered a very similar trend to that of non-Chinese top 50 (about 13 per cent in 2008 against 2 per cent in 2009), both in line with the trend of the overall provincial industrial output. Again, it is worth going into more detail on the main Guangdong industrial sector, that is, IT and electronics. Data show that while the top 50 non-Chinese electronic firms have suffered from a reduction in their output by 7.5 per cent in 2009, the top 50 Chinese electronic firms have increased by an astonishing 45.6 per cent.

To summarize, given the weight of the top 50 firms on the industrial output of the province and also considering that the electronic top 50 firms accounted for 40.5 per cent of the provincial output for the sector in 2009, we can generalize the results, asserting that the firms appearing to have faced the international crisis better are the Chinese top firms operating in the electronics sector. This could be partly explained by the recent change in the priorities of the government, moving from a strong orientation towards foreign direct investments (FDIs) to a heavy support of national companies (see also Section 4.5). Second, the success of Chinese electronic firms could also be explained by a preferential access to the growing domestic market, which has been less hit by the international crisis.

2.3 Firms' ownership

In China, it is possible to identify several typologies of firms according to their ownership. In particular, the NBS defines the following:

1 State-owned and State-controlled Enterprises refer to state-owned enterprises plus state-controlled enterprises. State-owned enterprises (originally known as state-run industrial enterprises or industrial enterprises owned by the whole people) are non-corporate economic entities registered in accordance with the Regulations of the People's Republic of China on the Management of Registration of Corporate Enterprises, where all assets are owned by the state. Included in this category are state-owned enterprises, state-funded corporations and state-owned joint-operation enterprises. Joint state-private industries and private industries, which existed before 1957, were later transformed into state-run industries and then into state-owned industries in 1992. Where no separate statistics on these enterprises are listed, they are included in state-owned enterprises. State-controlled enterprises are a subcategory of enterprises with mixed ownership, referring to enterprises where the percentage of state assets (or shares by the state) is larger than any other single share holder of the same enterprise. This subcategory illustrates the control of the state over a particular industry.
2 Collective-owned Enterprises refer to economic entities registered in accordance with the Regulations of the People's Republic of China on the Management of Registration of Corporate Enterprises, where assets are owned by collectives. Collective enterprises constitute an integral part of the socialist economy with public ownership. They include urban and rural enterprises with collective investment, and some enterprises registered in

industrial and commercial administration agencies as collective units where funds are pulled together by individuals who voluntarily give up their right of ownership.

3 Share-holding Corporations Ltd. refer to economic units registered in accordance with the Regulations of the People's Republic of China on the Management of Registration of Corporate Enterprises, with total registered capitals divided into equal shares and raised through issuing stocks. Each investor bears limited liability to the corporation depending on the holding of shares, and the corporation bears liability to its debt to the maximum of its total assets.

4 Enterprises with Funds from Hong Kong, Macao and Taiwan refer to all industrial enterprises registered as the joint-venture, cooperative, sole (exclusive) investment industrial enterprises and limited liability corporations with funds from Hong Kong, Macao and Taiwan.

5 Foreign-funded Enterprises refer to all industrial enterprises registered as the joint-venture, cooperative, sole (exclusive) investment industrial enterprises and limited liability corporations with foreign funds.

- Share-holding Corporations Ltd. with Foreign Investment refer to share-holding corporations Ltd. established with the approval of the Ministry of Foreign Trade and Economic Cooperation (formerly Ministry of Foreign Trade and Economic Relations) in line with relevant state regulations, where the share of investment from foreign investors exceeds 25% of the total registered capital of the corporation.
- Share-holding Corporations Ltd. with Investment from Hong Kong, Macao and Taiwan refer to share-holding corporations Ltd. established with the approval of the Ministry of Foreign Trade and Economic Cooperation (formerly Ministry of Foreign Trade and Economic Relations) in line with relevant state regulations, where the share of investment from Hong Kong, Macao or Taiwan businessmen exceeds 25% of the total registered capital of the corporation.
- Joint-venture Enterprises with Foreign Investment refer to enterprises jointly established by foreign enterprises or foreigners with enterprises in the mainland of China in accordance with the Law of the People's Republic of China on Sino-foreign Joint-Venture Enterprises and other relevant laws, where the share of investment, profits and risks is stipulated in the contract.

6 Enterprises categorized as 'Others' in this Yearbook refer to other types of industrial enterprises (units) except state-owned enterprises, collective-owned enterprises and individual operation, including joint-operation enterprises, private enterprises, share-holding companies, limited liability corporations, foreign-funded enterprises (Sino-foreign joint ventures, Sino-foreign co-operative enterprises and enterprises with sole foreign investment), enterprises with investment from Hong Kong, Macao and Taiwan (joint ventures

> with enterprises in the mainland, cooperative enterprises with enterprises in the mainland and enterprises with sole investment from Hong Kong, Macao and Taiwan) and other enterprises.
>
> (SBGP, 2011: 361–362)

On the basis of the above-mentioned definitions, the private sector can be identified as the sum of the following four categories:

1 share-holding co-operative industry;
2 share-holding industry;
3 foreign-funded industry;
4 industry with funds from Hong Kong, Macao and Taiwan.

Some could argue that the foreign-funded category also includes joint ventures (JVs) with Chinese state-owned enterprises (SOEs) that could even hold the majority of capital (up to 75 per cent). As a consequence, they should be more properly included in the public sector category (Qian and Stiglitz, 1996). We have, however, chosen to include them in the private sector for two main reasons. First, the weight of SOEs in the Chinese economy is decreasing, in particular in the JVs group. In fact, while in the first few years immediately after the opening up of Chinese boundaries to foreign capital, it was almost impossible for a foreign firm to establish a JV in China [apart from special economic zones (SEZs)] without a heavy presence of publicly owned firms (and with the requirement of Chinese management), these limitations have been progressively eliminated by more recent regulations (see also Section 4.4). Second, the co-participation of SOEs in foreign-funded JVs forces them to play in an open context, and therefore to manage the JVs according to private market principles (Qian and Stiglitz, 1996).

In 2000, the private sector as defined above represented about 53.8 per cent of the total number of ADS firms and 73.4 per cent of the gross industrial output of Guangdong province. These percentages have augmented over time, increasing to 83.5 per cent and 88.9 per cent, respectively, in 2010 (Table 2.5).

The development of the province has, however, been driven, especially in its first phases, by foreign-funded firms, which still have a relevant weight in the provincial industrial sector. In 2010, in total (including Hong Kong and Taiwan) they accounted for 35.4 per cent of the total number of industrial ADS firms of the province and produced 53 per cent of the industrial output. Data therefore confirm that foreign-funded firms have been, and still are, among the main forces driving the industrial development of Guangdong, even if their relative weight seems to be declining over time (in 2000, they accounted for about 43 per cent of total firms and 58 per cent of the industrial output). However, it is the 'Hong Kong, Macao and Taiwan – funded industry' that plays the most crucial role, accounting alone for about 25 per cent of the total number and total output of industrial ADS firms in 2010 (Table 2.6).

As far as the publicly owned sector is concerned, it is clear that the government has continued to play an important role in the last decade, contributing to the

Table 2.6 Number of industrial enterprises and output value by ownership in Guangdong province (ADS firms), various years

	2000	*2005*	*2008*	*2009*	*2010*
Total number of industrial enterprises (unit)	19,695	35,157	52,603	52,217	53,418
State-owned industry	2,383	1,033	631	588	567
Collective-owned industry	4,158	1,272	1,024	878	872
Share-holding co-operative industry	299	331	252	241	223
Share-holding industry	1,875	12,753	23,497	24,130	25,490
Foreign-funded industry	1,682	4,416	6,117	5,910	5,790
Industry with funds from Hong Kong, Macao and Taiwan	6,731	11,292	14,141	13,277	13,151
Others	2,567	4,060	6,941	7,193	7,325
Gross industrial output value (100 million RMB)	12,480.9	35,942.7	65,424.6	68,275.8	85,824.6
State-owned industry	1,450.9	2,068.8	2,877.3	3,654.9	4,595.8
Collective-owned industry	1,202.5	468.6	566.0	635.4	767.0
Share-holding co-operative Industry	106.9	103.7	118.0	168.2	175.7
Share-holding industry	1,780.6	9,256.5	21,385.9	23,728.3	30,626.8
Foreign-funded industry	2,527.1	11,167.5	19,104.8	18,758.9	23,705.9
Industry with funds from Hong Kong, Macao and Taiwan	4,747.3	11,708.0	18,690.8	17,395.5	21,813.3
Others	665.7	1,169.7	2,681.8	3,394.7	4,140.1

Source: Authors' elaboration on SBGP (2011).

Table 2.7 Percentage of FDIs in Guangdong on total China (actually utilized foreign capital), various years

Year	*Incoming FDIs (Guangdong per cent on China)*
2000	30.06
2001	27.67
2002	24.86
2003	29.11
2004	15.63
2005	19.38
2006	23.02
2007	22.91
2008	20.74
2009	21.70

Source: Authors' elaboration on SBGP and NBS data (various years).

industrial development of Guangdong province. However, the weight of government owned and controlled firms (including the categories defined by the NBS as 'state-owned and state-controlled industry' and 'collective-owned industry') has been shrinking noticeably over time, decreasing from 33.2 per cent of the total number of ADS firms in 2000 to 2.7 per cent in 2010 and from 21.3 per cent of the total

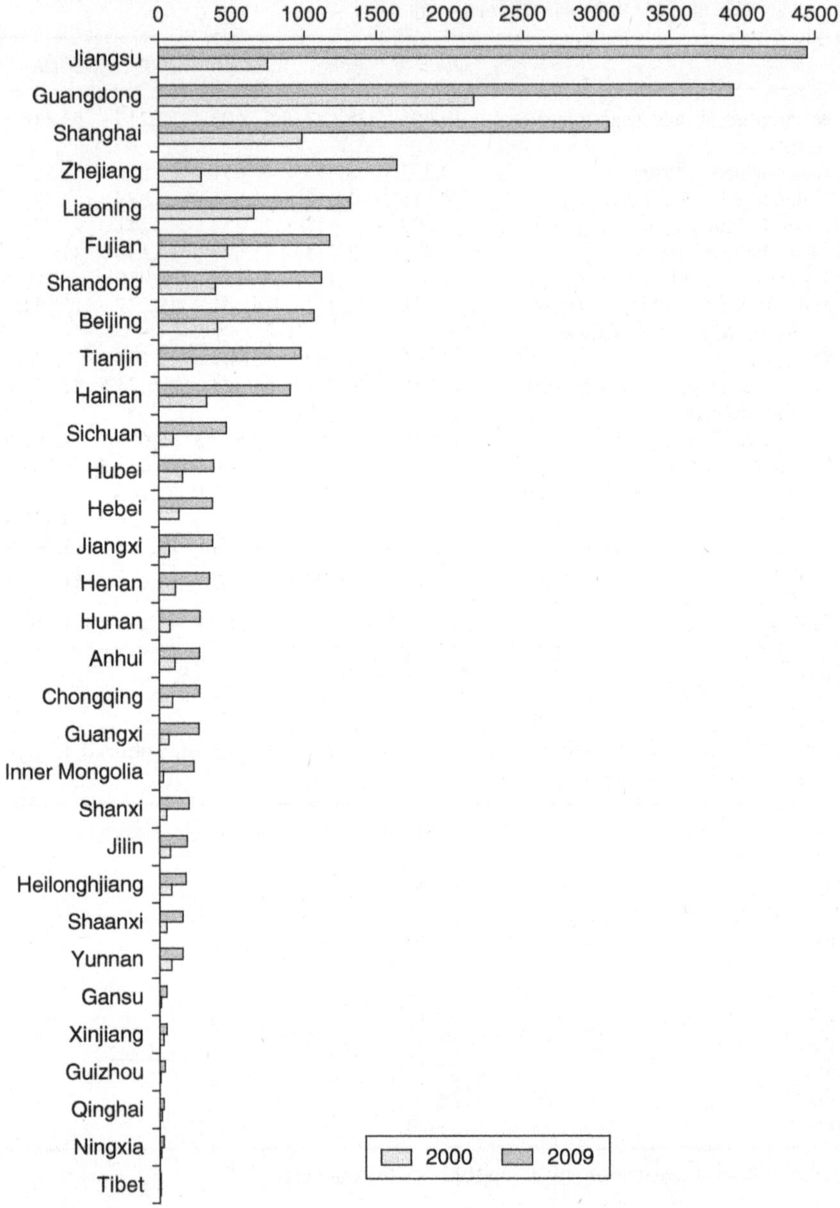

Figure 2.5 Regional distribution of FDIs in China (2000 and 2009, 100 million US$, total investment).

Source: Authors' elaboration on NBS data, China Statistical Yearbook, various years.

industrial output of ADS firms in 2000 to 6.3 per cent in 2010. It is relevant to specify that the sub-category 'state-owned industry' has diminished from 2000 to 2010 in terms of number of firms (– 76 per cent), but the output produced has boosted in the same period by an outstanding 216.8 per cent. This could be read as a signal of a wider restructuring process of the state-owned and state-controlled sector that seems to have led to a gradual concentration of production in a smaller number of possibly more efficient units (Hassard *et al.*, 2010; Zhu *et al.*, 2011).

2.4 An outward-oriented province

2.4.1 Foreign direct investments

Guangdong is among the Chinese provinces attracting the highest amount of FDIs: 21.70 per cent of the whole of China in 2009 (Table 2.7).

Figure 2.5 shows the relevant weight of the southern province of China in the country: in 2009, FDIs worth 19,535 million US$ flew into Guangdong, with China totalling 90,033 million US$ of FDIs. The relative weight of Guangdong, which is still very high at the national level, is, however, decreasing when compared to the beginning of the decade: in 1990, Guangdong represented 42.84 per cent of the total incoming FDIs. This signals the fact that the development process in China for the last 20 years has been spreading over a growing number of provinces (SBGP, 2005). Comparing the year 2000 data on total investment of foreign-funded firms with the 2009 figures, it can be noted that in less than a decade not only has the Jiangsu province been able to steal Guangdong's primacy, with FDIs growing by 493 per cent (against an increase for the same period for Guangdong of 'only' 82 per cent), but Guangdong is actually the Chinese province where FDIs have grown less. On one side, the reduction in the percentage of FDIs attracted by the Guangdong province can be read as a consequence of the increasing competition of the Yangtze River Delta (YRD) (Jiangsu is its leading province, surpassing Guangdong in 2004 for the first time in the attraction of FDIs). On the other, this declining trend is also due to the relatively recent orientation of the government towards an autonomous, domestic and better balanced industrialization of the country, in particular after the international crisis of 2008–2009 that has especially hit the export-oriented areas (see Section 4.5).

Despite this decreasing trend, the total amount of invested capital has constantly risen over time (21.7 million US$ in 2000, 28.9 million US$ in 2005 and 42.1 million US$ in 2010), with its sectoral distribution remaining, however, virtually the same, except for a growth in the weight of the manufacturing sector, increasing from 39 per cent of the total foreign invested capital in 2000 to about 59 per cent in 2010 (Table 2.8).

Guangdong, and especially the PRD, has for years represented an ideal destination for investors of some newly industrialized countries in Asia. As we will see in more detail in Chapter 4, this is also the consequence of a wider and earlier opening up of the Guangdong economy in comparison to other Chinese provinces.

Table 2.8 Total investment of foreign companies in Guangdong by sector, 2000 and 2010

	2010 Value (100 million US$)	*% Distribution (2010)*	*% Distribution (2000)*
Agriculture	35.25	0.84	1.04
Manufacturing sector	2,465.69	58.53	38.91
Mining	5.12	0.12	0.25
Production and supply of electric power, gas and water	282.57	6.71	6.48
Construction	95.64	2.27	2.56
Services			
Transportations and telecommunications	209.26	4.97	5.03
Information and Communication Technologies (ICT)	70.61	1.68	
Wholesale and retail trade	126.30	3.00	1.92
Hotels and catering	62.87	1.49	
Finance	21.55	0.51	0.09
Real estate	548.06	13.01	13.95
Leasing and business services	159.01	3.77	
Scientific research	61.47	1.46	
Water management, environment and public services	17.19	0.41	
Services to households and other services	15.78	0.37	0.07
Education	0.58	0.01	3.60
Health, social security and social welfare	3.15	0.07	0.24
Culture, sport and recreation	25.70	0.61	0.37
Other	6.81	0.16	0.59
Total	4,212.60	100	100

Source: Authors' elaboration on SBGP (2001, 2011).

Table 2.9 International trade (import–export, billion US$) – Guangdong, various years

Year	*Value*			*Growth rate*		
	Total import–export	*Export*	*Import*	*Total import–export*	*Export*	*Import*
1990	41.9	22.2	19.7	17.8	22.7	12.7
1992	65.8	33.4	32.3	25.2	23.6	26.9
1994	96.7	50.2	46. 5	23.4	34.3	13.4
1996	110.0	59.4	50.6	5.8	4.9	6.8
1998	129.8	75.6	54.2	– 0.2	1.4	– 2.5
2001	176.5	95.4	81.1	3.8	3.8	3.7
2002	221.1	118.5	102.6	25.3	24.1	26.6
2003	283.5	152.9	130.7	28.2	29.0	27.3
2004	357.1	191.6	165.6	26.0	25.3	26.7
2005	428.0	238.2	189.8	20.0	24.3	14.6
2006	527.2	302.0	225.3	23.2	26.8	18.7
2007	634.0	369.2	264.8	20.3	22.3	17.6
2008	683.5	404.2	279.3	7.8	9.5	5.5
2009	611.1	359.0	252.2	– 10.6	– 11.2	– 9.7
2010	784.9	453.2	331.7	28.4	26.2	31.5
Average annual growth rate 1990–2010				16.4	17.2	15.6

Source: Authors' elaboration on SBGP (2011).

In this process, investors from Hong Kong, Macao and Taiwan have benefited from relevant advantages: first, the geographic proximity and second, a shared language and a similar cultural basis (Shen *et al.*, 2000). Hong Kong is the most important source of FDIs, and between 1979 and 2010, Hong Kong firms have signed 111,515 investment contracts in Guangdong, representing 72.1 per cent of the total, with a total amount of utilized capital of 258,677.75 million US$ in 2010 (65.6 per cent of Guangdong's total) (SBGP, 2011). Hong Kong investments have mainly been directed towards the following manufacturing sectors: electronics, toys, clothes, footwear, plastic and food. Further investments have flowed towards trade, the construction industry and the development of infrastructures.

The remaining FDIs of Guangdong province come from the Virgin Islands (10.3 per cent of total utilized foreign capital in 2010), Taiwan (2.8 per cent), United States (2.6 per cent) and Macao (2.6 per cent) (SBGP, 2011).

2.4.2 Foreign trade

Guangdong accounts for the main import and export quota among the Chinese provinces, representing about 28 per cent of the total Chinese foreign trade in 2009. Despite a quite irregular trend of exports (Table 2.9), their average annual growth rate between 1990 and 2010 amounted to 16.4 per cent.

Table 2.10 Main import–export markets for Guangdong (%), 2000 and 2010

	Exports		*Imports*	
	2000	*2010*	*2000*	*2010*
Asia	53.5	55.3	77.1	78.7
Hong Kong and Macao	34.9	34.0	6.8	1.8
Japan	8.4	4.8	17.9	14.0
ASEAN	4.6	6.9	11.7	14.9
Taiwan	1.9	1.3	19.3	13.2
Africa	1.1	2.7	1.0	1.9
Europe	14.9	16.4	10.8	9.1
European Union	13.7	14.7	9.0	7.9
Latin America	2.3	4.5	1.1	2.9
North America	26.9	19.7	7.7	5.1
United States	25.7	18.5	6.8	4.4
Oceania and others	1.4	1.5	2.3	2.4

Source: Authors' elaboration on SBGP (2001, 2011).

This trend sharply reversed in 2009 as a consequence of the world economic crisis, with a sudden fall of 11.2 per cent in exports and 9.7 per cent in imports. However, the recovery seems to have been even more sudden: in 2010, exports registered an annual increase of 26.2 per cent and imports of 31.5 per cent.

The wide majority of Guangdong exports in 2010 were made of electric and electronic devices (56.7 per cent), followed at a great distance by textiles (8 per cent) and metal products (4.2 per cent) (SBGP, 2011). Most Guangdong exports are directed to Asian markets, but other advanced countries also account for interesting rates (Table 2.10).

The picture is rather stable over time, even if, since 2000, there has been a reduction in the relative weight of Hong Kong and Macao, Japan and Taiwan as regards imports, counterbalanced by an increased dependence from the Association of Southeast Asian Nations (ASEAN) countries. Also, the reduced importance of the American markets for both imports and for exports has to be underscored. In ten years, the weight of the United States on total imports has lost more than two percentage points, and more than seven on total exports.

2.5 The Pearl River Delta

2.5.1 The definition

The rapid development of Guangdong's manufacturing sector has been favoured by foreign investment, especially that flowing into the PRD region. The so-called Pearl River Delta Economic Zone (PRD-EZ) is part of the Guangdong province and it includes the prefectures of Guangzhou, Shenzhen, Zhuhai, Foshan, Jiangmen, Dongguan and Zhongshan, part of Huizhou (the urban district

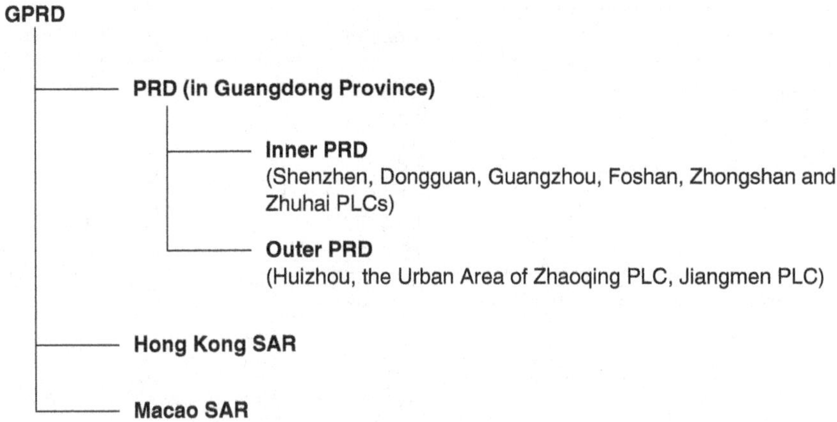

Figure 2.6 Administrative structure of GPRD.

Source: OECD (2010).

of Huizhou, Huiyang County, Huidong County and Boluo County) and part of Zhaoqing (the urban district of Zhaoqing, Gaoyao and Sihui). This definition of the PRD-EZ was formulated by Guangdong policy makers in 1984 and it is still the official definition used by the China NBS (also applied by Enright *et al.*, 2005). However, in several documents and statistics the entire prefectures of Zhaoqing and Huizhou are included in the PRD definition, which is also the one adopted for the data presented in this section.

Another definition is 'Greater PRD' (GPRD) (Figure 2.6), which also includes the Hong Kong SAR and Macao SAR (Barbieri *et al.*, 2009b).

Finally, some authors refer to the Pan Pearl River Delta (PPRD), 'broadly defined as that part of South China comprising the Pearl River Basin, which is drained by the river in parts of Guangdong, Guangxi, Yunnan and Guizhou, and other provinces south of the Yangzi River' (Yeung, 2005: 75; see also Yeung and Jianfa, 2008).

2.5.2 PRD development

Guangdong development is uneven across the territory: the PRD is by far the most advanced area in the province. While representing only 23.8 per cent of the territory, in 2009 it hosted about half of the Guangdong population and it accounted for more than 80 per cent of provincial GDP (9.4 of China's total) and for a remarkable 95.7 per cent of Guangdong's imports and exports (corresponding to 26.5 per cent of the national total) (Table 2.11).

In 2007, the real GDP of the PRD grew by an average of 7.35 per cent, in line with the provincial data (7.3 per cent).

Table 2.11 PRD, comparison with Guangdong and China (2009)

	Guangdong (%)	*China (%)*
Total land area	23.8	0.4
Population	49.7	3.6
GDP	81.4	9.4
Total value of import–export	95.7	26.5
Export	95.2	28.4
Import	96.4	24.1
FDI	86.3	19.4

Source: Authors' elaboration on NBS (2010) and SBGP (2010).

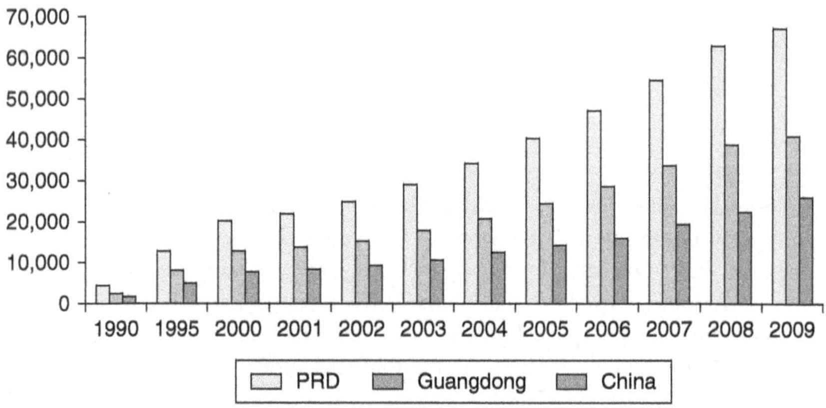

Figure 2.7 Per capita GDP in PRD, Guangdong and China (RMB), various years.

Source: Authors' elaboration on NBS (2010) and SBGP (2010).

To confirm the concentration of wealth in this region, the average per capita income of the PRD in 2009 was about 67,000 RMB (approximately 9,417 US$) – much higher than the 41,166 RMB (about 5,786 US$) of Guangdong province and than the national one of 25,575 RMB (around 3,595 US$). Figure 2.7 shows how the gap between the PRD and the whole province (as well as the entire nation) has been constantly growing over time in terms of per capita GDP.

Data included in Table 2.12 indicate that, on average, per capita GDP is much higher in PRD prefectures (with the highest figure – Shenzhen – being more than 32 times higher than the lowest value – Meizhou). PRD prefectures in 2009 also accounted for the highest density of enterprises, once again with Shenzhen on the top of the ranking with more than 4 firms per square kilometre, against a minimum value of only 0.03 firms per square kilometre registered by some non-PRD prefectures (Shaoguan, Heyuan and Meizhou).

Table 2.12 Some data at prefecture level

Prefecture	*PRD*	*Population (2009)*	*Firms' density (no. of ADS firms per km^2) 2009*	*2007 GDP (billion RMB)*	*2009 GDP (billion RMB)*	*Per capita GDP (RMB) 2009*
Shenzhen	Yes	2,459,600	4.31	680.2	820.1	333,428.2
Dongguan	Yes	1,787,300	2.35	316.0	376.4	210,597.0
Foshan	Yes	3,676,300	2.03	366.0	482.1	131,137.3
Guangzhou	Yes	7,946,200	0.96	714.0	913.8	114,998.4
Zhuhai	Yes	1,026,500	0.84	89.5	103.9	101,217.7
Zhongshan	Yes	1,478,600	2.80	126.8	156.6	105,911.0
Huizhou	Yes	3,243,600	0.17	111.8	141.5	43,624.4
Jiangmen	Yes	3,915,200	0.34	110.0	134.1	34,251.1
Qingyuan	No	4,088,200	0.04	60.2	86.2	21,085.1
Zhaoqing	Yes	4,136,900	0.07	62.0	86.2	20,836.9
Shantou	No	5,107,300	1.07	82.9	103.6	20,284.7
Yangjiang	No	2,756,700	0.08	40.5	52.7	19,117.1
Chaozhou	No	2,578,900	0.37	37.3	48.0	18,612.6
Shaoguan	No	3,255,400	0.03	48.1	57.9	17,785.8
Maoming	No	7,353,100	0.07	99.7	123.1	16,741.2
Zhanjiang	No	7,631,400	0.06	92.4	115. 7	15,161.0
Jieyang	No	6,491,100	0.35	58.6	81.6	12,571.1
Yunfu	No	2,758,000	0.06	27.6	34.5	12,509.1
Heyuan	No	3,489,800	0.03	33.0	40.6	11,633.9
Shanwei	No	3,406,100	0.07	28.9	39.0	11,450.0
Meizhou	No	5,073,600	0.03	41.2	51.9	10,229.4

Source: Authors' elaboration on SBGP (2010) data.

Table 2.13 Selected economic indicators of the main PRD cities (2009)

City	*Per capita GDP (RMB)*	*GDP growth rate (%)*	*Industrial output (100 million RMB, current prices)*	*Exports (100 million US$)*
Guangzhou	94,173	11.5	10,298	374
Shenzhen	92,772	10.7	15,416	1,620
Foshan	80,686	13.5	11,780	246
Zhuhai	69,890	6.6	2,405	178
Zhongshan	62,304	10.2	4,057	177
Dongguan	56,601	5.3	5,935	552
Huizhou	49,096	14.3	2,508	171
Jiangmen	48,837	10.4	1,819	79
Zhaoqing	47,453	11.9	522	20

Source: Authors' elaboration on SBGP (2010).

Cities with the highest levels of industrial production are located in the PRD area and include Guangzhou, Shenzhen, Foshan, Dongguan, Zhongshan, Huizhou, Zhuhai and Jiangmen. Many of them record outstanding numbers in terms of per capita GDP, among these are Guangzhou (94,173 RMB, i.e. 13,236 US$), Shenzhen (92,772 RMB, about 13,039 US$), Foshan (80,686 RMB, roughly equal to 11,340 US$) and Zhuhai (69,890 RMB, corresponding approximately to 9,823 US$) (see Table 2.13).

PRD is also the preferred part of the province for foreign investors. In 2010, FDIs (in terms of actually utilized capital) amounted to 90.5 per cent of the total, mainly concentrated in Shenzhen (21.2 per cent), Guangzhou (19.6 per cent), Dongguan (13.5 per cent) and Foshan (9.7 per cent of the total provincial FDIs) (SBGP, 2011).

2.5.3 The relation between PRD and Hong Kong

One of the strategic factors allowing for the development of the PRD region has undoubtedly been its relation with Hong Kong (Enright *et al.*, 2005; Hirsch and Rubini, 2006). As will be explained in more detail in Chapter 4, the Chinese reform programme has chosen the PRD area as initial target also because of its proximity to the former British protectorate. The idea was to use Hong Kong as a bridge connecting China to the external world; southern China would have been the laboratory in which to study the capitalistic approach of Hong Kong and the rest of China would have consequentially absorbed it. In fact, even if this has never been officially confirmed, the Guangdong area, since 1979, has welcomed a growing number of scholars and officials arriving from all over China to study the opening-up process (Chung *et al.*, 2001).

The relationship with Hong Kong has, however, been planned to be mutually beneficial and is effectively represented by the popular slogan 'front shop, back factory': the Hong Kong 'shop' had management skills, money and consolidated international relations, while the PRD 'factory' could count on low-cost land and labour coming from inland China (for more information on migrant workers in Guangdong, see Chapter 5) (Yeung, 2010). After the opening up of the Guangdong economy, Hong Kong firms have increasingly moved their plants to the province (and to PRD in particular), increasing their dimensions. At the same time, Hong Kong has raised and strengthened the role of its service sector (Shari and Huang, 2008).

The relation between the two areas has been further reinforced by the Closer Economic Partnership Agreement (CEPA), launched in 2003 by the provincial government and aimed at accelerating the integration between the two territories in terms of free trade, services and investment flows (Yeung, 2010).

The relations between Hong Kong and the PRD do not have only an economic nature. Many Hong Kong residents come from families rooted in Guangdong and this social linkage have caused over the years relevant population flows in both directions. As soon as China opened up to foreign contacts, these cultural relations were coupled with business relations, Hong Kong becoming the global platform for those having economic interests in Guangdong. For this reason, some commentators refer to the GPRD: the PRD cannot work without the logistical support of Hong Kong, while the latter exists and flourishes, thanks also to its proximity to Mainland China. The GPRD area outstrips, in terms of GDP, exports and incoming FDIs, the fiercest national competitors such as the YRD and the Bohai Rim (Barbieri *et al.*, 2009a, 2009b; Hirsch and Rubini, 2006).

2.5.4 Emerging challenges

In these last few years, the PRD has been facing double competition:

1 New areas, in terms of capacity to attract FDIs and innovative multinationals, are emerging in China, reducing the primacy of the PRD. In particular, the most fierce competitor in this sense is the YRD.
2 Emerging countries (such as India and Vietnam) and inland Chinese provinces (such as, among others, Hunan and Guangxi) have surpassed the PRD in terms of low labour costs, which for years was one of the main competitive advantages of the area.

The YRD includes Shanghai and the provinces of Zhejiang and Jiangsu.[5] Its economic development started relatively late (in 1984), when the cities of Shanghai, Ningbo and Wenzhou were declared open to foreign investment. Since then, its growth has been rapid and continuous (Table 2.14). The advantages of YRD, apart from the presence of Shanghai, are the availability of a qualified labour force, a widespread entrepreneurial spirit and a coordinated development of the different cities of the region, thanks to carefully planned supportive policies (Hirsch and Rubini, 2006).

Table 2.14 FDIs and exports (% of China total) in PRD and YRD (2000–2005)

	PRD		*YRD*	
	FDIs	*Exports*	*FDIs*	*Exports*
2000	36.1	43.0	27.5	28.7
2001	33.8	41.5	28.6	30.2
2002	28.8	42.2	33.3	31.2
2003	36.6	40.4	50.6	34.2
2005 (first half)	19.0	28.0	51.0	37.0

Source: Chen (2007).

The two deltas together account for the vast majority of foreign capital and exports. This is because both areas have based their development on their outward orientation. However, in 2002 YRD surpassed PRD in terms of FDI attraction and in 2005 in terms of export capacity (Table 2.13). The YRD seems to show an increased orientation towards advanced manufacturing technologies and high-tech productions, which allow higher value added (Chen, 2007; Hirsch and Rubini, 2006). This undoubtedly represents a concrete threat for the PRD's future development that the government is trying to face with the measures presented in the following section.

With regards to the second type of new PRD competitors, even if a low labour cost is still a key factor of Guangdong province's advantage, there are new areas in inland China (and abroad) that can offer even lower labour costs. This is due to the fact that in China the minimum wage is defined by law by each local administration. After having considered the different life standards in the districts, the Central Government has in fact allowed the provincial governments to define the minimum wage according to their own situations.[6] This decision, coupled with the increasing focus on the attraction of foreign investment, has caused a fierce competition among local governments, with a consequent push towards the reduction of minimum wages.

If, on one side, the use of such a low-cost labour force has represented – and still represents – a great potential for economic development, on the other, it is possible only at the expense of deficiencies in social welfare protection, exploitation, poor labour conditions and violation of human rights, especially of migrant workers (analysed in more detail in Chapter 5).

However, the recent trend emerging in the province, and in particular in the PRD area, seems to be different. According to several Chinese and non-Chinese sources, in fact, the area seems to be facing a growing problem of an insufficient workforce.[7] This could be explained by the coexistence of different phenomena: the growing need and insufficient offers for qualified workers; the reduced presence of migrant workers that have to face excessively bad working conditions and excessively low salaries; their growing requests in terms of safe working conditions, collective bargaining and so on. As a consequence, migrant workers have become increasingly selective and more mobile on the national territory (Hirsch and Rubini, 2006; Fan, 2008; Matthews and Baum, 2011). According to a study carried out by the Chinese Ministry for Labour and Social Security (MOLSS, 2004), the problem appears particularly serious especially for those firms characterized by the lowest wages and the worst working conditions.

This workforce scarcity, coupled with increasing waves of workers' protests, is therefore causing a steady rise in wages in Guangdong province and in particular in the PRD area. The Guangdong provincial government has in the last few years started a process of minimum wage increases, with the latest adjustment implemented in March 2011. According to it, the minimum monthly wage is set at 1,300 RMB (about 198 US$)[8] for Guangzhou; 1,100 RMB (about 168 US$) for Zhuhai, Foshan, Dongguan and Zhongshan; 950 RMB (145 US$) for Shantou, Huizhou and Jiangmen and 850 (approximately 129 US$) for the remaining prefectures. This new decision increases the minimum salary by about 19 per cent and makes Guangzhou the city with the highest minimum wage in the whole country (CB, 2011).

According to Chan (2010a), China could have reached the so-called 'Lewis turning point', that is, 'the point when the dualistic labour market in a country begins to break down and merge into one' (p. 514). These changes represent new challenges for the future competitive capacity of the PRD. It seems clear that it can no longer be exclusively based on low labour costs, because other areas are emerging as new pools of low-cost workforces and because Guangdong has started to go through a process of wage increases and workers' protection that cannot be reversed. With this trend, the risk for the PRD is to be squashed by this double competition, unable to increase the competitiveness and innovative capacity of its manufacturing base, on one side, and no longer competitive in terms of low cost of inputs on the other.

Investing more on the creation of a sustainable domestic consumption-led economy could be vital: continuing to build on export-oriented production based on low labour costs does not seem to be the best strategy for the future competitiveness of Guangdong and of the whole country (Chan, 2010a). In line with these needs, the provincial government is implementing measures to facilitate the presence of Chinese firms on the domestic market (see Section 4.5.3), while at the same time fostering the technological upgrading of the national industrial system (as illustrated in Section 4.5.2).

2.5.5 The recent policy measures

Given the key role played by the PRD in the development of the whole province, in these last few years it has been at the centre of several governmental programmes (see also Section 4.5). Among these, it is worth mentioning the 'Outline of the plan for the reform and development of the Pearl River Delta (2008–2020)' (otherwise referred to as Outline) and the 'Coordinated plan for cluster development in the Pearl River Delta 2004–2020' of the provincial government (hereinafter, Coordinated Plan) (Greater Pearl River Delta Business Council, 2006b; Li & Fung, 2006; Barbieri *et al.*, 2009a, 2009b).

The Outline confirms the role of the PRD as a pilot area to test specific strategies: 'first try, first implement'. Great importance is given to the increase in the innovative capacity of the region, especially in the high-tech sectors. This should be accomplished by supporting the circulation of knowledge and the technology transfer processes by means of strengthened linkages between firms and universities/research centres and by favouring the participation of local actors in international co-operation projects on innovation. The aim is to pass from the label 'Guangdong made' to the label 'Guangdong designed' (Organization for Economic Co-operation and Development (OECD), 2010; Yeung, 2010) (for an in-depth policy focus on innovation, see Chapter 7). A strengthened relation with Hong Kong and Macao is also foreseen, in order to favour the positioning of the whole area among the most competitive ones in the Asia-Pacific region (Yang, 2009).

The Outline identifies specific targets to be reached by the PRD. Among others (OECD, 2010; Yang, 2009):

- by 2012, per capita GDP equal to 80,000 RMB[9] (about 12,587 US$), with a doubled amount foreseen by 2020;
- by 2012, urbanization of more than 80 per cent of the area (85 per cent by 2020);
- by 2012, the service sector accounting for 53 per cent of the PRD GDP, reaching 60 per cent by 2020;

As regards industry:

- The PRD will focus its manufacturing sector on the following areas: nuclear and wind power facilities and devices, power transmission and distribution facilities, numerically controlled machine tools and ocean engineering equipment.
- By 2020, the advanced manufacturing activities should represent 50 per cent of the total industrial value added and high-tech industries should account for 30 per cent of total industrial value added.
- By 2020, the region is expected to develop ten China-based multinationals with annual sales of 20 billion US$, two or three mega-size auto-makers with output exceeding 100 billion RMB (about 15.7 billion US$) each and to host an extra-large petroleum and chemical industry, with two or three mega refineries and ethylene producers.

In line with the most recent Guangdong priorities (Section 4.5), the Outline also assigns great importance to the improvement of the social and welfare system (by 2012, the pension system should cover 95 per cent of urban workers, 80 per cent of migrants and 60 per cent of rural residents; for the same year, a social security system for all residents is also foreseen) and to environmental preservation (e.g. by 2020 the rate of reusable industrial water should reach 80 per cent) (OECD, 2010; Yeung, 2010).

Also, the Coordinated Plan identifies some main objectives to be reached by the industrial development strategy. Such a strategy has mainly to be based on two pillars:

(a) sectoral support: identification of the sectors to which most of the support should be directed;
(b) geographic support: identification of the ideal localization of specific industrial sectors.

In particular, regarding point (b), within the PRD, three areas are identified: the 'western PRD', including the prefectures of Zhuhai, Zhongshan and Jiangmen; the 'eastern PRD', including Shenzhen, Dongguan and Huizhou and, finally, the so-called 'central' prefectures of Guangzhou, Foshan and Zhaoqing (see also Section 6.3.1).

Since the western PRD still has a good availability of land and human resources, it is considered to be the best area to host traditional labour-intensive industries. However, among the priorities for this area, the Coordinated Plan also assigns the development of medium-high-tech sectors, thanks to the construction of new ways of communication and transportation. In fact, the plan itself aims at developing such new ways in a corridor going from Nansha (Guangzhou) through Zhongshan and Zhuhai to Macao, which will run parallel to the more consolidated corridor of Guangzhou – Shenzhen – Hong Kong. For the eastern areas, such as Shenzhen and Dongguan, the Coordinated Plan asserts that they should maintain their vocation to export and continue to support the development of the already strong manufacturing base built over the years. At the same time, they should also try to promote services linked to manufacturing activity, with particular focus on logistics and transportation (Barbieri *et al.*, 2009a, 2009b; OECD, 2010).[10]

Finally, the central areas are identified as the best ones to become the financial and tertiary hub in support of the whole Guangdong industry. In line with these indications, in these last few years these central areas have been concentrating their efforts on the development of a wide range of industry-related support services related to trade, funding availability and banking, professional consulting, training and so on. This has been done by means of direct support to firms, but also with improvements in telecommunications, tourism and entertainment in general.

An ambitious project aimed at further reinforcing the PRD regards Nansha, an island located 60 kilometre from Guangzhou. The project objective is to use Nansha to transform Guangzhou from a riverside city into a coastal city. During the 1990s, the government tried to drive foreign capital to the island to be used to build new infrastructures. Starting from 2000, the measures were then centred on the attraction and reinforcement of strategic sectors such as the chemical and petrochemical industry and the metallurgic industry.

The city will also become a multi-service centre, especially for high-tech activities, thanks mainly to the construction of the Guangdong–Hong Kong IT industrial park and of a deep-water port for large container ships (ICE, 2011).

As regards the policy measures specifically impacting the PRD, further changes in the area will also be induced by the Double Relocation Policy, which will be illustrated in more detail in Section 4.5.

Of course, PRD development is also affected by more general policies, designed for the whole province, also sketched out in Chapter 4.

3 The geography of industry in Guangdong

3.1 Guangdong territories

A study on the allocation of industry within the Guangdong territory needs first to shed some light on the administrative structure of the province. Article number 30 of the People's Republic of China's (PRC) Constitution (adopted in December 1982) rules the administrative divisions of the nation, identifying three levels.

According to such article:

> The administrative division of the People's Republic of China is as follows:
>
> 1 The country is divided into provinces, autonomous regions and municipalities directly under the Central Government;
> 2 Provinces and autonomous regions are divided into autonomous prefectures, counties, autonomous counties, and cities;
> 3 Counties and autonomous counties are divided into townships, nationality townships, and towns.
>
> Municipalities directly under the Central Government and other large cities are divided into districts and counties. Autonomous prefectures are divided into counties, autonomous counties, and cities.
>
> All autonomous regions, autonomous prefectures and autonomous counties are national autonomous areas.
>
> (NPC, 2004)

However, the enormous changes that have occurred in the PRC in the last few decades have brought about an extremely rapid economic and social evolution, which in many cases has been much faster than the adjustment of the underlying administrative structures. Over time, the vastness of the nation and the wide variety of cultural, geographic and historical backgrounds have led to many exceptions, particular cases and singularities.

While on some terms such as 'province' and 'prefecture' there seems to be a general agreement, the terms 'city-prefecture' and 'city-county' refer to concepts used less often, indicating respectively 'city at prefecture level' and 'city at county level'. The boundaries of such realities are often difficult to understand, in addition because their definition implies the distinction between rural and urban areas, which is in continuous evolution. The county, for example, is originally a typically rural administrative division, but within a county there can be growth of urban centres requiring an administrative recognition and a different regulation that are therefore named 'cities at county level' (for more details see, among others, www.china.org.cn).

The administrative division of the PRC is schematized in Figure 3.1. Each government level sets its own industrial goals according to its own situation and in compliance with the general guidelines set by the higher government levels (Qian and Stiglitz, 1996).

While analyzing the Chinese administrative divisions, in some cases difficulties arise due to the complexity of the Chinese language. Often the translations of Chinese words are different according to the utilized source (institutional, academic or statistical) and translations can sometimes also differ within the same source, in particular within the institutional context. Furthermore, there are ideograms that are used to identify similar but nevertheless different concepts: for example, the ideogram for city (市) is included in the construction of the name of at least four different territorial entities at two different administrative levels (Figure 3.2). For this reason, to talk about *city* in the Western meaning could be misleading and the term has to be put into the right context every time it is used.

Of course, it is not possible in this study to analyze in detail the administrative divisions of the PRC and their origin. Some of them are deeply linked to specific historical or geographic factors and an exhaustive list of the different typologies is not the aim of the present study. We will only clarify the administrative units currently present within Guangdong province.

Even if the Constitution is of course still valid, up until now for Guangdong we have identified four levels for which it is possible to obtain official statistics:

- the province level;
- the prefecture level;
- the county level;
- the municipality level.

Every level then contains different territorial entities. In this chapter, we present an analysis of the geographic distribution of industry at the prefecture level and, when possible, at the county level, referring to the scheme presented in Table 3.1.

Out of the 21 Guangdong prefectures,[1] 19 also have a third administrative level and are further divided into 23 city-counties, 41 counties, 3 autonomous counties and 54 districts. The remaining two prefectures, Dongguan and Zhongshan, have a different structure, since they have no county-level division. The first has 32 administrative units (4 townships and 28 towns) and the second administrates 24 units (5 district offices, 18 towns and 1 development zone)

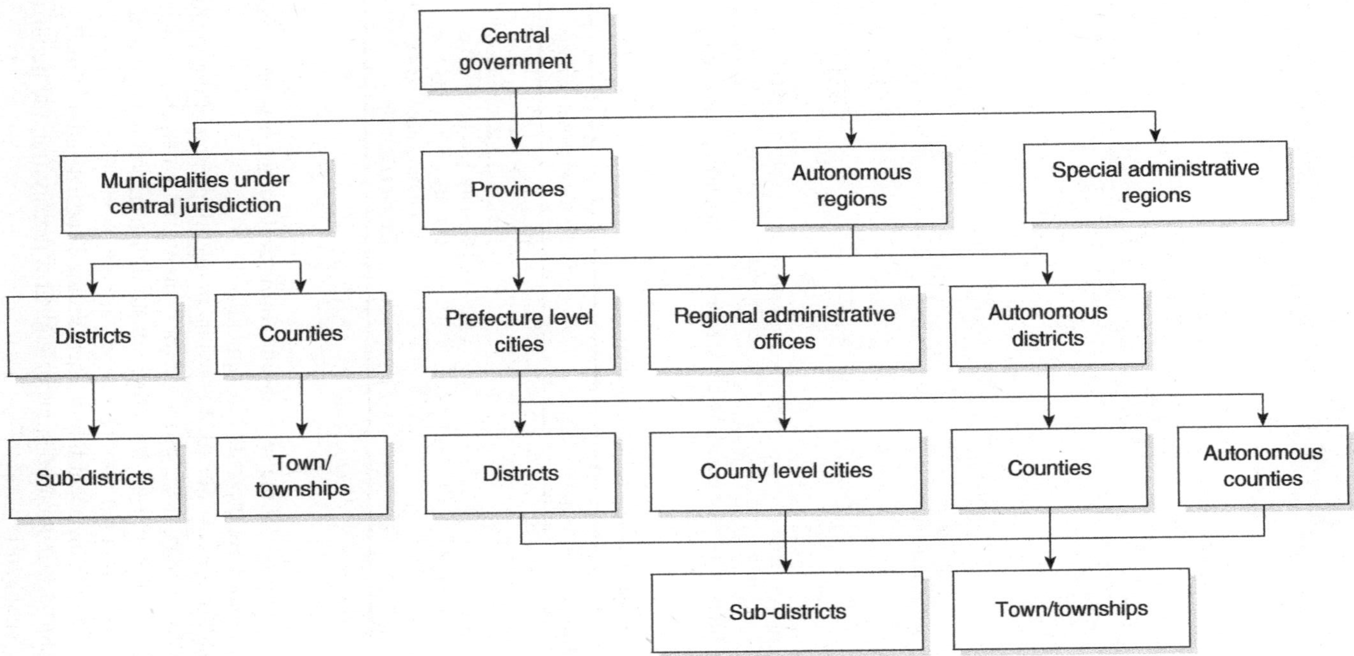

Figure 3.1 Structure of the government in China.

Source: Organization for Economic Co-operation and Development (OECD, 2010).

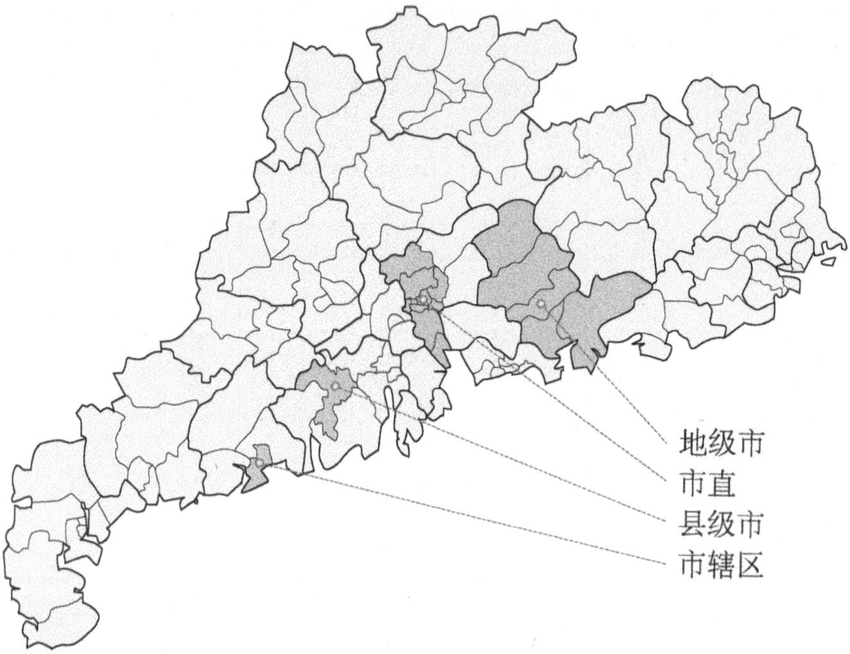

Figure 3.2 Four different uses of the ideogram for 'city' in Guangdong geography.

Source: Authors' elaboration.

Table 3.1 The administrative levels in Guangdong

Administrative level	*Entities in Guangdong*
Province level	Province (省)
Prefecture level	Prefecture-level city (地极市)
County level	County-level city (县级市)
	County (县)
	Autonomous county (自治县)
	District (市辖区)

Source: Authors' elaboration on SBGP (2005) and VV.AA. (2006).

(SBGP, 2007). The details of the second- and third-level administrative divisions of Guangdong province are presented in Appendix 1.

The following sections are aimed at drawing an overall picture of the localization of firms within Guangdong province (only industrial enterprises, no trade and services). We first of all start from the industrial distribution in the provincial territory in terms of output per prefecture and per county, moving on then to consider the allocation of firms according to their sectoral specialization. Finally, we see the geographic distribution of industry and firm density (i.e. the number of units per square kilometre).

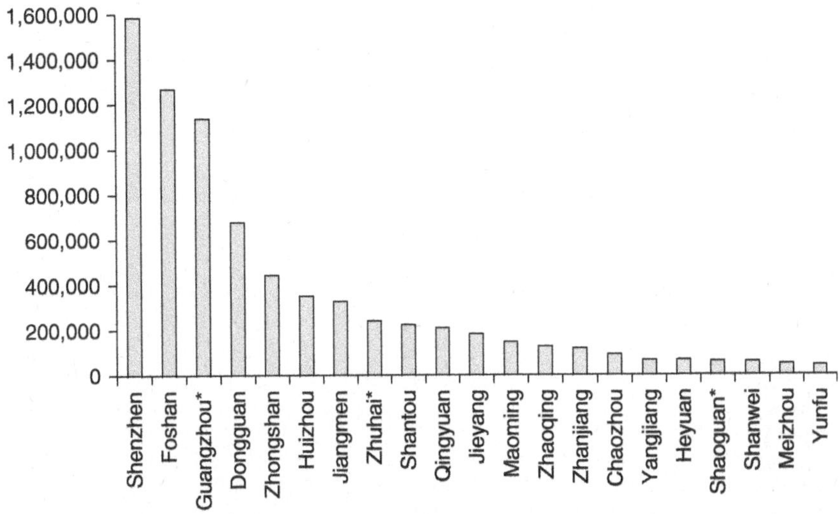

Figure 3.3 Output of industrial firms in Guangdong per prefecture, 2009. *No data available on industrial output of BDS firms.

Source: Authors' elaboration on data of the statistics bureaus of Guangdong prefectures, 2010.

3.2 Overview of location of firms among prefectures

3.2.1 Geographic distribution of firms according to industrial output

The study of the geographical distribution of industry in Guangdong starts with the allocation of industrial output. As shown in Figure 3.3, Shenzhen ranks first, accounting for 22.6 per cent of the provincial output. It is then followed by Foshan and Guangzhou. The industrial output dramatically decreases when comparing the third and the fourth positions: Dongguan output represents almost half of the output of Guangzhou.

Unfortunately, this is the only available information at the prefecture level on total industrial output. More detailed information is in fact published only for above designated size (ADS) firms. As already underlined, this is of course a limitation of this analysis, even if ADS accounts for the vast majority (more than 90 per cent on average in 2010) of the industrial output of Guangdong province. However, it has to be noted that there are many differences among prefectures. As illustrated in Table 3.2, while in Shenzhen and Qingyuan the weight of ADS firms in terms of output is about 97 per cent, in other prefectures small firms have a more important role, with below designated size (BDS) accounting, for example, for 37 per cent in Jieyang, 36 per cent in Chaozhou, 32 per cent in Shantou and 28 per cent in Meizhou. As it is reasonable to expect, these are all non-Pearl River Delta (PRD) prefectures, where industrial development is based

Table 3.2 ADS and BDS industrial output in Guangdong per prefecture, 2009 (%)

Prefecture	*ADS*	*BDS*
Guangzhou	–	–
Shenzhen	97	3
Zhuhai	–	–
Shantou	68	32
Foshan	92	8
Shaoguan	–	–
Heyuan	93	7
Meizhou	72	28
Huizhou	86	14
Shanwei	55	45
Dongguan	90	10
Zhongshan	91	9
Jiangmen	90	10
Yangjiang	77	23
Zhanjiang	86	14
Maoming	75	25
Zhaoqing	93	7
Qingyuan	97	3
Chaozhou	64	36
Jieyang	63	37
Yunfu	75	25

Source: Authors' elaboration on SBGP (2010).

more on small enterprises than on large foreign-funded firms. This data is coherent with the analysis carried out in the previous chapter and confirms the central role the literature (Bellandi and Di Tommaso, 2006; Barbieri *et al.*, 2009a, 2009b; Enright *et al.*, 2005) assigns the PRD regarding the industrial development of Guangdong province.

Having signalled the differences in the ADS weight among prefectures, the analysis continues using only the information on ADS firms, also reassured by the fact that the distribution per prefecture of the ADS industrial output (Figure 3.4) does not seem to show great differences from the overall picture traced in Figure 3.3. In fact, it also reveals that the PRD prefectures account for the vast majority of the observed variables. However, in several cases in 2010 there was a decrease in their weight on the provincial total, or a very slow increase.

Among these we find Shenzhen, whose incidence on the provincial total in terms of ADS industrial output has decreased from 24.23 per cent in 2008 to 21.6 per cent in 2010, Dongguan (10.14 per cent in 2008 and 9.02 per cent in 2010) or Zhuhai (4.73 per cent in 2008 and 3.47 per cent in 2010).

As already underlined in Chapter 2, the industrial development of Guangdong province is geographically unbalanced, historically favouring the PRD area. In 2009, in fact, the PRD accounted for more than 85 per cent of the total industrial

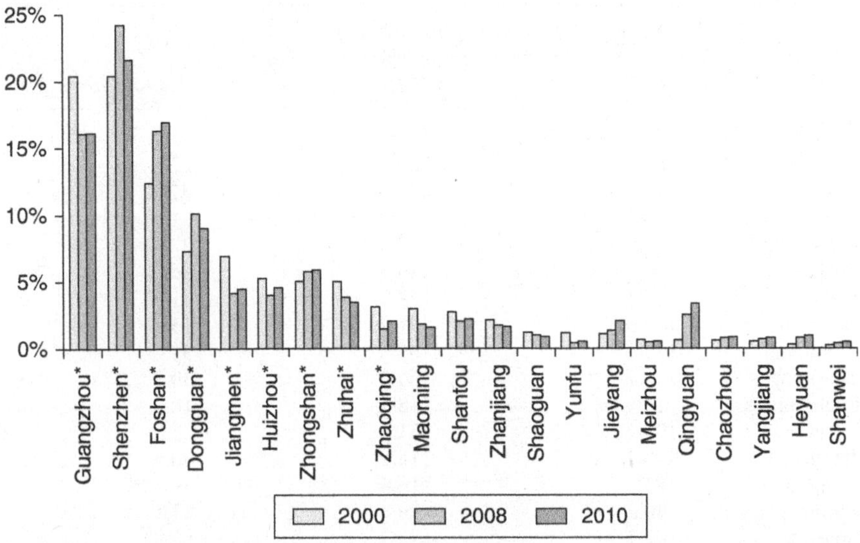

Figure 3.4 Weight of Guangdong prefectures in terms of ADS industrial output (2000, 2008 and 2010). *PRD prefectures.

Source: Authors' elaboration on SBGP (2010, 2011).

Table 3.3 ADS industrial output in Guangdong province per macro-areas (million RMB), various years

	2000	*2005*	*2006*	*2007*	*2008*	*2009*
PRD	1,069,483	3,161,471	3,908,991	4,789,500	5,619,757	5,815,582
East	58,476	146,736	179,021	229,485	299,535	358,506
West	70,849	156,013	197,835	234,194	278,768	263,148
Mountains	49,285	130,055	181,629	272,106	344,402	390,340
Total	1,248,093	3,594,275	4,467,476	5,525,285	6,542,462	6,827,576

Source: Authors' elaboration on SBGP (2010).

output of ADS firms. However, after strong growth until 2005, in these last few years its relative weight is slightly but steadily declining, losing three percentage points since 2005 (Table 3.3).

The decline in the growth rate of ADS industrial output in the PRD is counterbalanced by a relatively better trend in other zones of the province, such as the eastern part and the mountainous territories. This trend could in part be read as a consequence of the 2008 international crisis. As we already explained, for years the PRD has based its development on the promotion of export-oriented

Table 3.4 Average output of ADS firms in Guangdong per prefecture, 2009 and 2010

	Average ADS output (million RMB)		
Prefecture	*2009*	*2010*	*% Variation (2010)*
Qingyuan	262.9	355.1	35.1
Shenzhen	183.2	224.6	22.6
Zhuhai	173.5	220.9	27.3
Huizhou	160.7	210.7	31.1
Guangzhou	162.0	199.0	22.9
Foshan	150.0	189.1	26.0
Heyuan	147.1	179.1	21.8
Maoming	149.0	171.7	15.3
Zhanjiang	123.7	165.3	33.6
Zhaoqing	110.7	154.2	39.3
Shaoguan	116.4	138.3	18.9
Dongguan	104.7	131.2	25.3
Jiangmen	90.4	118.0	30.5
Yangjiang	83.5	116.4	39.3
Zhongshan	80.6	99.2	23.1
Shanwei	92.1	95.7	3.9
Meizhou	71.8	87.5	21.9
Yunfu	67. 6	77.2	14.2
Shantou	63.7	73.5	15.5
Jieyang	62.9	71.1	13.0
Chaozhou	51.2	58.1	13.4

Source: Authors' elaboration on SBGP (2010, 2011).

sectors that have been particularly hit by the crisis. But there is also another possible explanation: the slow decrease in the relative importance of the PRD for Guangdong industrial development could also partially be the result of the different policies implemented by the provincial government to rebalance the uneven territorial development. In Section 2.5, we have seen those specifically targeting the PRD, while we refer to Section 4.5 for a general overview of the relocation policy implemented at the provincial level.

The PRD's primacy is much less evident considering the average output per ADS firm, illustrated in Table 3.4. The average output in 2010 was higher in Qingyuan, Shenzhen, Zhuhai and Huizhou, where most productive ADS firms seem to be located. In this respect, it has to be mentioned that both Shenzhen and Zhuhai are special economic zones (see Chapter 4), centring their development on high-tech productions.

In light of the data illustrated in Table 3.4, two elements are worth being underscored. The first is the wide difference between the top and the bottom of the table, with Qingyuan ADS firms producing on average an output that is 6.1 times higher than that of the Chaozhou ones (and the gap is increasing: in 2009, Qingyuan ADS output was only five times higher than the Chaozhou one). The second is the 2010 annual variation in the average ADS industrial output. In all prefectures there is an increase; the average 2009–2010 growth rate amounts to a remarkable 23.5 per cent, with peaks of 39.3 per cent in Yangjiang and Zhaoqing, 35.1 per cent in Qingyuan and 33.6 per cent in Zhanjiang.

3.2.2 Sectoral specializations

Each prefecture of Guangdong province shows a very specific sectoral specialization (Table 3.5).[2] Some prefectures do not display distinct specializations, with the first sector accounting for less than 15 per cent of ADS output (Shantou, Heyuan, Jiangmen, Zhaoqing and Jieyang).

On the contrary, in other cases the ADS industrial output is particularly concentrated in a specific sector. Among these there is Maoming, where petroleum refining, coking and nuclear fuel processing accounted for 61.5 per cent in 2009 (even if the rate is decreasing over time) and Chaozhou, with 31.4 per cent of ADS industrial output related to non-metal mineral products.

Shenzhen instead is characterized by a particularly high specialization rate in the production of telecommunications machinery, computers and other electronic devices (almost 60 per cent of the total output of industrial ADS firms in 2009). For this reason, the city is considered to be the high-tech productive centre of Guangdong (and of China as a whole). Other prefectures in the same year display an analogous specialization, such as Huizhou (47.1 per cent), Dongguan (27.5 per cent), Zhuhai (26.4 per cent) and Shanwei (21.6 per cent).

However, in all of the above-mentioned prefectures specialized in the electronic sectors, the specialization rate in 2009 is lower than in 2004, with a remarkable decrease especially in Shanwei (down from 39 to 22 per cent) and in Huizhou (down from 63 to 47 per cent).

They all show impressive growth rates from 2004 to 2008, but the wind suddenly changes direction in 2009 (Table 3.5). The electronic sector has been among the most hit during the crisis, due to its export-oriented nature (even if with some exceptions, as illustrated in the analysis of the top 50 Guangdong firms described in Section 2.2). So, in several cases, it seems reasonable to hypothesize that the decrease in the information technology (IT) specialization rate is rather a consequence of the crisis the sector has been facing internationally in these last few years, than a sign of progressive de-specialization.

The sectors that seem to have better resisted the international crisis are the traditional ones, probably because they have been sustained by internal demand. Examples are the textile industry in Shantou (+21.6 per cent in 2009), plastic products in the same prefecture (+17.4 per cent) or metal products in Foshan (+20.9 per cent).

Contrary to the trend previously highlighted for electronics, some prefectures over time show an increased concentration of activities in the first sector of specialization (the production of transport equipment in Guangzhou, for example, has grown from 15.7 per cent of industrial output in 2004 to 24.7 per cent in 2009, while the production of electrical machinery in Zhongshan has grown from 16 per cent in 2004 to 22.7 in 2009).

Table 3.5 Output of ADS firms in Guangdong by main sectors (2004, 2008 and 2009)

Prefecture	*Sector*	*Output (2009) (million RMB)*	*Variance (2004–2008)*	*Variance (2008–2009)*	*Output (2004) (%)*	*Output (2008) (%)*	*Output (2009) (%)*
Guangzhou	Transport equipment	280,912	177.3	23.6	16.2	21.6	24.7
	IT hardware	127,661	51.9	34.0	12.4	9.1	11.2
	Raw chemical products	117,711	57.9	5.7	14.0	10.6	10.3
Shenzhen	IT hardware	904,490	134.3	−0.8	59.8	57.5	58.7
	Electric machinery and equipment	116,640	225.1	−3.6	5.7	7.6	7.6
	Production and supply of electric and heat power	67,152	128.8	7.9	4.2	3.9	4.4
Zhuhai	IT hardware	63,492	68.6	−19.3	36.9	31.5	26.4
	Electric machinery and equipment	60,369	132.0	12.8	18.3	21.4	25.1
	Raw chemical products	15,134	76.8	2.0	6.6	5.9	6.3
Shantou	Textile industry	17,459	225.0	21.6	8.1	10.8	11.4
	Plastic products	16,903	195.5	17.4	8.9	10.8	11.0
	Garment, footwear and headgear	15,215	144.9	21.2	9.4	9.4	9.9
Foshan	Electric machinery and equipment	249,488	181.0	7.6	24.8	21.8	21.3
	Metal products	103,379	301.7	20.9	6.4	8.0	8.8
	Non-metal mineral products	86,976	177.9	−4.6	9.8	8.6	7.4
Shaoguan	Ferrous metals smelting and pressing	14,727	87.5	−27.4	34.5	30.3	24.6
	Non-ferrous metals smelting and pressing	7,522	98.1	−11.0	13.6	12.6	12.6
	Production and supply of electric and heat power	7,072	126.6	−6.8	10.7	11.3	11.8
Heyuan	IT hardware	9,060	1,598.6	44.9	3.4	12.0	15.0
	Ferrous metals smelting and pressing	8,439	226.4	2.9	23.3	15.8	14.0
	Mining and dressing of ferrous metal ores	5,021	687.7	6.1	5.6	9.1	8.3
Meizhou	Production and supply of electric and heat power	7,929	222.9	23.4	12.7	19.3	22.6
	Non-metal mineral products	5,470	56.5	8.6	20.6	15.1	15.6
	Tobacco manufacturing	5,387	48.0	1.6	22.9	15.9	15.3
Huizhou	IT hardware	141,488	77.6	13.4	62.7	48.0	47.1
	Petroleum refining, coking and nuclear fuel processing	30,790	–	1,540.4	0.0	0.7	10.2
	Raw chemical products	25,650	1,795.0	−21.4	1.5	12.6	8.5
Shanwei	IT hardware	6,912	140.6	−0.1	39.4	26.8	21.6
	Textile industry	5,418	165.3	14.7	24.4	18.3	17
	Production and supply of electric and heat power	5,054	1,313.5	12.4	4.4	17.4	15.8

(*continued*)

Prefecture	*Sector*	*Output (2009) (million RMB)*	*Variance (2004–2008)*	*Variance (2008–2009)*	*Output (2004) (%)*	*Output (2008) (%)*	*Output (2009) (%)*
Dongguan	IT hardware	167,123	86.5	−5.77	36.8	26.7	27.5
	Electric machinery and equipment	60,794	145.1	−16.9	11.6	11.0	10.0
	Production and supply of electric and heat power	44,362	225.7	−3.6	5.5	6.9	7.3
Zhongshan	Electric machinery and equipment	92,015	210.2	9.4	16.0	22.3	22.7
	IT hardware	45,595	33.6	25.1	16.1	9.7	11.2
	Garment, footwear and headgear	27,675	77.7	12.3	8.2	6.5	6.8
Jiangmen	Metal products	42,230	108.2	8.2	14.2	14.4	14.4
	Transport equipment	34,879	217.4	9.5	7.6	11.8	11.9
	Electric machinery and equipment	29,712	70.1	10.6	11.9	9.9	10.1
Yangjiang	Metal products	16,614	264.4	12.8	26.2	32.9	32.9
	Processing of farm and sideline food	7,335	267.8	1.6	12.7	16.1	14.5
	Ferrous metals smelting and pressing	4,767	255.2	−1.2	8.8	10.8	9.4
Zhanjiang	Processing of farm and sideline food	22,659	89.3	−12.0	28.0	22.6	22.0
	Extraction of petroleum and natural gas	18,971	123.4	−23.5	22.8	21.8	18.4
	Petroleum refining, coking and nuclear fuel processing	16,191	263.3	−27.5	12.6	19.6	15.7
Maoming	Petroleum refining, coking and nuclear fuel processing	67,528	78.3	−14.5	71.6	65.8	61.5
	Raw chemical products	11,234	156.5	−0.4	7.1	9.4	10.2
	Production and supply of electric and heat power	5,361	294.5	−16.7	2.6	5.4	4.9
Zhaoqing	Metal products	16,171	139.2	20.7	10.4	13.9	13.7
	Smelting and pressing of non-ferrous metals	14,782	1,635.4	2.6	1.5	14.9	12.5
	Raw chemical products	11,234	198.8	56.9	4.4	7.4	9.5
Qingyuan	Smelting and pressing of non-ferrous metals	33,579	1,323.8	5.95	13.0	19.3	16.6
	Non-metal mineral products	29,906	974.9	30.3	12.5	13.9	14.8
	Recycling and waste disposal	20,033	14,106.9	62.1	0.5	7.5	9.9
Chaozhou	Non-metal mineral products	18,256	177.6	16.9	27.3	30.0	31.4
	Production and supply of electric and heat power	6,988	883.4	−14.3	4.0	15.6	12.0
	Production and supply of gas	5,207	43.9	35.7	13.0	7.4	9.0
Jieyang	Garment, footwear and headgear	15,653	183.0	43.9	15.2	12.3	13.6
	Plastic products	13,915	244.1	30.5	12.3	12.0	12.1
	Metal products	13,636	286.8	45.0	9.6	10.6	11.8
Yunfu	Non-metal mineral products	6,166	64.9	31.1	12.5	17.1	19.0
	Metal products	5,230	21.9	23.0	15.3	15.5	16.1
	IT hardware	3,628	192.6	21.5	4.5	10.9	11.2

Source: Authors' elaboration on SBGP (2005, 2010) data.

Three prefectures show particularly interesting specialization patterns: (1) Heyuan has progressively increased the weight of hardware production, which is now the leading sector, at the expense of more traditional and low-tech activities such as ferrous metal smelting and pressing and mining and dressing of ferrous metal ores. This process could have been favoured by the proximity to two IT-led prefectures such as Huizhou and Shanwei, coupled with the recent relocation policies implemented by the provincial government (see Section 4.5 for more information on the relocation measures and Chapter 7 for a focus on the innovation policies). (2) Meizhou is another prefecture that has quite radically changed the structure of its industrial sector over the last few years, shifting from a prevalence of tobacco products in 2004 to the production and supply of electric and heat power. This last sector has grown from 12.7 per cent in 2004 to 22.6 per cent in 2009; (3) Qingyuan seems instead to be heavily investing in sustainability. In particular, 9.9 per cent of its industrial production comes from recycling and waste disposal, which in 2009 was the third sector in terms of importance, while in 2004, it was virtually non-existent, accounting for only 0.5 per cent of prefectural output.

The data on firms' specialization in the different Guangdong prefectures presented in Table 3.5 also indicate that the weight of the so-called traditional sectors in the industrial output of ADS firms shows signs of a decline over time. In fact, while in 2004, the textile and garment sector was among the first three sectors of specialization in 7 out of 21 prefectures, in 2009, it ranked among the first three only in four cases.

Finally, to confirm the industrial vocation of Guangdong province, only two prefectures show a clear specialization in agriculture-related activities: in Zhanjiang, the processing of agriculture-related products is the first sector of specialization (accounting for 22 per cent of the total industrial output of the area), while in Yangjiang it ranks second, representing 14.5 per cent.

In Figure 3.5, we have highlighted with different colours the first sector of each prefecture. From the map it clearly emerges that proximity matters in the specialization patterns of the province. The IT sector is the main one in several prefectures of the PRD area, as well as in Heyuan. Even if the latter is not part of the official PRD definition, it is, however, very close to it in terms of geographic proximity and territorial continuity.

Another sector that seems to be geographically clustered is the heavy industry, which is prevalent in the north-eastern part of the province. The garment and textile industry is the first sector in two western prefectures (Jieyang and Shantou), while Zhanjiang is more specialized in agriculture-related activities. The analysis of data on the sectoral distribution of ADS industrial output per prefecture also allows us to identify the sectors that are more polarized in specific areas.

Guangzhou proves to be among the most prominent manufacturing hubs of Guangdong. It is in fact the leading prefecture for the production of transport equipment (67.6 per cent of provincial total), chemical products (36.7 per cent), ferrous metals (30.9 per cent), food (32 per cent), medicines (22.3 per cent), beverages (35.3 per cent), rubber items (21.69 per cent), gas (26.3 per cent) and tobacco products (44.1 per cent).

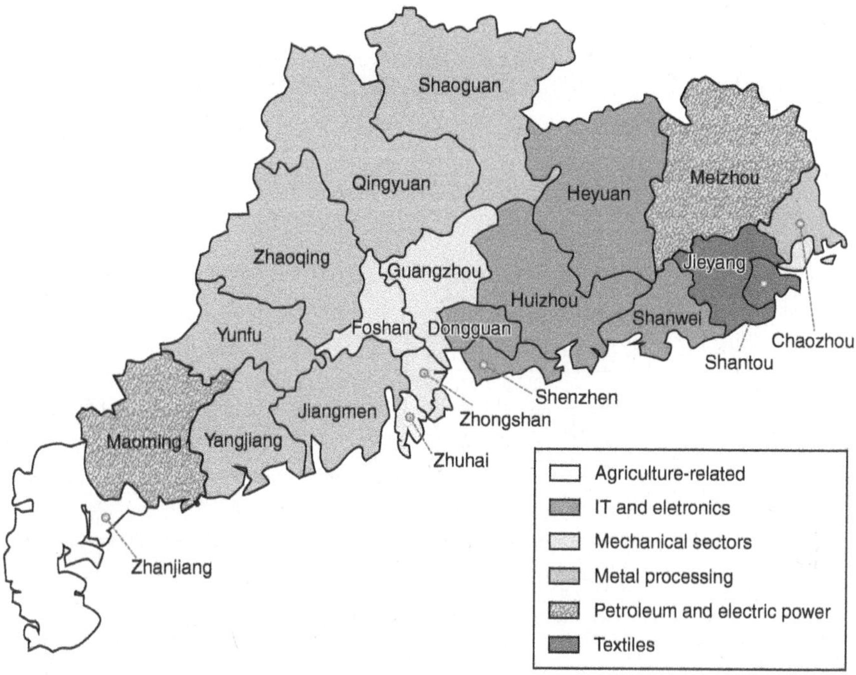

Figure 3.5 The leading industrial sector in terms of ADS industrial output per prefecture, 2009.

Source: Authors' elaboration on SBGP (2010).

Shenzhen once again emerges as the most important prefecture for the production of high-tech items, accounting in 2009 for 57.5 per cent of the provincial production of computers and electronic equipment and for 37.3 per cent of office machines.

Another well-consolidated area of Guangdong province is Foshan, which is the leading prefecture, especially in traditional sectors, such as electric devices (33.9 per cent of provincial total), metal products (31.8 per cent), plastic products (23.9 per cent), non-metal mineral products (37.3 per cent), garment (15.6 per cent), textiles (24.1 per cent) or furniture (30.3 per cent). Other interesting areas are Qingyuan, which accounts for 44.5 per cent of provincial recycling and waste disposal, and Heyuan, Guangdong's leader in mining and dressing of ferrous (48 per cent) and non-ferrous metal ores (32.8 per cent) (SBGP, 2010).

3.2.3 Geographic distribution of industry according to the number of firms

The geographic distribution of industrial activities in Guangdong province can also be studied considering the number of industrial firms, which are again available only for ADS enterprises.

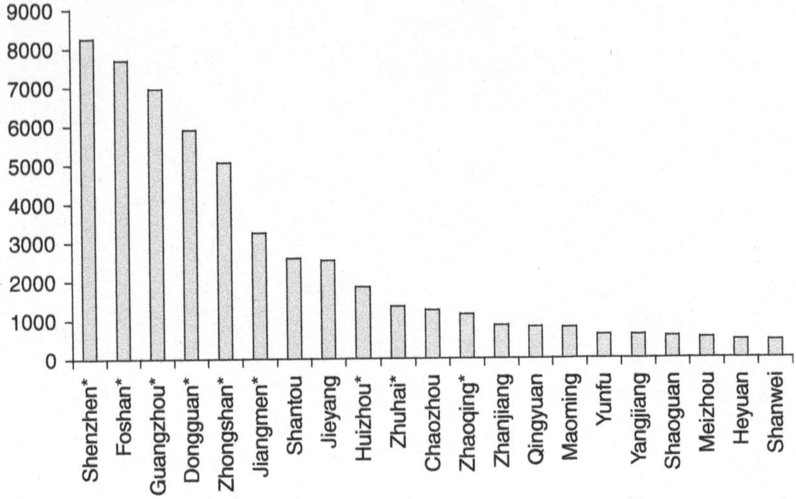

Figure 3.6 Number of ADS firms in Guangdong per prefecture, 2010. *PRD prefectures.

Source: Authors' elaboration on SBGP (2010).

As illustrated in Figure 3.6, in 2010, more than 8,000 ADS firms were located in Shenzhen, confirming the industrial vocation of the city. To draw a complete picture, it would have been extremely interesting to have had the data on the total number of industrial enterprises for this prefecture. The only numbers that have been possible to find are those available in an official document of the local government, which asserts that in Shenzhen there were 152,000 firms in 2006 (22,000 foreign owned, 40,000 domestically owned and 90,000 private firms) (Shenzhen Government, 2006). While highlighting the large number of BDS, the existence of so many firms in the prefecture could also be a consequence of the presence of many foreign multinational headquarters.

Ranking second in terms of number of ADS firms in Guangdong province is Foshan, followed by Guangzhou, Dongguan, Zhongshan and Jiangmen. These prefectures are all located in the PRD, which hosts 80 per cent of Guangdong ADS firms. These numbers once again confirm the wide gap that still seems to exist between PRD and non-PRD areas in terms of industrial development, despite the government attempts to rebalance the situation (see Section 4.5).

Moving on to consider the county level, the data show that in 2008, the majority of ADS firms were located in urban districts and cities, while counties only hosted 8 per cent of large firms (Figure 3.7). Again it would have been very interesting to complete the analysis with the total number of firms. It is in fact reasonable to expect a higher number of BDS firms in rural areas.

More information can be obtained from the analysis of the evolution over time of the number of ADS firms by county. The total number of ADS firms in

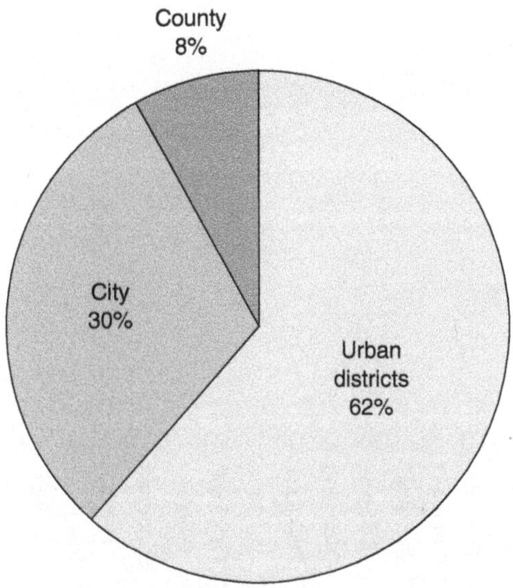

Figure 3.7 Territorial distribution of ADS firms at county level in 2008.

Source: Authors' elaboration on data of the statistics bureaus of Guangdong prefectures, 2009.

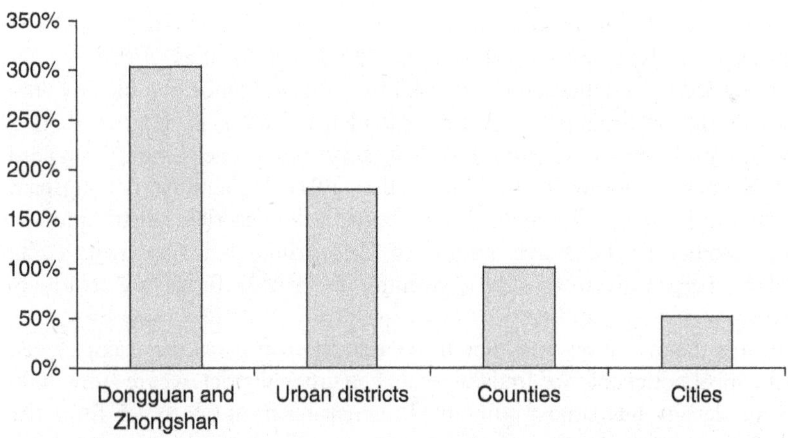

Figure 3.8 Average growth in the number of ADS firms by county, 2000–2008.

Source: Authors' elaboration on data of the statistics bureaus of Guangdong prefectures, 2009.

Guangdong province has noticeably increased since 2000, growing from 19,695 to 52,603 in 2008. As illustrated in Figure 3.8, however, such an increase has been much higher in the Dongguan and Zhongshan prefectures (+300 per cent),

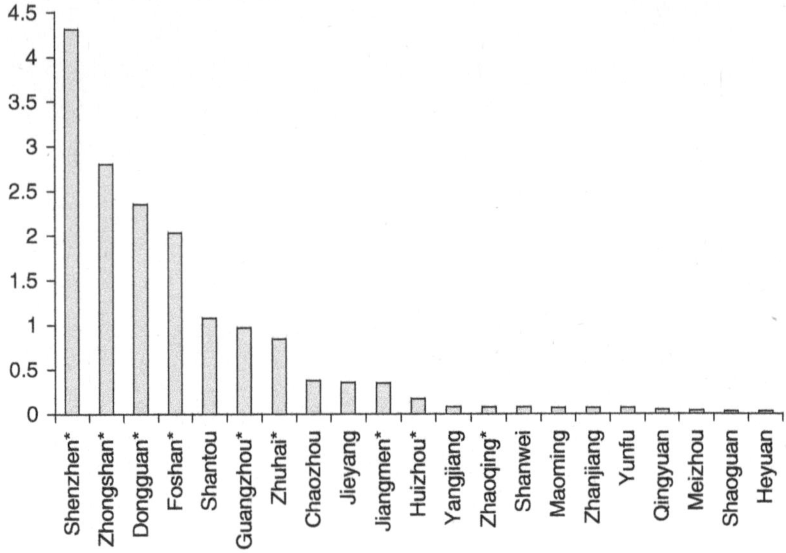

Figure 3.9 Density of ADS industrial firms (number of firms per square kilometre) per prefecture in 2010. *PRD prefectures.

Source: Authors' elaboration on SBGP (2011).

followed by urban districts and counties, with an average growth of 179 and 101 per cent, respectively, against a rise of 'only' 52 per cent in cities.

More detailed information on the distribution of firms can be obtained by analysing the density of firms per prefecture, calculated in terms of number of ADS units per square kilometre (Figure 3.9). Not surprisingly, once again the record goes to Shenzhen, followed by three other PRD prefectures (Zhongshan, Dongguan and Foshan). The main difference with the described distribution of firms by number is the lower weight of Guangzhou and Jiangmen, while Zhongshan emerges given the high concentration of ADS firms in a relatively limited area.

As regards the evolution over time of the density of firms at the county level, among the most noticeable we find the Shenzhen urban district, where from 2000 to 2008 the density has almost quintupled, increasing from 0.9 to 4.5 firms per square kilometre. Only in 13 cases has the density decreased, but the change is never dramatic. The highest contraction is the one registered by Lianshan county, in the Qingyuan prefecture, where firms' density has decreased from 0.02 to 0.006 ADS firms per square kilometre. Table 3.6 lists the counties with the highest (> 50 per cent) increase in the number of ADS firms per square kilometre for the period considered.

Table 3.6 Counties with the highest 2000–2008 variation in industrial ADS firms' density (number of industrial firms per square kilometre)

County	*Prefecture*	*Density (2000)*	*Density (2008)*	*Density change (2000–2008) (%)*
Xuwen county	Zhanjiang	0.002	0.019	775.0
Huidong county	Huizhou	0.012	0.078	531.0
Jiedong county	Jieyang	0.048	0.295	512.2
Chaoan county	Chaozhou	0.097	0.501	414.6
Shenzhen UD	Shenzhen	0.939	4.572	386.9
Xinfeng county	Shaoguan	0.005	0.024	380.0
Zhongshan	Zhongshan	0.597	2.821	372.8
Heyuan UD	Heyuan	0.073	0.333	357.1
Yangdong county	Yangjiang	0.032	0.131	312.1
Qingxin county	Qingyuan	0.015	0.059	292.7
Fogang county	Qingyuan	0.019	0.076	292.0
Jieyang UD	Jieyang	0.631	2.434	285.6
Haifeng county	Shanwei	0.018	0.070	284.4
Qingyuan UD	Qingyuan	0.150	0.570	279.5
Foshan UD	Foshan	0.567	2.078	266.8
Yun'an county	Yunfu	0.007	0.024	262.5
Dongguan	Dongguan	0.675	2.415	258.0
Jiexi county	Jieyang	0.025	0.084	235.3
Shantou UD	Shantou	0.400	1.194	198.7
Lufeng city	Shanwei	0.017	0.051	193.1
Puning city	Jieyang	0.101	0.270	168.1
Yangchun city	Yangjiang	0.014	0.037	166.7
Zijin county	Heyuan	0.005	0.013	161.1
Huizhou UD	Huizhou	0.171	0.432	153.1
Jiangmen UD	Jiangmen	0.413	1.038	151.1
Yunan county	Yunfu	0.013	0.032	148.0
Lianping county	Heyuan	0.008	0.021	147.4
Boluo county	Huizhou	0.056	0.138	145.9
Heshan city	Jiangmen	0.146	0.353	141.8
Longchuan county	Heyuan	0.009	0.021	132.1
Gaozhou city	Maoming	0.022	0.051	130.6
Shanwei UD	Shanwei	0.030	0.068	128.0
Lianjiang city	Zhanjiang	0.033	0.075	127.7
Wuchuan city	Zhanjiang	0.045	0.101	126.3
Dongyuan county	Heyuan	0.007	0.015	122.2
Maoming UD	Maoming	0.105	0.232	120.7
Yunfu UD	Yunfu	0.066	0.135	106.0
Longmen county	Huizhou	0.015	0.031	105.9
Suixi county	Zhanjiang	0.021	0.043	104.8
Chaozhou UD	Chaozhou	0.796	1.592	100.0
Heping county	Heyuan	0.009	0.017	90.5
Yingde city	Qingyuan	0.011	0.020	90.2
Yangxi county	Yangjiang	0.021	0.040	87.1
Yangshan county	Qingyuan	0.008	0.014	86.2
Ruyuan county	Shaoguan	0.013	0.023	82.1
Zhuhai UD	Zhuhai	0.457	0.826	80.9

(continued)

Table 3.6 (continued)

County	*Prefecture*	*Density (2000)*	*Density (2008)*	*Density change (2000–2008) (%)*
Yangjiang UD	Yangjiang	0.218	0.365	67.3
Raoping county	Chaozhou	0.053	0.088	65.6
Enping city	Jiangmen	0.052	0.087	65.2
Shixing county	Shaoguan	0.008	0.013	61.1
Xinyi city	Maoming	0.028	0.044	60.0
Zhaoqing UD	Zhaoqing	0.373	0.593	58.9
Pingyuan county	Meizhou	0.024	0.037	54.6
Zengcheng city	Guangzhou	0.430	0.660	53.5
Huazhou city	Maoming	0.034	0.051	51.9
Fengshun county	Meizhou	0.014	0.022	51.3
Sihui city	Zhaoqing	0.160	0.241	50.5
Luhe county	Shanwei	0.008	0.012	50.0

Source: Authors' elaboration on data of the statistics bureaus of Guangdong prefectures, 2001 and 2009.

4 Industrial development policy in Guangdong

4.1 The main steps of the Guangdong industrial development process

During the last four decades of its economic history, the country has experienced a dramatic change in its internal equilibrium, which has been coupled with an era of great transition for the global competitive and productive system. The national economy has gradually opened up to the market economy beginning with very specific areas, where policy makers have decided to 'test' the effects of such a radical change.

Guangdong province has been the first of these pilot areas (together with Fujian) and one of the most active in China.

In this chapter, and in the following ones, we show how the current industrial structure of Guangdong province, its strong orientation towards exports, the importance of the private sector and the massive presence of foreign direct investments (FDIs) are rooted in an explicit industrial development policy. A policy that was carefully planned and implemented by the central national government in the first phases and by the central provincial authorities in more recent years (on the role of policy for development see also Chapter 8).

Analyzing the Guangdong development process, we have identified three main phases, each one characterized by specific policy objectives and strategic choices:

Phase 1: The experimentation phase.
Phase 2: The outward-oriented growth.
Phase 3: The recent choices: going beyond growth.

In this chapter, we trace and analyze the main features of each phase, starting with a brief overview of Guangdong's economy before the implementation of the open-door policy.

4.2 Phase 0: Guangdong before 1978

Given its history as a trading centre and treaty port, its distance from Beijing and its proximity to the 'Western world', represented by Hong Kong and Macau, from 1949 to 1978 Guangdong was tightly controlled by the central government. In these three decades, the province suffered as a result of the subordination of provincial interests to national priorities. Due to the restrictions imposed by the United States after the Korean war, in fact, Beijing moved the industrial development to the inland parts of the country, with little capital assigned to Guangdong (Chung, 1998). The third five-year plan (1966–1970) allocated 71 per cent of state investment in the inland part of the province, at the same time moving firms previously located in Shanghai and in coastal areas to the mountains (Démurger *et al.*, 2002).

As a consequence, before the implementation of the open-door policy, Guangdong was among the less advanced provinces of China, with an economic growth always below the national figures: the average growth rate of the province in the period 1952–1978 was 3.1 per cent, against a national growth of 3.9 per cent (Lachang and Yehua, 2007).

To summarize, among the reasons for this low economic performance, the following can be listed (OECD, 2010; Maruya, 1998):

1 agriculture prevailed due to the subtropical climate and the availability of water and rich soil;
2 mainly rural population had a very poor education;
3 for political reasons, the borders of China with Hong Kong and Macao were virtually closed in 1949;
4 in the late 1960s, an inefficient resource allocation decided upon by the central government favoured heavy industry, causing the province's economic stagnation.

4.3 Phase 1: the experimentation years and the launch of the open-door policy

The path giving birth to the 'New China' unfolded in 1978: in December, during the eleventh plenary assembly of the communist party, Deng Xiaoping (who was at that time vice president of the People's Republic of China) presented his plan to implement the modernization process necessary for the nation to compete on the global stage. According to it, China needed to increase the incoming flows of foreign capital and know-how and to open its doors to investments coming from outside the country, allowing a renewal of the system, thanks to new investment, knowledge and technology (Ota, 2003; Chung *et al.*, 2001). To this aim, in 1979, Deng Xiaoping launched the so-called *open-door policy*, that is, a government support policy favouring the modernization of the Chinese socialist economy which was based on opening up to the global capitalistic market. Among the foreseen aims there were the growth of contacts with foreign investors, the decentralization of the decision-making processes in order to improve the capacity to react to market forces and, finally, the progressive legalization of land ownership transfers.

In talking about the opening-up process of the nation's economy, Deng Xiaoping declared:

> (...) I am of the view that we should allow some regions, some enterprises, some workers and farmers, because of hard work and good results achieved, to be better rewarded and improve on their livelihood ... [T]hey will engender powerful demonstrative effects on their neighbours and lead people in other regions, work units to follow their examples. In this way, the national economy will, wave-like, surge forward, with all the people becoming relatively well-off.
>
> (Deng Xiaoping, as quoted in Yeung *et al.*, 2009: 222)

As a first step in the implementation of the open-door policy, in 1979, the central government delegated to Guangdong and Fujian provinces a set of economic powers (the so-called 'special policies, flexible measures'), in a sort of tax contracting process assigning to the governments of the two provinces more authority in managing their own economy. However, no political privilege was assigned, with the appointment of the provincial leader kept tightly under the control of Beijing (Chung, 1998; Démurger *et al.*, 2002). The central government selected Guangdong as a pilot area to experiment with the opening up of the economy and the delegation of the administrative decision power necessary to implement it for two main reasons: (1) its strategic location, being close to the Hong Kong and Macao special administrative regions (SARs). According to national government planners, this proximity would have favoured the diffusion throughout the province of a high entrepreneurial spirit, which would contribute to the enrichment of the area with knowledge and best practices coming from the rest of the world (Barbieri *et al.*, 2009a; Yeung and Chu, 1998; Enright *et al.*, 2005); (2). As previously underlined, at the end of the 1970s the province had limited economic power at the national level, unlike other already developed and potentially more 'dangerous' areas such as Shanghai. It was therefore less risky for 'testing' the opening-up process (Chung, 1998).

In this new relationship with the central government, Guangdong signed a five-year fiscal contract obliging the provincial government to transfer to Beijing a limited lump sum every year, remaining then responsible for the management of the exceeding (or for gathering the missing) part. This contract strongly motivated the provincial leaders to increase revenues and to look for FDIs. Guangdong province was assigned the authority of managing foreign investment and trade (except for some export quotas which were still under central control) (Chung, 1998).

The delegation of decision-making power on economic issues from the central government has been gradual, resulting from a continuous process of mutual adjustments and compromises. The final result has the local government playing a very important role, preferring indirect rather than direct intervention (Qian and Stiglitz, 1996). However, the dialogue and coordination with the central government remains strong.

This process of autonomy delegation and the open-door policy were launched simultaneously, enabling Guangdong province to favour the inflow of FDIs, reinforcing its bargaining position with the central government (Chung, 1998) and leading the province to the second phase of its development: the outward-oriented growth.

4.4 Phase 2: outward-oriented growth

4.4.1 The role of special economic zones

China started to open its boundaries to foreign investment in 1979, when the 'Law of the People's Republic of China on Chinese-Foreign Joint Ventures' was promulgated (Fu, 2000; Pearson, 1991; Ng and Tuan, 2001; Chandra, 1999; Kamath, 1990). The aim of the law was to attract foreign capital to support growth while at the same time keeping the process under control: 'selectively absorb the good things and boycott the bad things from abroad' (as reported by Carter, 2011: 61).

This aim was pursued by allowing the establishment of equity joint ventures (EJVs)[1] with a minimum participation of 25 per cent of foreign capital, but headed by Chinese managers strongly linked to the government (Pearson, 1991). Even if, in principle, foreign capital was allowed to account for up to 99 per cent of the total joint venture (JV) value, in practice, in most cases the foreign presence was purposefully limited to minority quotas. Applications for wholly foreign-owned enterprises (WFOEs)[2] were rejected (Fu, 2000).

As the first attempt to open up China to foreign capital, the law's implementation in the first few years was rather difficult, leaving many signs of uncertainty and vague interpretations (Fu, 2000).

A substantial step forward in the promotion of FDIs in the country was made at the beginning of the 1980s when Guangdong province entered into the second phase of its development, what we called the outward-oriented growth. The main aim of this phase was to acquire foreign knowledge, capital and technologies. This was done by means of a carefully planned FDI attraction policy based on the creation of special economic zones (SEZs).[3] In 1980, three SEZs were established in Guangdong province (in Shenzhen, Zhuhai and Shantou) and one in Fujian province (Xiamen).[4] What makes these areas 'special' is the fact that 'foreign investment and other economic activity in the zones were allowed to operate under an institutional framework different from that used in the rest of China' (Fu, 2000: 33; on this aspect also see Sit, 1985). Table 4.1 compares in brief some of the conditions allowed in the SEZs and in the rest of China.

All SEZs were localized in proximity to strategic sources of foreign capital: close to Hong Kong (Shenzhen), Macao (Zhuhai) and facing Taiwan (Shantou[5] and Xiamen) (Ota, 2003; Chu, 1998).

Table 4.1 FDI treatment in SEZs and in the rest of China: some selected aspects

	China	*SEZs*
Allowed typologies	EJV (minimum 25% foreign capital). Direction of JV only to Chinese managers (up to 1990) WFOE formally authorized in 1986 but only if exporting at least 50% of their output or producing high-tech goods WFOE fully authorized after China's entry in WTO	EJV, CJV[a], WFOE (but with a local partner for workforce and raw material procurement)
Approval	By the Ministry of Foreign Economic Relations and Trade (central government) for projects exceeding 3 million US$. For lower valued projects, local approval (with some exceptions such as Beijing and Guangzhou allowed to approve projects up to 10 million US$)	Independent SEZ approval for light industry projects valued up to 30 million RMB and heavy industry projects valued up to 50 million RMB
Access to Chinese market	Formally not forbidden, almost impossible in practice	Products to be sold on the international market
Income tax for foreign-invested companies	30% + 3% local tax (against 50% of domestic firms) up to the 2008 New Corporate Income Tax. The new law sets a 25% tax rate for all companies, allowing a 10% reduction only for high-tech firms	15% for all foreign firms, despite of their sector up to the 2008 New Corporate Income Tax. The new law sets a 25% tax rate for all companies, allowing a 10% reduction only for high-tech firms
Profit repatriation	50% extended to 100% in 1979, provided that the firm has a reserve fund amounting to 50% of registered capital. If not, only 90% of profits can be repatriated	100%
Profit repatriation tax	10%	0%
Duration of JVs before being nationalized	10 years (extended to 50 years in 1986); currently no more foreseen	Unlimited

Source: Authors' elaboration on Fu (2000), Sit (1985), Chandra (1999), Kamath (1990), Lemoine (2000) and Koehler (2011).

Note

a CJV: contractual joint venture. The foreign partner provides technology (and in some cases a share of capital) and the Chinese one provides land, labour, inputs and so on. The participation share of each partner in profit/losses is decided *a priori* in the contract.

The SEZs were designed as 'laboratories' in which to experiment with an accelerated economic development and the controlled import of foreign technologies and capital. In particular, the main aims of the establishment of SEZs are (Chu, 1998; Ota, 2003; Fu, 2000; Chen *et al.*, 1995; Stoltenberg, 1984; Kamath, 1990) as follows:

1 to observe and understand capitalism;
2 to test different policies;
3 to acquire capital, modern technologies and management methods;
4 to accelerate exports;
5 to create local job opportunities, especially for young people;
6 to generate foreign exchange to finance China's import needs;
7 to promote competition among regions;
8 to facilitate the future return process of Hong Kong, Macao and Taiwan into China, by favouring a graduated reduction of income gaps with mainland areas.

If successful in testing the opening-up process, the SEZ experiment would have then been expanded to the rest of the country. As declared by the head of the Guangdong provincial SEZ administration:

> (...) This high concentration of activity in a small area offers a greater administrative control and makes economic planning more tractable. The SEZs are a testing ground for integrated development in infrastructure, regulation and law, industrial projects, construction, tourism and foreign investments.
>
> (As quoted by Sit, 1985: 75)

Deng Xiaoping himself stated that 'a special economic zone is a medium for introducing technology, management and knowledge' (as quoted by Kamath, 1990: 109).

These aims were mainly to be reached by attracting FDIs. Within the SEZs, foreign investors had the chance to benefit from a favourable fiscal climate, the possibility to hold foreign currency, a cheap rent for land use and several other financial incentives and trade privileges (Jin, 2007; Chung *et al.*, 2001; Wang, 2010; Ota, 2003). Furthermore, on one side, the availability of a highly qualified labour force and on the other, the growing presence of low-cost migrant workers coming from the rural areas of the province into the Guangdong territories have played an important role in the attraction of foreign-funded firms (see Chapter 5 for more details). All of this in the absence of trade unions.

The central government assigned a special authority to SEZs, entitling them to decide their own development policy, from industrial production to Research and Development (R&D) promotion, from education to social well-being (excluding railways, postal and telecommunication, banking, civil aviation and national defence). They were encouraged to experiment with policy innovation, with the guarantee of full recognition for well-functioning initiatives. To increase their autonomy and minimize the risks of political interferences, they were purposefully located far from Beijing (Yuan *et al.*, 2010; Yeung *et al*, 2009; Ge, 1999).

While the central government granted the coastal regions a growing amount of decisional autonomy, in 1983, the inland provinces started to suffer from the increasing competitive gap and began to ask the central government for the partial reintroduction of a system of centralized policies. For this reason, the government adopted a new strategy of inter-provincial cooperation, encouraging JVs and trade between the inland and the coastal areas: firms located in the coastal areas had the opportunity to reinvest their profits in inland areas, creating new flows of wealth across the country. As a consequence, the whole nation became dependent on the most developed areas, with a simultaneous growth in the role played by foreign firms within the Chinese economy (Chung *et al.*, 2001).

In January 1984, Deng Xiaoping visited Guangdong province, in order to personally support the projects implemented within the SEZs. This visit had an immediate effect on local development, with the number of buildings under construction in Shenzhen doubling in number in only one year (Wang and Meng, 2004). Another consequence of the visit, and in light of the success of the first SEZs, was the extension of the status of SEZ to 14 urban coastal centres and to the Hainan Island. Guangzhou was declared an 'open coastal city' and in 1985, the Pearl River Delta (PRD) was officially designated an 'open economic region' (along with the Yangtze River Delta and the Golden Triangle Delta) with the aim of obtaining an accelerated economic development and of knowing in advance what was happening on the international scene (Jin, 2007; Barbieri *et al.*, 2009b; Lachang and Yehua, 2007; Ota, 2003; Fu, 2000).

In 1988, the central government authorized the establishment of two other SEZs, in the Pudong district (Shanghai) and in Hainan, which was at the same time also separated from Guangdong and declared an autonomous province (Guo and Feng, 2007; Fu, 2000; Chen *et al.*, 1995; ICE, 2011).

4.4.2 Shenzhen, China's first SEZ

Shenzhen was chosen by the central government in 1980 to establish China's first SEZ. It therefore represents the pilot case through which the government began to experiment with the effects of the process of opening up the economy. For this reason, Yeung *et al.* (2009) define it as the most 'special' of the four SEZs.

Shenzhen is located in the southern part of Guangdong province, in the heart of the PRD, bordering Dongguan to the north and northwest, Huizhou to the north and north-east and Hong Kong to the south. It has a total area of 1,985 square kilometres and it includes eight districts: Bao'an, Futian, Longgang, Luohu, Nanshan, Shekou, Yantian and Guangmin New Area. It is 100 kilometres from Guangzhou and 60 kilometres from Dongguan.

In Shenzhen, revolutionary changes such as the selling of state-land-use rights, the establishment of a stock exchange or the personnel system reform have been tested. Shenzhen was the first to commercialize residential land and to set up public auctions for rights to use state-owned land. It abrogated the voucher quota for food purchase in 1984 (ten years before the national abolition). In the same year, the municipal government started to link wages to employees' efficiency. Shenzhen was the first city in China to allow the presence of foreign banks in 1982 and to establish a stock exchange in 1990. In 1986, it started the reform process of state-owned enterprises (SOEs), and four years later also allowed the presence of private domestic and foreign investors in former SOEs. It was also among the first cities to apply different corporate tax rates for foreign and domestic firms (11 and 23 per cent, respectively) (for a comprehensive overview of the implemented reforms, see Yuan *et al.*, 2010; Lai, 2006; Yeung *et al.*, 2009). These reforms were possible, thanks to the special status and advantages given to the city by the central government: a ten-year exemption from the submission of tax revenues to the central and provincial governments and the same political status as the capital, granted to Shenzhen in 1981. In 1992, the central government granted it legislative power (Yeung *et al.*, 2009; Zeng, 2011).

This set of government choices has had intense effects on the development of the city, as testified by its very rapid growth.

In 1979, that is, only a year before being transformed into an SEZ, Shenzhen was no more than an agriculture-based village, with an irrelevant contribution to gross domestic product (GDP; less than 1 per cent) and a per capita GDP below 90 US$ per year. There were only 20,000 residents with low education levels and poor living standards. The manufacturing sector was practically inexistent: there were less than 30 small enterprises whose total output did not reach 10,000 US$. In Shenzhen, there was almost no infrastructure, nor qualified or semi-qualified employment. The only advantage of the area was its proximity to Hong Kong, Macao and Taiwan and a low resistance to any kind of structural change because of its simple social structure and the absence of internal conflicts (Ng and Chu, 1985; Ge, 1999; OECD, 2010; Yuan *et al.*, 2010).

Before proceeding with the establishment of the SEZ, the government decided to start with the strengthening of the Shenzhen infrastructure system: almost 48 per cent of the capital investments in the area in 1979 were financed by the central government. In August 1980, the National People's Congress (NPC) officially declared a 3.3 square kilometre portion of Shenzhen (Shekou) an SEZ. The first aim was to facilitate JVs between the China Merchant Steam Navigation Co. (a Chinese firm based in Hong Kong) and foreign firms to develop and manage the infrastructural system and to deal with other matters such as project approval, workforce recruitment and transportation (Yuan *et al.*, 2010; Sit, 1985). In that same year the development of Shenzhen started to increase, followed by decades of steady growth in all of the economic and social indicators.

4.4.2.1 Urban development

In 1980, Shenzhen's SEZ expanded from 3 to 10 square kilometres; its population grew immediately, reaching 300,000 inhabitants. The core of local development was Luohu, the area closest to the railway station neighbouring Hong Kong (which is currently the biggest land border checkpoint in the whole of China).

The aim of the first development phase of the SEZ was to stimulate the expansion of the urban centre to a medium size. Such an expansion was instead faster than expected, with Shenzhen growing during the first years by 12 square kilometre per year. The foundations of more than 300 skyscrapers were immediately laid, almost competing with the Hong Kong skyline (Chung *et al.*, 2001; OECD, 2010). Lai (2006) reports the completion of one floor of a skyscraper that was under construction in three days.

In 1982, Shenzhen already had 800,000 inhabitants; due to this demographic boom, the SEZ area was extended to encompass an area of 60 square kilometres.

During the period 1982–1983, the Guangzhou Planning Institute designed a path for the development of Shenzhen focused mainly on light industry imported from Hong Kong. Meanwhile, the population continued to rise steadily, thanks also to the flow of workers coming from the northern provinces which represented an important factor in the city's development and growth as well as the solution to the local manpower scarcity. As a consequence, planners had to continuously adjust the estimations of the number of inhabitants, and soon permanent residents were outnumbered by temporary residents.

In 1984, Shenzhen started its second development phase: the SEZ doubled its area, reaching 122 square kilometres and, for the first time, government authorities officially recognized the presence of a temporary population.

In 1985, Shenzhen's population grew to exceed 1 million inhabitants: 800,000 permanent residents and 300,000 floating workers (Chung *et al.*, 2001). This figure is even more impressive if we consider that official sources in 1984 foresaw about 250,000 inhabitants for the following year (Stoltenberg, 1984). In 1985, policy makers planning Shenzhen's growth were forced to introduce a variable named 'quick changes' within their planning activities, due to the impossibility to exactly plan the development process in such a rapidly evolving context. In 1989, the population reached 1.5 million, and the SEZ area increased to 150 square kilometres. In the same year, Shenzhen became the officially recognized laboratory for the real estate market in communist China. In fact, the law on the transfer of land-use rights was first applied in Shenzhen as a pilot project, launching a speculative development period in the real estate sector. Hong Kong became the reference model for Shenzhen development. In order to show the difficulty in predicting Shenzhen development within a free market context, in the subsequent years the word 'plan' was replaced by the term 'prevision' (OECD, 2010; Barbieri *et al.*, 2009b; Hirsch and Rubini, 2006).

During the 1990s, six new development zones were established, surrounding the city of Shenzhen; in 1996, the Shenzhen urban area accounted for about 3.5 million inhabitants, growing to 10.8 million in 2007 (with migrants accounting for 83 per cent of the total population) (Jin, 2007; NBS, 2008; Guo and Feng, 2007). In 2010, the Forbes magazine included Shenzhen among the top five most crowded cities in the world (Xiao, 2010).

Until July 2010, the SEZ included Luohu, Futian, Nanzhan and Yantian. In that year the government decided to massively increase the dimension of the SEZ, from 396 to 1,953 square kilometres, by officially including all the remaining

Table 4.2 Industry and GDP growth and composition in Shenzhen, 1979–2008

Year	*Industrial value added (million US$)*	*Industrial growth rate*	*GDP (billion US$)*	*Contribution of industry to GDP growth*	*Primary sector (%)*	*Secondary sector (%)*
1979	3.4	32.5	–	–	–	–
1980	5.4	34.9	0.04	6.5	29.6	25.9
1985	149.7	41.4	0.6	61.9	6.2	46.1
1990	945.6	29.3	2.5	58.9	4.1	44.8
1995	4,942.1	26.1	12.4	44.6	1.5	50.1
2000	14,116.6	31.3	32.1	61.1	0.7	49.7
2005	36,419.2	24.4	72.6	63.4	0.2	53.2
2008	53,054.6	12.4	114.5	–	0.1	48.9

Source: Yuan *et al.* (2010).

districts (and therefore making the SEZ comprise the total Shenzhen area) (Xinhua, 2010).

4.4.2.2 Economic development

Shenzhen over time demonstrated itself to be one of the cities with the most rapid development not only of Guangdong but of the whole of China, with a yearly growth rate of 15 per cent in 2008. Furthermore, Shenzhen has the highest per capita GDP in the province after Guangzhou: in 2009, it amounted to 92,772 RMB, equal to about 13,039 US$ (it was 606 RMB in 1979) (Yuan *et al*, 2010; SBGP, 2010).

Shenzhen industrial output is the highest among all provincial cities (1,541 billion RMB in 2009 – about 217 billion US$) and industry accounts for a growing share of GDP formation and GDP growth (Table 4.2).

Being an SEZ, the current industrial activity of Shenzhen is strongly oriented towards exports. In 2008, they amounted to about 180 billion US$.

FDIs have also grown tremendously in the last four decades. In 1979, the amount of utilized foreign capital was 0.005 billion US$, while in 2008, it was 4.03 billion US$, mainly directed towards the manufacturing sector. By the end of 2008, 164 out of 500 of the world's top multinationals had invested in Shenzhen (Yuan *et al.*, 2010; Zeng, 2011).

Many traditional manufacturing activities are located in Shenzhen but, as already mentioned, the development of the city has been heavily based on the attraction of high-tech firms, especially after 1995, when the local government decided to foster the development of technology-intensive sectors. From 1991 to 2007 the total output of Shenzhen high-tech industries grew from 0.34 billion US$ to 111.42 billion US$, while exports of high-tech products increased from 11.37 billion US$ in 2001 to 79.37 billion in 2008 (Yuan *et al.*, 2010). Among the high-tech sectors, electronics is the leading one: in 2008, it accounted for 91 per cent of the total output value of high-tech industries (Wang and Pei, 2010).

The Shenzhen industrial sector has gradually transformed its structure from one of small firms to one of large enterprises and multinational companies and from one comprising subcontractors to one with independent firms gradually establishing their own brands (Guo and Feng, 2007). We have seen that the Shenzhen government has been particularly effective in designing measures to attract foreign-funded firms. As a consequence, several multinationals operating in technology-intensive sectors have established their branches in Shenzhen, such as IBM, Intel, Siemens, Ricoh, Toshiba, Epson, Xerox and Hitachi, among others (Yeung *et al.*, 2009; Zeng, 2011).

4.4.2.3 Recent policy measures

Recently, government measures have been mainly directed to improve the efficiency and quality standards of the Shenzhen logistical sector, so as to further facilitate the capacity to attract multinationals. The heavy investments in infrastructure have provided the area with an urban metro system, the Guangzhou–Shenzhen Express, the Shenzhen–Shantou and Shenzhen–Huizhou national highways, the Yantian port (the second largest in the country for container shipments), the Bao'an international airport (ranking fourth at the national level) and about 12 border checkpoints (Jin, 2007; Guo and Feng, 2007; OECD, 2010).

Lots of efforts have been made towards the reinforcement of the political independence of the area, while at the same time reducing the role played by the government in microeconomics. This has been done by means of the creation, in 2004, of government departments that are independent from national ministries. Thanks also to this change, the network of industrial relations appears in recent years to be more horizontally structured, that is, with more relations among firms and less hierarchical control at the bureaucratic level (DSTGG, 2006a; Vogel, 1989).

Despite the Shenzhen success story of amazing and constant development, Yuan *et al.* (2010) also underline the future challenges that the area will have to face in the coming years: (1) policy changes following China's inclusion in the World Trade Organization (WTO); (2) decreased effects of institutional reforms due to the diffusion of the pilot initiative across the whole country; (3) problems of unsustainability in the development process, requiring a shift to an intensive growth model; (4) lagging social development, with particular reference to education, science and technology, culture, healthcare, environment, social security and so on; (5) increasing resource scarcity and environmental degradation; and (6) cultural conflicts. A recent trend related to the transfer of a growing number of high-tech companies outside Shenzhen is highlighted in a survey carried out by Wang and Pei (2010). The main reasons given for this phenomenon are the rise in costs (in particular of labour costs as a result of the new labour law), the search for new markets and resources, an increasingly limited availability of land and energy, financing difficulties and a deteriorated living environment. Even if this is only a limited survey, it seems to stress the possible emergence of a new path in the future development of Shenzhen.

Table 4.3 Industry distribution of the main activities in the three SEZ prefectures in terms of output (2009)

	Shenzhen		*Zhuhai*		*Shantou*	
Sector	*Value (100 million RMB)*	*%*	*Value (100 million RMB)*	*%*	*Value (100 million RMB)*	*%*
Communication equipment, computers and other electronic devices	9,044.9	71.7	635.0	35.0	42.8	4.5
Electric devices	1,166.4	9.2	603.7	33.3	73.7	7.8
Production and supply of electric power and heat power	621.5	4.9	135.9	7.5	142.9	15.2
Instruments and devices for cultural and office use	440.3	3.5	107.6	5.9	8.1	0.9
Plastic products	421.6	3.3	60.6	3.3	169.0	17.9
Metal products	316.8	2.5	35.0	1.9	25. 7	2.7
Raw chemical products	196.7	1.6	151.3	8.4	96.3	10.2
Textile garment, footwear and headgear	171.2	1.4	30.6	1.7	152.2	16.1
Farm and sideline food	155.0	1.2	30.4	1.7	57.6	6.1
Textiles	86.7	0.7	22.3	1.2	174.6	18.5
Total	12,621.0	100	1,812.3	100	942.86	100

Source: Authors' elaboration on SBGP (2010).

4.4.3 Guangdong SEZs in recent years

Different from what happened in other parts of the world, the Chinese SEZs have been able to move towards higher value-added productions, with strong linkages to foreign firms located all around the world. This has been possible, not only thanks to the wide variety of incentives for firms, but also, and most of all, thanks to the growing administrative independence granted to these areas, which has allowed them to establish direct contacts with firms and institutions all over the world (Bolognini, 2000).

Table 4.3 presents a synthetic overview of the current structural composition of output in the three Guangdong SEZs. As we have seen, in Shenzhen there is a strong preponderance of electronics, which accounts for more than 70 per cent of total activities. Also, Zhuhai sees a prevalence of the electronic sector (35 per cent), but the production of electric machinery and components also plays a relevant role (33 per cent). The Shantou SEZ shows instead a rather different composition, with a focus on more traditional sectors such as clothing and textiles, accounting for 18.5 per cent and 16.4 per cent of the total, respectively, and plastic products (about 18 per cent).

Table 4.4 FDIs and exports in Guangdong SEZs, various years

	Shenzhen	*Zhuhai*	*Shantou*
Exports (billion current US$)			
1978	0.01	0.01	0.25
1990	8.15	0.49	0.84
2000	34.56	3.65	2.60
2006	135.96	14.84	3.48
2007	168.54	18.48	3.91
2008[a]	163.78	19.73	3.28
Utilized FDI (million current US$)			
1978	5.48	–	1.61
1990	389.94	69.1	98.09
2000	1,961.45	815.18	165.61
2006	3,268.47	824.22	139.60
2007	3,662.17	1,028.83	171.62
2008[a]	3,929.58	1,138.49	–

Source: Zeng (2011).

Note
a Preliminary figures.

As regards the outward orientation of the Guangdong SEZs, Table 4.4 presents data on FDIs and exports. For both variables, the three areas show great increases over the three decades, both in exports and in their capacity to attract foreign capital. However, they are far from representing a homogeneous reality. Shenzhen, by far, outnumbers the others, its export value in 2008 being 8.6 times higher than Zhuhai's and its FDIs being 3.5 times higher. Zhuhai ranks second both in terms of exports and in terms of attracted foreign capital, followed by Shantou, whose figures are much lower as a consequence of its previously mentioned specialization in traditional sectors.

The open-door policy, mainly implemented by means of the SEZs, rapidly began to demonstrate its effects on the province as a whole: in the mid-1980s, more than 50 per cent of prices were market-determined, and in 1991, the percentage reached 90 per cent. The weight of SOEs has been reduced: they accounted for 63 per cent of the total industrial output in 1980, for 39 per cent in 1990 and for 18 per cent in 1994.

Being left free to decide its own industrial and economic priorities, the province started to promote agriculture and light industries that drew the development of heavy industry, resulting in growth rates illustrated in Chapter 2 (Maruya, 1998).

4.4.4 Opening process: more recent policy tools

The open-door policy has not been implemented only by means of the SEZs. Several other types of development zones with different incentives and various levels of autonomy have been gradually established throughout China, and especially in Guangdong.

In 1991, several high-tech zones were established. The underlying idea was to distribute high-tech activities in Guangdong according to the model of 'three nodes and one belt'. Shenzhen, Guangzhou and Zhongshan have been assigned to become the high-tech nodes, with a high-tech belt going from Guangzhou to Shenzhen (Lachang and Yehua, 2007).

Table 4.5 summarizes the main development zones currently located in the province. As is possible to note, many areas host more than one type of development zone; for example, Guangzhou is an open coastal city but it also hosts, among others, an economic and technological development zone (ETDZ), an export processing zone (EPZ), a high-tech development zone (HTDZ) and a duty-free zone.

The different development zones grant different levels of incentives. As an example, Table 4.6 summarizes the main preferential policies of Guangzhou's development zones.

The ETDZs are approved by the central government and can apply favourable fiscal policies, such as national and local tax reductions or tax holidays for foreign investment (Zhang, 1999). These zones are then further divided into several areas with different functions. The main aims are to favour the attraction of FDIs in harmony with local firms, to offer incentives for the introduction and diffusion of advanced technologies, and to support the use of advanced managerial techniques.[6] While SEZs are planned as independent cities, ETDZs have limited autonomy in policy making and administration (Siu-Wai and Bo-Sin, 2005; OECD, 2010). Within an ETDZ, an administrative committee, usually selected by the local government, controls the economic and social management of the zone on behalf of the local administration. By April 2010, there were 10 ETDZ in the PRD. They are usually located in the suburbs of a major city (Zeng, 2011).

The HTDZs are also approved by the central government and are specifically aimed at favouring service firms using new technology to increase the value added of their customers. Their first aim was to implement the 'Torch Programme' launched by the Ministry of Science and Technology in the late 1980s. Its main objective was to use the technological capacity of research institutes, universities and large- and medium-sized firms to develop new and high-tech products and to accelerate technology transfer processes (Zeng, 2011).

The free trade zones (FTZs) were established to test free trade before China's inclusion into the WTO. They are approved by the Duty Office and have three main objectives: export processing, foreign trade and logistics and bonded warehousing. Even if they are physically located inside China, they function as if outside China's customs regulations. Companies located in FTZs can benefit from tax refunds on exports, import duty exemptions and a concessionary value-added tax (Zeng, 2011).

EPZs are also approved by the Duty Office, and were created to develop export-oriented productions and to increase foreign exchange earnings (Zeng, 2011).

Table 4.5 The main development zones of Guangdong province

Location	*Type*
PRD	
Guangzhou (6)	Export processing zone
	Economic and technological development zone
	New and high-tech industrial development zone
	Duty-free zone
	Nansha development zone
	Huadu overseas Chinese economic development trial zone
Shenzhen (6)	New and high-tech industrial belt
	New and high-tech industrial development zone
	Shatoujian duty-free zone
	Futian duty-free zone
	Yiantian duty-free zone
	Export processing zone
Jiangmen (4)	Taishan Chuandao Island comprehensive trial holiday development zone
	Taishan Guanshai Bay overseas Chinese investment trial zone
	High and new technological industrial development zone
	Xinhui Jinguzhou economic development trial zone
Huizhou (4)	Daya Bay economic and technological development zone
	Zhongkai high and new technological industrial development zone
	Lingzhou Island economic development trial zone
	Huiyan Sanhe economic development trial zone
Zhaoqing (3)	Seven-star-rock holiday resort
	Xijiang River aisle economic development trial zone
	New and high-tech industrial development zone
Zhuhai (3)	Duty-free zone
	High and new technological industrial development zone
	Wanshan Sea exploitation trial zone
Foshan (2)	High and new technological industrial development zone
	Xiqiao Mountain holiday resort
Zhongshan (2)	Torch High and new technological industrial development zone
	High-tech ex-oriented agricultural development trial zone
Dongguan (1)	Songshan Lake new and high-tech industrial development zone
Eastern area	
Shantou (6)	Duty-free zone
	Nanao Island economic development trial zone
	Zhenghai Laiwu economic development trial zone
	High and new technological industrial development zone
	Chaoyang economic development trial zone
	Zhenghai Linghai industrial garden
Chaozhou (4)	Chaozhou economic development trial zone
	Chaoan Anbu economic development trial zone
	Raoping Taiwan businessmen investment trial zone
	Chaozhou Sanbaimen port economic development trial zone
Jieyang (4)	Economic development trial zone
	Jiedong economic development trial zone
	Guangdong provincial Xianmei people-owned technological garden
	Huilai seashore economic development trial zone

(*continued*)

Table 4.5 (continued)

Location	*Type*
Shanwei (4)	Honghai Bay economic development trial zone
	Haifeng old district economic development trial zone
	Lufeng Xingdu economic development trial zone
	Lufeng East Sea economic development trial zone
Western area	
Maoming (7)	Shuidong economic development trial zone
	Xinyi helping the poor economic development trial zone
	Maonan economic development trial zone
	Huazhou Linjiang economic development trial zone
	Gaozhou Golden Mountain economic development trial zone
	Nongken Nanshan Mountain economic development trial zone
	Petrochemical industrial zone
Yangjiang (6)	Hailing Island economic development trial zone
	Jinglang Island economic development trial zone
	Yangjiang port economic development trial zone
	Yangdong Dongping seashore economic development trial zone
	Nongken Golden Bay economic development trial zone
	High and new technological industrial development zone
Zhanjiang (6)	Economic and technological development zone
	East Sea Island economic development trial zone
	Xuwen Haian economic development trial zone
	Lianjiang Jiuzhou River economic development trial zone
	Wuchuan economic development trial zone
	Mazhang economic development trial zone
Mountainous areas	
Shaoguan (6)	Yuebei industrial development zone
	Renhua Danxia trial holiday development zone
	Wengyuan Guandu economic development trial zone
	Shixing forestry economic development trial zone
	Lechang economic development trial zone
	Qujiang economic development trial zone
Meizhou (4)	Economic development trial zone
	Fengshun economic development trial zone
	Wuhua economic development trial zone
	High and new technological industrial development zone
Heyuan (3)	High and new technological industrial development zone
	Heyuan helping the poor economic development trial zone
	Zijin guzu economic development trial zone
Qingyuan (1)	High and new technological industrial development zone
Yunfu (1)	Liudu economic development trial zone

Source: www.thegprd.com (accessed 3 September 2011).

Finally, SEZs should not be confused with industrial parks. The latter are authorized by the local (provincial or municipal) government. They generally include only part of a city and are not autonomous from an administrative point of view. In contrast, SEZs are entitled by the central government with a high

Table 4.6 Incentives and preferential policies in Guangzhou development zones

Status	*ETDD* *State-level development zone*	*HIDZ*	*EPZ*	*FTZ*
Duty and VAT for self-use equipment and spare parts	Exemption for the 'encouraged industries' identified by the national government		Exemption	
Duty and VAT on office appliances	No exemption		Exemption	
Duty and VAT on raw materials and parts	Exemption for processing trade enterprises only		Exemption	
Licenses for equipment, raw materials and office appliances of processing trade	Free of license only for processing trade of 'encouraged industries'		Free of license for all processing trade projects	
Domestic sales for finished products with duty-free raw materials	Levy on finished products			Only levy on imported raw materials and parts
VAT refund for finished products made with domestic raw materials	VAT refunded after shipment departure of finished products		Immediate VAT refund upon entering the area for domestic raw materials	VAT refunded after shipment departure of finished products
Ratio between export and domestic sales	• Decided by investors as long as their projects are in compliance with national industry guideline and are excluded from export license and quota management • High flexibility for the ratio between export and domestic sale		More than 70% export required	No restrictions

(*continued*)

Table 4.6 (continued)

	ETDD	*HIDZ*	*EPZ*	*FTZ*
Status	*State-level development zone*			
VAT rate	13 per cent for agriculture-related projects, 17 per cent for the remaining			
Real estate tax rate	• Exemption for 3 years • Exemption for 5 years for hi-tech companies, 1.2% afterwards		• Exemption for 3 years • Exemption for 5 years for hi-tech companies	
Guarantee deposit system	Conduct the system by categorizing enterprises into type A, B, C and D		Not available	

Source: Guangzhou Economic and Technological Development District (GETDD), Guidebook of Preferential Policies, http://eng.luogang.gov.cn/guidebook/procedure.jsp?catid=93|115 (accessed 19 December 2011).

Note: ETDD, economic and technological development district; HIDZ, High-Tech Industrial Development Zone.

degree of autonomy in designing and implementing their own economic policies. China's SEZs are usually located in strategic positions, while location is not so important when considering industrial parks. In short, industrial parks can be seen as support components of SEZs (Guo and Feng, 2007).

4.4.5 Refining the opening up of the economy in the 1990s

The opening-up process which started in the 1980s has been further refined and reinforced during the 1990s. At the beginning of this decade, Guangdong's economic growth accelerated and the eighth five-year plan (1991–1995) set the average annual GDP growth rate to 19 per cent.

The plan also introduced a price system differentiating the rules according to the nature of goods: some had a fixed price, while others had to follow the rule of variable prices. At the same time, huge amounts of money were invested in the strengthening of infrastructural networks, especially in the country's inland areas. Finally, with an average yearly growth rate of 27 per cent, the PRD gained the title of *China's gold coast.* In 1992, Deng Xiaoping visited the PRD for the second time, reasserting the importance and the status of SEZs as a tool to implement the open-door policy; once again, his visit was followed by a period of frantic development.

A new 20-year economic and social development programme was issued in Guangdong in July 1994, with the broad aim of driving the province in the attempt to catch up with the Asian Newly Industrialized Economies (NIEs) (and in particular Korea) in terms of per capita GDP (Maruya, 1998).

The ninth five-year plan (1997–2000), which was also the first of the post–Deng Xiaoping era, represented the end of China's transition from a planned economy to a socialist market economy (Chung *et al.*, 2001). Among the foreseen policy objectives was the shift from an extensive to an intensive economy, the reinforcement of the agricultural sector, the acceleration of SOEs' reform and the strengthening of the entrepreneurial system, both in China and abroad. The eastern regions were required to further specialize in export-oriented industry, while 60 per cent of Chinese governmental resources were invested in the development of the central and western areas. Furthermore, the government pushed the coastal provinces to invest in the inland regions, in exchange for a constant flow of human resources. Finally, policy makers started to think about a general implementation of the open-door policy, extending those privileges originally implemented only in specific areas, such as the PRD, all over the country (Barbieri *et al.*, 2009b; Maruya, 1998).

4.4.6 2000s: the 'going abroad' strategy

The last phase of the opening-up process began in this decade, with the implementation of the 'going abroad' development strategy in 2000. According to this strategy, the central government encourages national enterprises to invest overseas. This choice has been driven by a set of factors (Zhang, 2002; Rossi and

Table 4.7 Distribution of China's ODI flows per final destination, 2004–2010 (million US$)

Flows	*2004*	*2005*	*2006*	*2007*	*2008*	*2009*	*2010*
Asia	3,014.0	4,484.2	7,663.3	16,593.2	43,547.5	40,407.6	44,890.5
Africa	317.4	391.8	519.9	1,574.3	5,490.6	1,438.9	2,112.0
Europe	157.2	395.5	597.7	1,540.4	875.8	3,352.7	6,760.2
Latin Amer.	1,762.7	6,466.2	8,468.7	4,902.4	3,677.3	7327.9	10,538.3
North Amer.	126.5	320.8	258.1	1,125.7	364.2	1,521.9	2,621.4
Oceania	120.2	202.8	126.4	770.1	1,951.9	2,480.0	1,889.0
Total	5,498.0	12,261.2	17,634.0	26,506.1	55,907.2	56,529.0	68,811.3

Source: Authors' elaboration on data of the Statistical Bulletin of China's Outward Foreign Direct Investment, 2010.

Burghart, 2009; Zhu, 2005; Wang M.Y., 2002; Boisot and Meyer, 2008; Luo *et al.*, 2010; Liu *et al.*, 2005):

1 An over-capacity in the production of several goods (about 40 per cent of textile industrial capacity and 60 per cent of colour TV in the mid-1990s), not absorbable by the domestic market alone.
2 An increasing dependence on foreign countries for the provision of natural resources and raw materials.
3 Growing unemployment due to the restructuring of SOEs.
4 Huge amounts of foreign reserves, causing strong pressure on the RMB foreign exchange rate (as a consequence of the open-door policy, by 1999 China held more than 15 billion US$ in foreign exchange reserves, ranking second worldwide) (Wang M.Y., 2002).
5 The necessity to increase the competitive capacity of Chinese companies, facilitating their access to new technologies, in order to help them face the growing competition of foreign firms on the international, but also on the domestic market.
6 The firm belief of the PRC's President Jiang Zemin that globalization cannot be stopped and that China cannot afford to be left behind.

Within this framework, large Chinese firms have been encouraged to set up businesses in foreign countries. During the first phase of the 'going abroad' strategy, firms (especially SOEs) have invested mainly in developing countries where they had a competitive advantage over other foreign firms (Zhang, 2002). In more recent years, both private and public firms have also directed their interests towards advanced markets, as shown in Table 4.7.

The flow of Chinese firms' investments abroad has increased from 2004 to 2010 by a remarkable 1,150 per cent, confirming China's new role as one of the most important players on international markets. By the end of 2010, there were 16,000 Chinese companies established overseas in 178 countries, accounting for 5.2 per cent of global capital flows, ranking fifth worldwide. This increase has also been possible, thanks to the capacity of the central and provincial governments to create a favourable environment and to support Chinese firms going abroad and dealing with complex issues such as double taxation, duty-free exports of their products to China and so on. (GPLTB, 2009). For example, in July 2004, the national Ministry of Commerce issued the 'Guiding catalogue of countries and industries for overseas investment', listing 67 sectors in which Chinese companies would receive favourable treatment when investing abroad. In 2009,the same ministry published an investment guide with information on more than 160 countries (Zhao, 2009).

Thanks to these policies, Chinese firms have learned the international business practices and increased their capacity to respond to target markets, being able to also raise their technological know-how (Zhang A., 2002).

Since 2004, China's outward directed investments (ODIs) have mainly been directed towards the service sector, and in 2006, China began to invest relevant amounts of capital in the financial sector (Rossi and Burghart, 2009). This is confirmed by a look at the 2010 sectoral distribution of ODI flows (Figure 4.1).

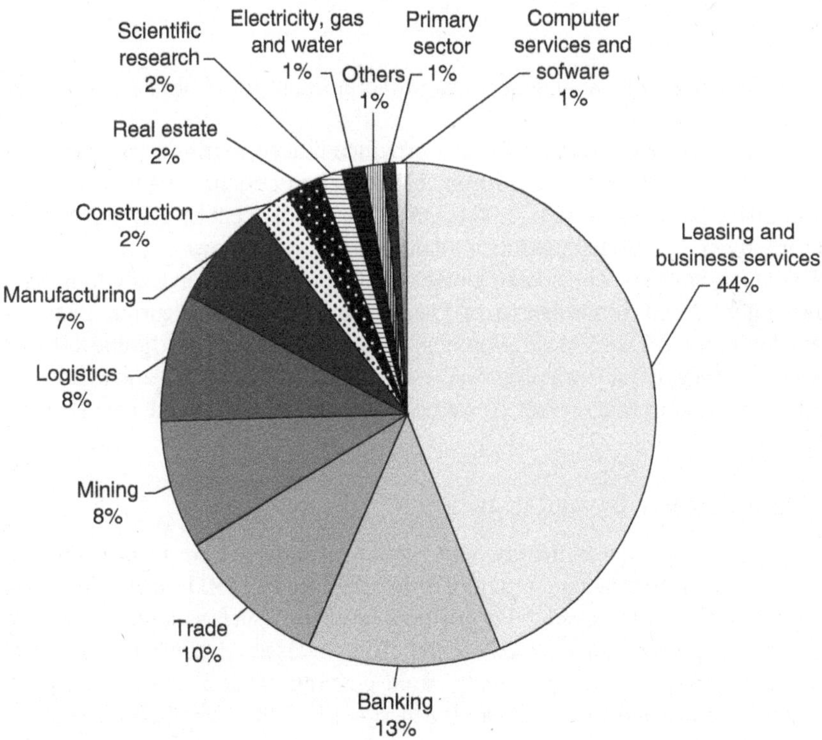

Figure 4.1 Distribution of China's ODI according to the sector of destination, 2010.

Source: Authors' elaboration on data of the Statistical Bulletin of China's Outward Foreign Direct Investment, 2010.

Table 4.8 Distribution of China's ODI flows by province (first ten positions), 2004–2010, non-finance part (million US$)

Area	*2004*	*2005*	*2006*	*2007*	*2008*	*2009*	*2010*
Total	5,498.0	12,261.2	17,634.0	26,506.1	41,859.2	47,795.25	60,182.3
Central total	4,525.2	10,203.7	15,236.9	21,252.7	35,982.8	38,192.8	42,437.0
Provincial total	972.8	2,057.5	2,397.1	5,253.4	5,876.3	9,602.5	17,745.4
Zhejiang	72.3	158.2	215.3	403.5	387.7	702.3	2,679.2
Liaoning	41.4	30.2	97.0	128.3	106.0	757.9	1,935.7
Shandong	75.2	159.0	126.7	189.3	474.8	704.4	1,890.0
Guangdong	138.9	207.1	630.0	1,141.0	1,242.5	923.0	1,599.8
Shenzhen	*150.6*	*92.0*	*452.9*	*924.3*	*763.8*	*414.5*	*608.8*
Shanghai	205.6	666.8	448.6	522.7	337.1	1,208.7	1,584.7
Jiangsu	57.3	108.3	124.0	519.0	493.8	850.6	1,371.2
Anhui	6.1	19.0	34.1	50.8	60.5	57.8	813.7
Beijing	157.4	113.1	56.1	153.0	473.0	451.9	766.1
Sichuan	5.1	26.7	28.3	291.2	81.1	107.4	691.0
Fujian	15.9	42.5	95.8	368.5	161.7	365.8	535.0

Source: Authors' elaboration on data of the Statistical Bulletin of China's Outward Foreign Direct Investment, 2010.

Leasing, business and banking services in fact account for about 57 per cent of the total.

As regards Guangdong, in 2010, the province ranked fourth in terms of ODI flows (Table 4.8). It has increased from 138.9 million US$ in 2004 to 1,600 million in 2010. In the same year, it accounted for 3.8 per cent of the central total and for 9.0 per cent of the provincial total.

This trend has to be considered along with China's recent tendency to remain increasingly 'closed' to foreign firms. One of the features of the current phase of Guangdong's (and China's) development – that we have called 'going beyond growth' – we see, in fact, is a progressive closure to foreign capital and a growing attention to the domestic market, as we will see in more detail in the next section.

4.5 Phase 3: going beyond growth

The analysis carried out in the previous sections illustrates how, historically, the great success of Guangdong province originated in the PRD area, which has benefited first from the availability of local resources (such as land, a low-cost labour force, power and so on), second from overseas capital (Hong Kong, Taiwan, foreign), but also specifically from government-designed support policies (Di Tommaso and Rubini, 2006; Barbieri *et al.*, 2009a, 2009b; Eng, 1997).

In Section 2.5, we have emphasized that the great success characterizing the PRD for many years has recently started to show some weaknesses: especially in the central zones, the metropolitan areas and those strongly export- and FDI-oriented areas (such as Shenzhen and Dongguan), which are currently beginning to encounter congestion problems as well as land scarcity, rising labour costs and pollution. These problems have to be faced while other areas of China are starting to grow (such as the Yangtze River Delta), inducing Guangdong (and in particular the PRD area) to re-think a shift in its industrial development policy. In fact, as already underlined, it no longer seems sustainable to continue to base the future development of the PRD only on advantages such as the use of low-cost resources.

In particular, we have identified four main trends in the priorities of the current government initiatives:

1 increasing attention towards technological upgrading, as a tool to maintain high growth rates;
2 'go domestic' policies, as a reaction to the international market crisis;
3 measures to manage the dualisms that currently characterize the province, from a territorial, economic and social point of view;
4 large governmental investments in welfare and quality of life. The new priority for development is not simply 'to grow', but to make such growth sustainable from a social perspective.

4.5.1 Managing dualisms

Aware of growing unbalances in its territory, in recent years the Guangdong government has placed particular attention on how to encourage firms to move to more remote marginal areas, in order to relieve congestion in the PRD while also stimulating the development of the province's lagging peripheral territories. In particular, in late May 2008, the Guangdong government launched the so-called *Double Relocation Policy*, with the long-term objective of favouring harmonious development within the different parts of the province. There are two main action lines (Li&Fung, 2008; OECD, 2010):

1 The relocation of labour-intensive, resource-consuming processing industries from the central PRD to less developed areas, such as northern Guangdong, and western and eastern PRD.
2 Workforce relocation from agriculture to the manufacturing and service sectors, concentrating on the skilled labour force in the central PRD. This action is the basis for promotion of the technological upgrading of the industrial sector in the central PRD (see next section).

The government has invested more than 40 billion RMB (about 5.5 billion US$)[7] in the implementation of the Double Relocation Policy. Its specific measures include improvements in transportation infrastructure to increase the accessibility to marginal areas, the creation of new industrial parks, training of the labour force and so on. In particular, for industry relocation the plan has foreseen the *ad hoc* creation of 'Industry-transfer demonstration parks' to host the sectors

Table 4.9 Identified priorities for Guangdong industrial development (2001–2010)

Sector	*Classification*	*Foreseen localization*
Electronics and informatics, automotive, mechanics, pharmaceuticals	High- and medium-tech	PRD
Petrochemicals, paper production	Heavy industry	Coastal areas
Traditional: household appliances, textiles, food, building material	Low-tech, resource-based	Internal and mountainous areas

Source: Greater Pearl River Delta Business Council (2006a), GDICC (2007a) and OECD (2010).

moving from their original locations. The main requirement is 'that all industries accepted by these parks be developed into one or more clusters, with one dominant sector and several supporting sectors' (Wang and Yue, 2010: 194). By January 2011, the parks alone have absorbed about 426,000 people, more than 60 per cent of which are coming from Guangdong (HKTDC, 2011).

Specific measures are also foreseen to redistribute migrant workers, facilitating labour migration from the lagging non-PRD areas to the PRD (and increasing the enrolment of students coming from these areas in PRD schools). Firms located in the new industrial parks are encouraged to hire local people and the government will provide free polytechnic education for the most rural poor.

The provincial government hopes with these measures to raise the Guangdong non-agricultural employment rate in the province to 80 per cent, with a great reduction of the labour-intensive manufacturing activities in the PRD (OECD, 2010).

However, it is important to underline that the Double Relocation Policy is only the most recent step of an older and wider idea of industrial development (structural adjustment and land-use management) pursued by Guangdong policy makers since the beginning of 2000.

This is affirmed by, for instance, by the so-called 'Specialized Town Programme' (local concentrations of firms operating in specific sectors, formally promoted by the Guangdong government), described in detail in Chapter 6.

The territorial re-location strategy of industrial sectors was also among the goals of the tenth (2001–2005) and eleventh (2006–2010) five-year Guangdong development plans. As synthesized in Table 4.9, they outlined the extended transfer of high labour-intensive industries to the inland areas of Guangdong province. The objective was to use the resulting space in the PRD to increase the number of firms manufacturing higher value-added products, while at the same time promoting the development of traditional and handcrafted productions in the internal rural and mountainous areas.

In particular, in order to favour such a transfer, the plans included massive investment in infrastructure in less developed regions, with more than 158 infrastructure projects in total. Among these included a new rail, water and airline transportation system in the eastern and western regions, new large-scale power stations in the coastal areas and new nuclear and wind power plants. The core cities in these newly developed areas are Shantou, Zhanjiang, Maoming, Shaoguan and Meizhou (GDICC, 2007).

More recently, relocation objectives were also among the aims of the already mentioned 'Outline of the Plan for the Reform and Development of the Pearl River Delta (2008–2020)' and 'Coordinated Plan for Cluster Development in the Pearl River Delta 2004–2020' of the Provincial Government (see Section 2.5).

As will be described in more detail in Chapter 6, there are already visible traces confirming that the previously described guidelines are being followed. By promoting specialized towns, the process of territorial relocation of industrial sectors has already begun. For example, in these last few years there has been a flourishing of towns specialized in tourism in Zhaoqing, Foshan and Jiangmen and of towns specialized in logistics and services in Dongguan and Guangzhou. The official acknowledgement of a town specialized in petrochemicals in Nanhai took place in 2008 (on the coastal area of the Maoming prefecture). In the same year, a new town specialized in pharmaceuticals (in the prefecture of Zhuhai) was recognized, while in 2011, another such town was officially acknowledged in Meizhou. Resource-based and agriculturally specialized towns together with – when possible – services and tourism have been recognized in the hinterland areas. In this sense (as will be explained in more detail later on), the government's formal acknowledgement of specialized towns can be easily seen, in light of the government's general strategic framework, as one of the tools used to reach specific policy objectives, and not simply as formal acknowledgements of existing and consolidated realities (Barbieri *et al.* 2009a, 2009b).

4.5.2 Technological upgrading

Another problem tackled by Guangdong policy makers is the need to raise the competitive capacity of the whole industrial sector of the province.

In particular, during several meetings we had the occasion to hold with local and provincial policy makers, a shared view clearly emerged: there is a great need to increase and show the value of the intangible content of local industrial productions especially considering that, as we have seen in Chapter 2, low-cost factors alone can no longer be considered a winning strategy (Wang and Yue, 2010).

The industrial policies currently designed and implemented are focused on favouring the local promotion of brands and on supporting investment in research, design and innovation (for a deeper analysis of Guangdong innovation policies, see Chapter 7).

While critically reviewing the strengths and weaknesses of the provincial industrial sector, the Department of Finance of Guangdong province underlines that Guangdong enterprises are characterized in many cases by a rather high level of technical knowledge and can do pretty well in confronting the problems linked to the concrete production process. What seems instead to be lacking is the capacity to evaluate the production chain as a whole and to take into proper consideration the importance of investing in 'intangible' areas such as research, design, innovation, branding, marketing and so on.

This has impelled the government to design an industrial policy strategy based on the promotion of higher value-added productions on one side, and on the other side, on the support of a restructuring process for the traditional industrial sectors located in the central and eastern part of the PRD.

In particular, the creation of industrial parks as foreseen by the Double Relocation Policy is meant to be not only a means to reduce territorial unbalances, but also a way to favour the technological upgrading of industries.

The same can be said for the specialized town programme (Chapter 6), which has been focusing on factors such as the exploitation of proximity, external economies and collaboration among actors as a way to increase competitiveness, innovation and knowledge flow among firms.

This does not mean that the numerous traditional industrial clusters, such as textiles in Foshan, that have been ingrained in the territory for many years, are doomed to disappear. On the contrary, it means that it is necessary to concentrate the most to align their production with international standards and to strengthen the reliability and the diffusion of local brands. The decision taken in 2006 by the provincial government to choose Dalang (Dongguan, wool textiles), Chenghai (Shantou, toys) and Fenxi (Chaozhou, ceramics) as pilot towns for the creation of brands at the local level goes in this very direction, for example. In particular, the Dalang town government announced a three-year programme for the registration and promotion of the brands 'Dalang' and 'Dalang Wool Textiles' at the international level providing an initial funding of about 1 million RMB (approximately 120,470 US$) to cover primary costs, such as hiring experts, designing the brand and planning the overall marketing strategy. The government intervention to support branding is particularly important if we consider that the costs linked to the creation of an international brand are not sustainable for a single firm in China (especially for smaller ones). On the contrary, the creation of local or town brands allows the firms in the cluster to jointly benefit from a common marketing strategy, undoubtedly reaching external economies that would have otherwise been impossible to obtain by the individual actors (Barbieri *et al.*, 2009a, 2009b).

A deeper analysis of the measures implemented by the provincial government in support of innovation and technological upgrading is presented in Chapter 7.

4.5.3 'Go domestic'

The recent economic crisis is having implications on the current and future practices of governments in industrial development and on the debate over industrial policies all around the world. In many countries industrial policy interventions, even sector-specific and selective ones, are back on the policy agenda or are at least widely and explicitly debated (see also Chapter 1).

In areas such as Guangdong province, which are strongly oriented towards exports, the crisis is particularly felt because of the sudden decrease in international demand (as shown by the analysis of the 50 leading firms in Guangdong presented in Section 2.2).

Governments (at different levels) are called upon to design policy interventions that are able to overcome future crises and hopefully able to make the country less exposed to future external shocks. With regards to Guangdong province, the current internal debate seems to point to the need to redirect industrial production towards mainland China's domestic market. As asserted by the governor of Guangdong province Huang Huahua on March 2008: 'We are now abandoning the [exporters] [but] selling domestically is good for the country, good for the collective, and good for the people' (as reported by Roberts, 2008: 1).

However, such a market is far from being united and homogeneous. Before being able to sell within China it will be necessary to overcome some obstacles that currently hinder the full exploitation of the opportunities provided by the national market. In brief, some of them are (HKTDC, 2009):

- regulation varies across provinces, and companies therefore have to deal with a wide variety of offices and institutions;
- in some inland areas there are not even offices providing general assistance to firms;
- there is still a lack of understanding of the mainland market in terms of trends, customer preferences and so on;
- to establish a distribution network in China implies a huge investment in terms of resources and knowledge;
- firms have to deal with fierce and increased competition, both from foreign companies also wishing to exploit the opportunities of the Chinese market, but most of all from national firms, increasingly supported by the local and central government.

4.5.4 'Make people happier'

The recent evolution of international markets, coupled with the rise in citizens' requests for better living standards, seems to have affected the priorities of provincial policy makers. The building of a harmonious society is increasingly cited as the long-term objective in official government documents (see, among others, DSTC, 2011a, 2011b).

In this framework, the Guangdong government has issued the twelfth five-year development plan (2011–2015). For the first time, the government has lowered the expectations of GDP growth to 'only' 8 per cent, declaring as final goal of the plan that of 'making people happier'.

In brief, the specific targets to be reached are the following (Yan, 2011):

- minimum annual GDP growth rate: 8 per cent;
- minimum annual per capita GDP growth rate: 7 per cent;
- weight of the service sector on the provincial economy: 48 per cent;

- focus on innovation with R&D expenditures amounting to 2.3 per cent of GDP (see Chapter 7);
- increased integration among the different regions of the province;
- 8 per cent annual increase of the per capita disposable income for urban and rural residents;
- improvements in the welfare system, with particular reference to education, health, culture and sports (with the average life expectancy reaching 76.5 years);
- reduction of energy consumption, CO2 emissions and pollution;
- reinforcement of the cooperation with Hong Kong and Macao.

With this plan, the government confirms the intention to tackle the four aspects that we have highlighted for the current development of the province. In the next five years, the Guangdong government will mainly focus its actions on the promotion of domestic demand, on the reinforcement of its infrastructure system, on the growth of its competitive capacity on international markets and on the reinforcement of its industrial system, focusing in particular on increasing the weight of the service sector.

5 Migration policies and the role of migrant workers in Guangdong industrial development

5.1 Migration flow management in Guangdong's industrial development strategy

Among the main factors behind the stunning economic development of Guangdong province, we can undoubtedly list migration flows. One first important flow involves those that have moved elsewhere from the province. In the few decades before the beginning of the open-door policy, more than 20 million Chinese people had moved from Guangdong to south-eastern countries and to North America. Furthermore, today more than 5 million Cantonese live in Hong Kong and Macao. These migration flows have favoured the creation of a network of relationships between the involved regions, with a relevant impact on the economic growth process of Guangdong province, thanks to money transfers and to direct investment made in the home country by migrants living abroad. Existing studies estimate that more than 80 per cent of foreign direct investments (FDIs) in Guangdong come from Chinese living abroad [Istituto per il Commercio Estero (ICE), 2002].

A second migration movement began instead to emerge after the beginning of the industrial development process. In this phase, Guangdong started to attract massive flows of labour force (in particular, non-specialized workers employed in simple activities on assembly lines) coming from other provinces, especially from the poorest areas of inland China and from rural areas (Zhao, 2003). Undoubtedly, this phenomenon has also led to the rise of social problems and tensions, especially in situations where the number of migrants widely outstrips the number of permanent residents. This is, for example, the case of Qingxi, specialized in the production of electronic items, where in 2006, there were about 30,000 permanent residents and more than 300,000 migrant workers (Hirsch and Rubini, 2006). In the remaining part of this chapter, the analysis will concentrate on this second migrant flow.

In Chapter 4, we have seen that one of the main tools used by the provincial government to open up the economy has been the attraction of FDI. Foreign firms started to move to Guangdong, thanks to a series of favourable conditions characterizing the province, one of which has been the abundance of a low-cost labour force. In order to guarantee the availability of this resource, the internal population movements have been driven by the central and provincial governments by means of a careful management of migration policies. As we will see in the following sections, by changing the regulation of residence certificates, the government has been able to favour, or hinder, the movement of the population across the country, according to the need to increase the availability of low-cost labour in the rapidly industrializing areas of the country. In this sense, therefore, migration policies are an important part of the long-term industrial strategy of the government.

5.2 China's migration policies: the evolution of the *hukou* system

In China, migration flows have been driven and ruled by the legislation adopted by the central and provincial government. During the Maoist period, the central state directly allocated jobs and workers, allowing low mobility and severely controlling migration. In this framework, since 1958, Chinese people have been classified according to a household or residential registration system (*hukou*)[1] that defines their connection to the administrative area in which they live. First, according to this system every individual has to register in one and only one place of permanent residence. Second, the system classifies the whole population as either 'urban' or 'rural' according to its location. In most cases, the status is inherited from one's parent (from the mother up until 1998). This classification gives citizens access to different state benefits. In particular, during the first few years of application, the population registered in rural areas only had the right to cultivate land (since it was presumed to be mostly self-sufficient), while those possessing a non-rural *hukou* could receive subsidies for rice and grain rations, oil, clothing, sugar, and could have access to jobs, housing, education and health services in their home town.

With a rural *hukou* it was impossible to survive in cities, since the state controlled the provision of all necessities in urban areas and, until 1985, the *hukou* was the only document allowed for identification purposes. Up until the late 1990s, the conversion of a rural *hukou* into an urban *hukou* (as a result of a permanent migration) first required approval from the central state, followed by registration from the local authorities, which issued a local *hukou*. The first step has then been abolished. Using the *hukou* system as an institutional barrier to internal migration, for decades the central government has been able to control and limit the movement of rural populations towards urban areas (Woon, 1999; Pieke and Mallee, 1999; Fan, 2008; Shen, 2011; Zhang, 2010; Chan and Buckingham, 2008).

The economic reform at the end of the 1970s favoured the inflow of technology and know-how that caused an increase in agricultural productivity, creating a surplus of peasants. In order to facilitate their employment within cities, reform of the *hukou* system gradually took place starting in 1978, partially loosening the administrative control system that bound farmers to rural areas and citizens to urban and industrial production areas (for a detailed review of the changes in the system, see Chan and Buckingham, 2008). Since then, the registration system and its rules have been modified several times. For example, local peasants have been allowed to move to the lowest areas of the urban hierarchy, as long as they paid for food and accommodation, obtaining the so-called self-supplied food grain town *hukou* or to accept certain jobs in cities but without urban entitlements (Tassinari and Tomba, 1996; Fan, 2004, 2008; Chan, 2010b).

In June 1985, a new system of 'temporary residence permits' was introduced. According to this system, rural migrants over the age of 16 were allowed to move to urban areas for more than six months if they obtained the required documents from their home town and if they asked public security offices for a temporary residence permit. The permit had to be renewed every year after paying specific fees and it did not give access to subsidies, housing assistance or education for children. Consequently, many migrant workers preferred not to register in the area, maintaining illegal status and worsening their already difficult situation (Woon, 1999; Garcia Carrillo, 2004).

In the late 1980s, in an austerity period during which the local governments were in dire need of funds and temporary workers sought to avoid expulsion, many cities started to sell *hukou* to migrants in exchange for very high fees. Since the 1990s, some large cities (such as Shanghai and Shenzhen) have introduced the practice of selling temporary workers, with specific skills, temporary urban registration certificates, called '*blue-stamp*' *hukou*. They are valid only in the urban area where they are sold and the price varies according to the prestige of the area.[2] Blue cards do not guarantee any type of subsidy, but they give children access to the education system and can be converted into a permanent *hukou* after a specific period of time. This experiment started without the prior approval of the central government, but it was subsequently legalized everywhere, except for major cities. This was possible because a certain degree of internal worker migration is considered a necessary element for the process of industrialization and modernization of the country (Woon, 1999; Roberts, 1997; Fan, 2008; Hirsch and Rubini, 2006).

In 1997, a scheme was launched by the central government to grant urban *hukou* in small cities and towns with the requirement being that a person has a permanent place to stay and a stable job. In 1998, new guidelines were introduced regarding the possibility for children to choose from which parent to inherit the *hukou* (prior to this date they inherited it from the mother) and regarding the possibility to obtain an urban *hukou* for: (1) rural residents who have lived in a city for more than one year and whose spouses hold an urban *hukou*; (2) elderly parents whose only child lives in a city; (3) people who have made investments, established firms or purchased a house; (4) people who have stable jobs and accommodation and who have lived in a city for more than one year.

However, each city government is free to either adhere to such guidelines or to restrict the criteria. In most large cities, only a small minority of migrants meeting requirements for very high skills can obtain local *hukou* and therefore access urban benefits (Fan, 2008).

As we have seen, with time the control of management of the *hukou* system has shifted from the central government to the city and town governments, which are now fully entitled to outline the admission criteria and the number of new *hukou* that can be accepted every year. Even if some provinces and large cities have eliminated the distinction between non-rural and rural *hukou*, the *hukou* location still defines one's access to resources, with wide differences between small cities and towns on one side, and large cities on the other (Fan, 2008; Chan and Buckingham, 2008).

5.3 Definitions and taxonomy

While talking about the migration flows in Guangdong, and in China in general, it has to be specified that the definition of migration is not always clear and that it often varies according to different sources, creating several problems and difficulties in data interpretation. According to some commentators, the term 'migration' requires a change of *hukou* (*de jure* definition of migration). According to others, instead, the term migration refers to a variation in permanent residence, with or without a change in the official residence certificate (de facto migration) (Yeung and Chu, 1998). Furthermore, the terms 'floating population' or 'temporary migration' usually refer to migrants not possessing a regular residence certificate in their new location; finally, the term 'permanent migration' is used for migrants possessing a regular certificate of local residence (Fleisher and Yang, 2003; Liang and Ma, 2004; Hirsch and Rubini, 2006).

To simplify, it is possible to classify migrants into two categories: permanent and temporary migrants (or 'floating' population). Permanent migrants can then be further divided into two groups: (a) 'formal' migrants who underwent an organized transfer or one approved by the state, which would provide them with the registration documents and (b) 'non-planned' permanent migrants who have purchased their registration documents in the destination area.[3] In this case, migrants have not changed their registration. They can be further divided into two groups: the so-called *zanzhu* with a temporary residence permit which at least partially protects them from expulsion and the so-called *sanwu* who do not have any permit, live in very large cities in the coastal area of the country and have no legal documents, no stable job and no stable residence (Woon, 1999).

If workers have not been living in their *hukou* location (township, town or street) for at least six months and therefore do not possess registration documents in the place of destination, they are called temporary migrants – or floating population – without taking into account the duration of their stay in another city (Woon, 1999; Fan, 2008). Woon (1999) defines the category of temporary migrants as de facto migrants. However, as already underlined, other authors give a wider definition of 'de facto migration', including within the category not only those migrating without changing *hukou*, but also all of those changing their permanent residence, without taking into account the fact that they may or may not modify their *hukou* (Yeung and Chu, 1998). The non-*hukou* migrants are supposed to stay within their destination for limited periods of time, and this is why they are called 'temporary'. However, several authors underline that often the real status of these workers is all but 'temporary': they are no longer peasants but they are also not urban citizens and they continue moving from one (scarcely paid) job to another (Myerson *et al.*, 2010; Zhang, 2010; Chan and Buckingham, 2008).

5.4 Migrants' conditions

As has been said before, the criteria to obtain an urban *hukou* (and therefore access to the related services and rights) today vary from city to city and are usually stricter in the larger ones, where the government provides local residents with a wider range of public services. Some commentators underline that even if the *hukou* system has been reformed, little has been done in practice to facilitate migrants' acquisition of local *hukou* registrations. Today, the *hukou* system is no longer used as a tool for resource allocation (having been almost totally replaced by market forces), but it is still a means by which to manage specific groups of people (Zhang, 2010; Wang, 2004). Most cities, especially the larger ones, in fact, grant local permanent *hukou* only to the very rich, to the highly educated or to those who have an immediate relative (usually spouse or children) who is an existing urban resident. This leaves aside the wide majority of migrants coming from the country's rural inland regions, whose rights and interests are often violated and who in many cases have to face related problems both in the place where they live and where they work. These people are still far from being able to enjoy the living standards of local residents, in terms of housing, employment, education, health and so on. They have to pay high fees for the education of their children (schools are free for permanent residents), and they often live in overcrowded conditions because they are excluded from social housing. They are usually employed in marginal, temporary and dangerous jobs that are refused by the local population. They have poor social protection and no social security. When they have accident insurance, the coverage is partial and much lower than that granted to urban workers. According to the National Bureau of Statistics, about 14 per cent of migrants have a pension scheme, but this requires high payments and working in a specific locality for at least 15 years before being eligible for any pension. At the beginning of the 2000s, a compulsory social insurance scheme, including pension, injury compensation, health services, maternity leave and an unemployment pension, was introduced to increase the protection of migrant workers. However, it is available only for workers with written contracts, which includes only a very low percentage of migrants (Chan, 2010a, 2010b; Ngai *et al.*, 2009).

The typical migrant worker is between 16 and 30 years old, unmarried, capable of handling quick and repetitive assembly work for 10–12 hours per day, 28–29 days per month, respectful and able to live for long periods in dormitories or barrack-type shelters. Workers are usually fired after 15–20 years, when age no longer permits them to work at the same rhythm. It is then very difficult for them to find a new occupation and they are not entitled to access urban unemployment benefits (Chan, 2010a, 2010b).

Local residents and governments tend to exclude migrant workers from the political, cultural, educational and social life of the cities; in this way, they are banished and consequently live in isolated factory or industrial area communities (Zhang, 2002; Shen, 2011; Chan and Buckingham, 2008; Florence, 2007). They are blamed for overloading the urban infrastructure, increasing crime, violating birth control policy, worsening urban unemployment and so on (Fan, 2008). Even if there are different attitudes among public governments towards migrant workers depending on the individual prefectures, most workers in general do not have formal contracts or social protection in terms of working hours.

> Few of the nonstate-owned factories have organized labor unions and thus workers lack an appropriate channel through which to voice their concerns. Even factories that have a branch of the government-sanctioned labor union (*All-China Federation of Trade Unions*), do not always improve their working environment because, in many cases, these labor unions don't really represent the workers' interests.
>
> (Zhang, 2002: 31)

All this, coupled with poor legal protection of their rights, makes it very difficult for them to obtain the full payment of wage arrears (Shen, 2011; Chan and Buckingham, 2008).

The migrants' difficulties have been exacerbated by the recent international crisis: given their lack of social and work protection they have been the first to be fired. About 20 million migrants were unemployed in early 2009 (about 40 per cent of global unemployment caused by the crisis) (Chan, 2010b). The central government has first encouraged them to go back home to farm or start a new enterprise. This solution has, however, proven to be unrealistic because of the following reasons: (a) most of them did not know how to cultivate land and did not have access to farmland; (b) there was not enough arable land for everyone; (c) there was no market in the countryside for starting other activities; and (d) most of them did not have the capital or the managerial skills required to start a new enterprise. Given the impossibility for rural migrant workers to follow the central government's indications, the second solution adopted was to support local authorities in organizing massive vocational training courses for these workers, in order to increase their skills and favour their re-insertion into working society. No data are available on the effects of this measure (Chan, 2010b).

The situation seems to be slowly changing in response to growing waves of migrant workers' protests and to the international response to recent accidents they have experienced.[4] For example, in 2007, a national law was approved, which indicated the need to increase migrant workers' protection by means of written contracts and by granting them the same treatment as given to local workers. However, its implementation is decided at the local level and depends on the decision of each city government, whose main aim in many cases is not to improve migrants' living and working conditions, but to increase the wealth and prestige of the city by attracting the best people (Chan and Buckingham, 2008).

5.5 Migrant labour in Guangdong and the Pearl River Delta

The almost infinite supply of workers coming from rural and poor areas of the country has been fundamental in meeting the development needs of the industries located in the coastal areas. The large flow of migrants from rural and inland areas and the consequently copious availability of low-cost labour – of course coupled with other advantages related to geographic location and policies implemented by local governments – has been one of the main driving forces behind the competitiveness of Guangdong province and the development of its big cities (Fan, 2008; Matthews and Baun, 2011). According to some authors, in the long run this phenomenon could also favour the growth of inland areas of the country, thanks to workers' remittances going to their place of origin and to the knowledge workers can acquire and bring back to their home town (Si-ming and Yat-ming, 1998; Pieke and Mallee, 1999).

In order to have an idea of the extent of the migration phenomenon in Guangdong province, it is possible to refer to the statistics of the fifth National Census of Population of China, according to which the 'floating' population of the province amounted to 21 million people in 2000 (about 150 million in the whole country, 12 per cent of the total population) (Hirsch and Rubini, 2006; Fan, 2008; Chan, 2010a). Statistics related to migrant labour are not precise, even if, according to several sources, the migrant workers employed in the assembly lines of the Pearl River Delta (PRD) industries amount to about 12 million (Chan, 2004). This discrepancy in numbers results, on one side, by the aforementioned manifold definitions of 'migrant workers' and, on the other, by the different boundaries given to the PRD area (see Section 2.5.1 for more on the PRD definition). For example, including, or not including, the migrant workers of the Shenzhen area generates great changes in the final estimation (Hirsch and Rubini, 2006).

> The cross-county and cross-district floating population in the fifth National Census of Population refers to the population whose registration location is different from their residence, and their residence is under the jurisdiction of other counties, city-counties or city-prefectures, outside and inside the province.
>
> [National Bureau of Statistics of China (NBS), 2003: 82]

In other words, these categories include all the people crossing administrative boundaries at the county level or at a higher level, even if they remain in a specific location for a relatively short period. This group, therefore, includes artisans, daily commuters, tourists, visitors and so on. Furthermore, sometimes official statistics vary according to the way in which they define the 'rather short period', which can last three days, three months, six months or a year (Woon, 1999).

With regards to the implementation of the *hukou* system in Guangdong province, the government sells blue-stamp *hukou* only to *sanwu* migrants: some counties sell them to all applicants while in others if the worker is female, she earns the right to buy a blue card only after 5 years of marriage to a resident (Hirsch and Rubini, 2006).

In 2009, the Guangdong government announced its intention to modify the *hukou* system in small cities in order to facilitate the assignment of urban *hukou* to rural migrants with a stable job, so as to favour the flow of migrant workers in the area (Qi, 2009). In particular, at the end of 2010, the government introduced an indexed rating system according to which educational background, skills, social security records and participation in charity activities increased a worker's rating, while crimes and violation of the family planning policy decreased a worker's points. Migrants with more than 60 points (85 for Guangzhou applicants) are eligible to apply for an urban *hukou* in the city they live in, their minor children are also eligible and even spouses can be registered in some cities. The number of rural-to-urban workers is decided every year by the city government (Mueller, 2010; Yue and Haoyuan, 2010).

5.6 Final remarks on migration policies

Guangdong's industrial development is unique: it has been heavily driven and carefully designed by national and provincial policy makers, who have decided to use the area as a pilot case study of their policies. Such policies would be subsequently extended to the rest of the nation if proven to be successful.

There have been several tools used to implement such a strategy and to foster the industrial development of the province. We have seen in Chapter 4 that the gradual transfer of administrative power from the central to the provincial government has gone arm in arm with the attraction of foreign capital, technology and knowledge, with the reinforcement of infrastructures and – as we will see in more detail in the following chapter – with the promotion of industrial clusters.

The development of Guangdong province, and in particular of the PRD, has also been based on the availability of a low-cost workforce from inland China. The ability to keep this flow constant over time and to maintain costs at low levels has been strongly linked to the *hukou* system described in this chapter. The government has managed the registration system so as to adjust the migration flow according to the new emerging industrial needs. This has also implied a gradual transfer of autonomy in the management of the *hukou* system from the central to the provincial and local government, in order to make it more flexible as to local specific aims. Cities have introduced new systems for administering *hukou*, allowing them not only to increase their financial gains, but also to select the 'desirable' migrant workers according to characteristics such as their education level, their compliance with laws and regulations and so on.

As we have also seen, this evolution in the registration system has not necessarily implied an improvement in the protection of workers' rights or in their working and living conditions. However, it is reasonable to assume that the growing waves of protests that seem to be arising all over the province will lead to further refinement of the registration system and to changes in the migrant labour legislation.

6 Local development policy in Guangdong

The 'specialized town programme'

6.1 Introduction

In Guangdong, as anticipated in Chapter 4, the government played a strong role in industrial development. In particular, great attention was placed on how to shape the 'geography' of the Guangdong industry by influencing the location of firms within the province's territory.

In brief, we may say that this active policy was mainly focused on meeting two targets: (1) manage the dramatically fast – and often chaotic – development of the Pearl River Delta (PRD) area and (2) encourage the development of the other lagging areas. In this context, the Guangdong government planners thought that encouraging the agglomeration of specialized firms in a few specific locations could serve as one of the tools used to achieve the two aforementioned targets and more generally to promote industrial development, competitiveness, innovation and technological upgrading. While doing so, Guangdong authorities have explicitly referred to academic international literature and to government practices diffused in several countries around the world.

Although in several cases, the agglomeration of (similar or complementary) firms has been a spontaneous process, Guangdong policy makers have decided to accelerate and guide this process by means of specific policy measures. In 2000, the provincial government launched the so-called 'one city, one product' programme to promote and encourage the growth and development of 'specialized towns' (STs): spatial agglomerations of firms all operating in the same sector or *filiere*. These STs differ from any other experience of industrial agglomeration because they have all received official recognition from government authorities, as explained in more detail in the following pages.

6.1.1 The genesis of the target towns

Guangdong province has a relevant number of sectoral agglomerations of firms, called 'STs'. They are far from being a homogeneous category: there are in fact relevant differences in the way they arose, developed and appear today (Di Tommaso and Rubini, 2006).

Some STs are no more than rural villages, others can be considered medium-sized cities or suburbs of big metropolises.

The literature identifies two main categories (Wang, 2009; Wang and Yue, 2010; Bellandi and Di Tommaso, 2005; Barbieri *et al.*, 2009b):

1 *Exogenous clusters*: Their development has been mainly pushed by the capacity of the territory to attract foreign direct investment (FDI) and to favour the relationships between foreign firms and existing enterprises. Dongguan is among the Guangdong prefectures with the highest number of these types of agglomerations (Wang, 2009).
2 *Endogenous clusters*: Their birth is due to local factors. Some of them derive from the consolidation of ancient productive systems. In other cases, their development has been pushed by the privatization of town and village enterprises (TVEs) (see Appendix 2 for more details).

As far as their internal structure is concerned, in some cases it is possible to clearly identify large, leading – mainly Chinese – firms, while in others small and medium firms prevail, cooperating with each other with no leading actors, similarly to what has been described in the literature analysing the Italian industrial district model (Becattini, 1989; Piore and Sabel, 1984). Finally, some STs are mere agglomerations of firms not willing to collaborate with each other, because they have been forced to locate to a specific area by private or public initiatives in the absence of a clear collective strategy (Bellandi and Di Tommaso, 2005; Di Tommaso and Rubini, 2006; Barbieri *et al.*, 2009b).

Even if their backgrounds differ, what makes STs similar is the formal recognition given to them by the provincial government.

The experience is unique: each potential ST is studied by a group of government experts who eventually award the town the label 'ST'. After this formal recognition, a number of financial and preferential policies are granted in order to (further) encourage agglomeration and specialization. In particular, government recognition and policy advantages are expected to increase competitiveness, innovation and market visibility.

In this way, the promotion of clusters in Guangdong becomes an explicit industrial policy model: a tool used by the government to address more general industrial development aims (Barbieri *et al.*, 2009a, 2009b; Organization for Economic Co-operation and Development (OECD), 2010).

6.1.2 The government programme

The phenomenon of the Guangdong STs is still widely neglected by the international English-speaking academic debate. While on the contrary, it is instead an emerging issue within Chinese academia. There are in fact several authors studying in particular the evolution of STs in the Guangdong province [Chen and Cheng, 2005; Li, 2002; Huang *et al.*, 2006; Li, 2006; Zhao, 2007; Wang and Yue, 2010; Wang J., 2002, 2004; Tang *et al.*, 2005; Lu, 2006;

Zhang and Ling, 2003; Department of Science and Technology of Guangdong Government (DSTGG), 2003, 2006a; Huang and Hu, 2007, citing only some]. However, most of the relevant material needed to understand the experience of the STs has to be found within the Guangdong government's official documents, which describe the details of the on-going practices. It was the DSTGG that first introduced the idea of the ST, and it remains at the centre of its current industrial policy promotion strategy. The support to STs originated at the end of 1980, when the Chinese government launched the '*Spark Plan*' (DSTGG, 2003; Bolognini, 2000; Barbieri *et al.*, 2009a, 2009b). The programme was aimed at increasing the technological innovation capacity in several rural areas of the country. The underlying idea was that strengthening the innovative capacity of the agricultural sector would have had positive spillover effects on the whole economy, therefore favouring a parallel growth of industrial productions (Di Tommaso and Rubini, 2006).

The Spark Plan, managed by the State Science and Technology Commission, initially consisted of three main parts (Bolognini, 2000):

1. a training component to provide about 200,000 young managers with the basic knowledge about the best techniques to be used in their local environment;
2. a fund to finance research institutes in order to develop 100 complete technologies to be used in agriculture;
3. the creation of 500 small 'demonstrative' TVEs to diffuse the transfer of knowledge, the management techniques and the quality controls in the rural areas.

The Spark Plan also included the creation of several investment areas, the so-called 'Spark Technology Investment Zones', where firms could benefit from the availability of funds coming from government subsidies and bank loans. These investment zones represented the seed from which several Guangdong STs originated. This occurred, for example, in the case of Datang, in the Shaoguan prefecture, with Zhangcha and Pingzhou in the Foshan prefecture and Fenxi in the Chaozhou prefecture.

While studying these investment areas, some DSTGG experts and officials realized that in most cases each area tended to specialize in a specific sector, what has been called 'one city, one product' (Lu, 2006; Wang and Yue, 2010). Given that the town was the prevailing administrative unit among these agglomerations, they were defined as STs (Lu, 2006; Barbieri *et al.*, 2009a, 2009b). These cases, coupled with the recognition of some analogous international industrial agglomeration cases considered to be successful all over the world (such as industrial districts, firm clusters, local systems of innovation, etc.), have been the basis for a new strategy in which Guangdong policy makers have started to design measures to actively support these types of industrial agglomerations. Particular relevance has been given to the initiatives designed to increase the innovative capacity of firms (see Chapter 7).

In this framework, in 1998, the DSTGG launched a specific programme to support an initial group of STs, subsequently extended to several other cities. Since then, the department officially acknowledges as STs those meeting the following criteria:

- The town has to be a 'township' from an administrative point of view or, less frequently, a 'county' or an 'urban district' (on the administrative divisions in China and in Guangdong, see Section 3.1) and at least 30 per cent of its industrial output (or employment) has to be concentrated in one industry (defined in specific sectoral terms, analogously to our three-digit classification systems). This industry is called 'specialized sector'. It has to be underlined that one city can have more than one specialized sector. For example, Dalang, in the Dongguan prefecture, is officially acknowledged as a town specialized in the production of knitwear articles and in the provision of services to firms.
- The annual value of the industrial output has to exceed 2 billion RMB (equal to about 315 million US$, at the November 2011 exchange rate).

The officially recognized STs are then entitled to receive a subsidy of 300,000 RMB (equal to about 47,200 US$)[1] from the DSTGG, provided that an additional part be financed by the local government in the proportion of 1 (province): 10 (city): 50 (town) (Wang, 2009; Wang and Yue, 2010).This money has to be mainly used to establish an innovation centre, whose aim is to help firms in the development of new technologies and in the upgrading of their production and to favour the establishment and consolidation of relationships among actors. The activity of the innovation centres is not only directed to the single firm, but it aims to favour an improvement in the reputation of the whole productive system of the town, possibly supporting the development of a common and easily recognizable brand (Arvanitis and Qiu, 2004; Wang J., 2004; DSTGG, 2003, 2006a).

In its official document *Thoughts and strategies for the development of clusters in Guangdong and for brands creation* (2005), the Department of Finance of the Guangdong government underlines the priorities that should be tackled while defining the industrial development strategy, implemented by means of industrial cluster promotion:

- to foster not only the development of STs per se, but also the collaboration among STs, in order to limit territorial overlapping and intra-provincial competition;
- to create *ad hoc* support centres specialized in quality control;
- to favour the creation of brands at the local level so as to increase the capacity of firms and STs to compete effectively on the international market;
- to increase the diffusion of knowledge on the rules for patenting and for the protection of intellectual rights.

The officially recognized STs are one of the main tools used by the local and the provincial government to foster industrial development. For this reason, in the next section, we study their establishment, location and evolution over time in order to know more about the strategic choices made by policy makers and their effectiveness.

6.2 Studying specialized towns

6.2.1 Building the 'China and Italy Research and Learning Project (CIRLP) database'

From the official documents, it emerges quite clearly that the declared targets of the 'one city, one product' policy are the ones described in the previous section. What is much more difficult to do is to quantify and qualify the real relevance of the experience of the STs. Official statistics at the town level, as a unit of analysis, are not easily accessible, too often fragmented and not homogeneous. This is also due to the dramatic impetus of industrial development and the rapid urbanization that quickly make administrative borders obsolete. Even apparently simple information such as the population becomes nearly impossible to quantify in STs due to the presence of floating and temporary workers, coming from different areas of Guangdong and China (see Chapter 5).

Based on this premise, beginning in 2001, we have started to promote fieldwork and data collection at the ST level. This activity has led to the creation of the 'CIRLP Database, University of Ferrara' (since then constantly updated) on which the analysis presented in these sections is based. The continuous evolution of the phenomenon of STs, along with the heterogeneity of available data, has induced us to continuously compare and verify information, using several official sources when possible.

In particular, data were initially gathered directly from the official statistics provided to us by representatives of the DSTGG, which is, as already mentioned, the main governmental body overseeing the design and implementation of the policy supporting the development of STs. Nevertheless, these first data were mainly useful in sketching a general framework and in identifying some required context variables [such as temporary and permanent population, output, gross domestic product (GDP), etc.]. Unfortunately, they did not allow for a detailed analysis of the different aspects related to performance, evolution and growth of STs. For this reason, we have decided to integrate the information first provided by the DSTGG with more specific sources. First, we have consulted several other official documents, publications and websites. Other relevant data sources have been the Research Development Centre of Guangdong province and the South China University of Technology, with which our research group has steadily collaborated since the beginning of our research. Given the important role played by local institutions in the development of STs and the mainly local dimension of the phenomenon, we have started to collect data and information from local governmental bodies. When possible, we have also relied on field case studies and interviews to relevant stakeholders (mayors, town chiefs, party representatives,

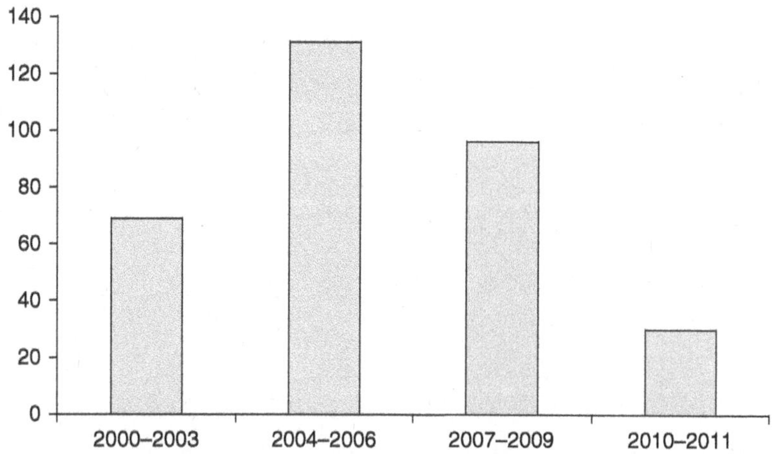

Figure 6.1 Number of newly recognized STs according to the acknowledgement period.

Source: Authors' elaboration.

entrepreneurs, policy makers in charge of the innovation centres, and so on). Finally, we have promoted an extensive phase of cross-checks, in order to minimize the risk of mistakes, inconsistencies and non-reliable information.

By the end of 2011, the 'CIRLP Database, University of Ferrara' included all the 326 officially recognized STs. It should be noted that the total amount is in constant evolution and the number of officially acknowledged STs increases almost day to day.

6.2.2 Relevance of specialized towns in the provincial economy

The relevance of the STs phenomenon we are studying can be better understood by studying and elaborating on the information provided by the official government and by statistical sources.

All the available information of the 'CIRLP Database, University of Ferrara' confirms the steady growth that has characterized STs over the years. In terms of the number of acknowledged towns (Figure 6.1), the most fruitful period has been the 2004–2006 triennium, with 131 STs, while in the most recent years, we see a relative (and natural) decrease in the number of newly recognized STs.

However, the weight of STs on the provincial economy has continuously risen over time (Table 6.1). In the time span of only nine years (from 2001 to 2010), STs have increased from representing 3.66 per cent to 28.5 per cent of total provincial GDP, and from 2 per cent to more than 33 per cent of the Guangdong population. The increase is equally impressive in terms of number of firms (from 14,800 in 2001 to more than 950,000 in 2010) and industrial output of the

Table 6.1 General data on STs in Guangdong (2001–2010)

Year	*2001*	*2002*	*2003*	*2004*	*2005*	*2006*	*2007*	*2008*	*2009*	*2010*
Number of STs	21	50	71	103	159	201	228	277	296	309
% of provincial GDP	3.66	7.23	9.26	12.09	20.83	23.24	24.94	29.49	27.93	28.47
Population (10,000 persons)	148	351.5	549.9	850.3	1,358.1	1,708.63	2,037.24	2,644.74	2,791.50	2,907.81
% of provincial population	2.0	4.6	7.1	10.9	17.2	21.2	25.0	32.0	33.4	—
Number of firms (10,000 persons)	3.92	9.79	13.47	16.4	23.9	36.7	41.4	42.9	35.5	37.2
Number of firms in the specialized sector (10,000 persons)	1.48	3.39	4.3	4.8	10.1	12.2	10.3	12.3	8.5	9.5
% of firms in the specialized sector on total number of firms	37.8	34.6	31.9	29.3	42.3	33.2	24.9	28.7	23.9	25.5
Industrial value of specialized sectors (100 million RMB)	422.4	1,271.4	1,780.3	2,693.7	4,683.1	5,607.4	9,731.4	9,777.7	10,549.0	13,255.6

Source: Authors' elaboration on Guangdong Science and Technology Statistics (www.sts.gd.cn; Statistical Bureau of Guangdong Province (SBGP), 2010).

specialized sector (from 42 billion RMB in 2001 to more than 132 billion nine years later) (Table 6.1).

All numbers indicate that STs have also been affected by the 2008–2009 international crisis, with reductions in 2009 compared to the previous year in terms of weight of STs on provincial GDP (−1.56 per cent), number of industrial firms (−17.2 per cent) and number of firms in the specialization sector (−30.9 per cent). However, as regards the productive capacity, STs have also been able to increase the value added of their production in 2009 (+7.9 per cent). In 2010, however, all figures start to grow again, with a remarkable +25.7 per cent in the value added of the specialized sector.

Data also indicate a continuous focus on innovation. From 2001 to 2009, the number of high-tech firms has increased by more than 2,200 per cent, with a slow but constant growth in their prevalence among the total number of specialized firms. Furthermore, there has also been a steady increasing flow of local government funds directed to science and technology and an amazing boom in the number of accumulated patents, which has jumped from 2,852 in 2001 to almost 154,000 in 2009 (Table 6.2) (for a more detailed analysis of innovation in STs, see Chapters 7 and 8).

It is also interesting to look at the analysis of the structure of the specialized industrial sectors in terms of typologies of firms (Table 6.3). The only available data is for 2005, but it is, however, useful in drawing an overall picture of the structure of the firms involved. The first eye-catching feature is the large prevalence of private firms, which in 2005 accounted for almost 77 per cent of the total number of firms operating in the specialized sector, for 50.5 per cent of industrial output, for 57.5 per cent of employment and for more than 56 per cent of high-tech staff.

In most cases, these private firms are mainly small and medium sized, with a relatively low presence of foreign-funded firms, when compared to the rest of the Guangdong industrial sector (as illustrated in Chapter 2).

6.2.3 Analyzing the evolution of the specialized town programme: geography

An analysis of the evolution of the official recognition process of STs by the Guangdong government confirms that such acknowledgements in the province, especially in recent years, have been used as an active tool of the relocation strategy, which was described in Chapter 4. In fact, Figure 6.2 shows that after the first wave of acknowledgements, STs have flourished, especially outside the PRD region.

According to our dataset 'CIRLP Database, University of Ferrara', of the first seven acknowledged STs, six were located in the PRD [and of the remaining, one was in Shantou, which hosts one of the three Guangdong special economic zones (SEZs)]. Furthermore, while in 2003, 62 per cent of STs were located in the PRD and clearly near the Hong Kong and Shenzhen SEZ, by the end of 2011, only 40 per cent of officially recognized STs were in the PRD. After the end of the first phase (2003-ongoing), in fact, the government acknowledged the majority of

Table 6.2 Data on technological development of STs (2001–2009)

Year	*2001*	*2002*	*2003*	*2004*	*2005*	*2006*	*2007*	*2008*	*2009*
Number of STs	21	50	71	103	159	201	228	277	296
Number of science and technology staff (10,000 persons)	10.69	18.78	26.01	48.16	–	–	–	–	–
High-tech firms	68	257	336	513	688	971	1,222	1,517	1,608
% of high-tech firms in the specialized sector	0.2	0.3	0.2	0.3	0.3	0.3	0.3	0.4	0.5
Funding of town government to science and technology (10,000 RMB)	13,527	29,525	41,132	60,004	61,283	46,738	65,544	98,606	101,863
Accumulated patents	2,852	16,289	23,006	46,101	49,285	68,964	108,416	111,642	153,857

Source: Authors' elaboration on Guangdong Science and Technology Statistics (www.sts.gd.cn; SBGP, 2010).

Table 6.3 Typologies of firms in STs according to capital ownership (2005)

	Collective firms	*Private firms*	*Hong Kong/ Taiwan firms*	*FDI*	*Total*
Number of firms in specialized sectors	998	77,278	2,805	886	10,0728
Total industrial value (100 million RMB)	288.00	2,366.19	741.73	410.25	4,683.13
Tax (100 million RMB)	5.55	60.53	20.36	19.37	116.35
Employees (10,000 persons)	12.36	213.22	55.22	30.00	370.71
Science and technology staff (10,000 persons)	1.04	13.66	5.29	2.98	24.11

Source: Guangdong Science and Technology Statistics (www.sts.gd.cn; SBGP, 2010).

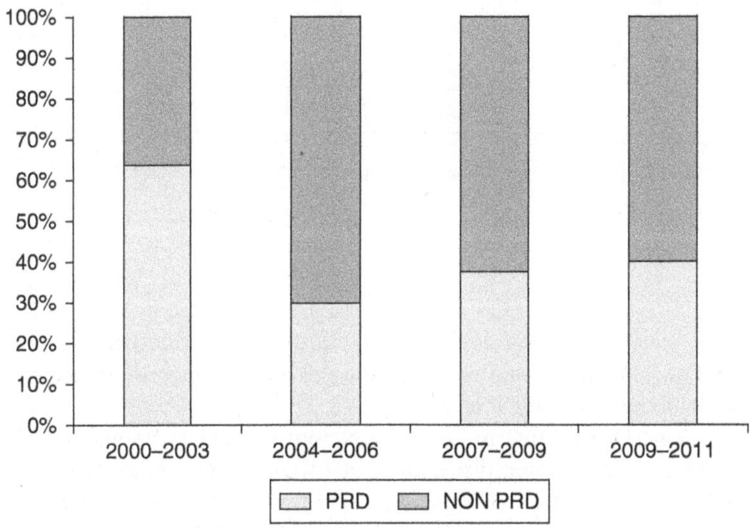

Figure 6.2 Distribution of STs among PRD and non-PRD territories.

Source: Authors' elaboration.

new STs in prefectures such as Meizhou, Zhangjiang, Yunfu and Jieyang, which are not included in the PRD. This is evident in Figure 6.3, which compares the prevalence of each prefecture within the total number of acknowledged STs in 2003 and in 2011.

In a previous study (Barbieri *et al.*, 2009b), we underscored a negative correlation between the number of newly acknowledged towns and the density of firms in the prefecture. To us this seemed to indicate a precise intention to use the 'one city, one product' programme to grant specific support not simply outside the

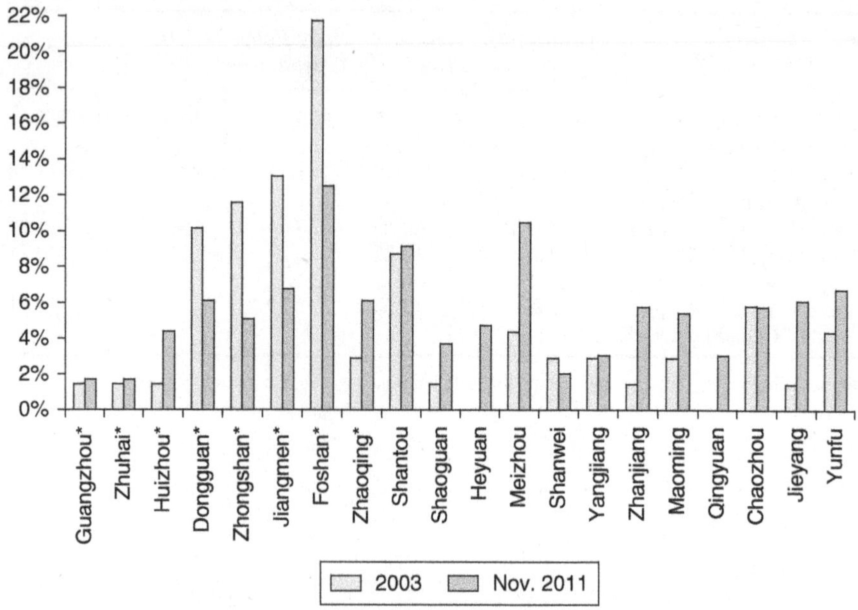

Figure 6.3 Distribution of STs among Guangdong prefectures (%, 2003 and 2011).

Source: Authors' elaboration.

Note: * indicates PRD prefectures.

PRD, but more specifically towards the areas with the lowest firm density (normally the rural areas of the inland region of the province), which in general are also the areas with the lowest GDP level.

Figure 6.4 clearly shows that in 2011 the picture seemed to be much more balanced in terms of geographic distribution of officially recognized STs. The first map shows that the very initial phase of programme implementation was mainly directed to the PRD area, while in subsequent years, the main increases in terms of number of STs have been registered in more peripheral prefectures.

Another clear concentration of STs is easily detectable in the eastern part of the province, close to the Shantou SEZ.

As we can also note from Figure 6.4, up until the end of 2011, Shenzhen hosted no STs while Guangzhou hosted only five. This is probably because these are the two prefectures with the highest level of industrial and urban development, and no specific industrial sector prevails. However, in saying this we have to also underscore the already underlined clear vocation of the Shenzhen area for the electronic sector, and for high-tech firms in general (see Chapter 3). Given the already heavy presence of enterprises in these territories, it is reasonable to expect that the provincial government would have no interest in using the STs tool to further push their industrial development.

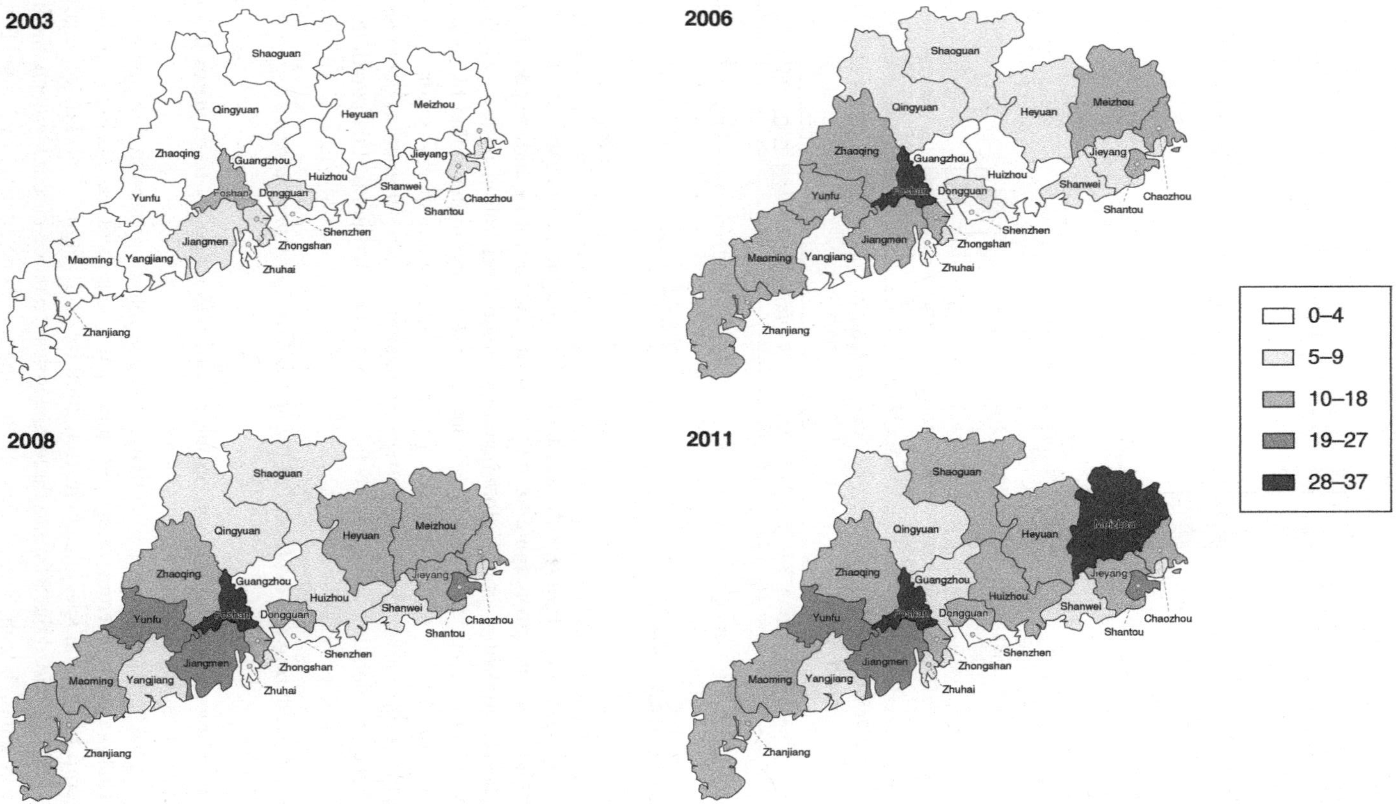

Figure 6.4 Evolution in the number and location of recognized STs in Guangdong province.

Source: Authors' elaboration and Barbieri et al. (2009a, 2009b).

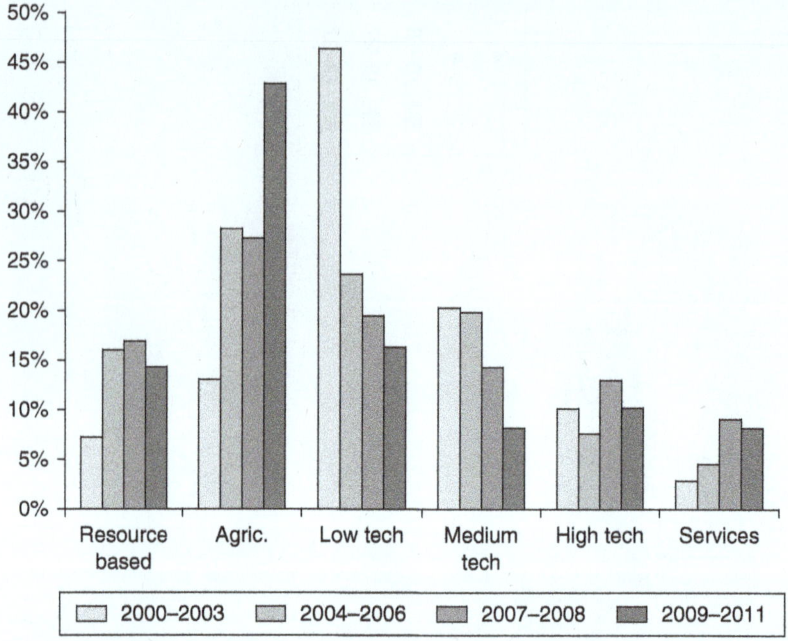

Figure 6.5 Distribution of newly recognized STs in Guangdong according to the sector. Each category only includes the new STs recognized in the considered period.

Source: Authors' elaboration.

These trends seem to indicate that the STs programme is used as a policy tool to influence the geographic location of firms and to follow and support the more general guidelines of the aforementioned double relocation policy (see Section 4.5). Our perception on the development of the programme is that by searching, in these areas, for locations that already demonstrate a specialization (or sometimes simply a vocation for a certain production), the government encourages further agglomeration and connects this to innovation and industrial upgrading.

6.2.4 Analyzing the evolution of the specialized town programme: sectors

Other interesting information on the role of STs as policy tools arises from the analysis of the specialization sectors.

Looking at the sector of activity, it is possible to group the 326 towns in our database into different categories, and then to compare the evolution of STs in terms of sectoral specialization from 2000 to 2011 (Figure 6.5). For our analysis, we have divided the STs into three categories: resource-based, low-tech, medium-tech and high-tech. This classification is the same one adopted by United Nations

Industrial Development Organization (UNIDO) (for more information, see UNIDO, 2002, Technical Annex).

Figure 6.5 illustrates the distribution over time of newly recognized STs, according to sectoral category. This representation allows us to spot possible changes in the structural distribution of STs.

The first three years of implementation of the 'one city, one product' programme show a large prevalence of low-tech sectors (about 46 per cent of the total number of STs). Over time, the weight of this category has progressively decreased, beginning already during the second wave of recognition (2004–2006), when low-tech STs accounted for only 24 per cent of the total.

The medium-tech sectors have also seen a reduction over time: they represented only about eight per cent of the STs recognized in the period 2009–2011, against 20 per cent in the period 2000–2006. This reduction seems to have been compensated for in two ways: on one side with an increase in the weight of services (tourism, business services, logistics, etc.) and high-tech activities, and on the other with a strong growth in the number of agriculture-related and resource-based (such as, e.g. paper production, food processing, stone extraction, etc.) STs. In the case of services and high-tech activities, the growth in the number of STs is slower, probably because it requires heavier investment in the training and attraction of a skilled workforce and advanced technologies.

These changes can be better understood by lining up the data on the sectoral specialization of STs with those of their geographic distribution presented in the previous section. As we have seen, in the most recent years the Department of Science and Technology of Guangdong province has formally acknowledged many new STs in the hinterland areas of the province, which have a rural and mainly agricultural vocation. This has not been done by chance: in this way, the provincial government has used the formal recognition of STs as a direct tool to reach specific industrial aims set by the general policy framework. This goes hand-in-hand with the simultaneous promotion of high-tech manufacturing activities of the tertiary sector, in coherence with the double relocation policy described in Chapter 4. The choice to move from the acknowledgement of purely manufacturing STs to new sectors, and in particular to services and tourism, reflects instead the need to diversify Guangdong's production specialization. This has also been clearly expressed during the interviews we have had the chance to carry out with representatives from the provincial government (and in particular from the DSTGG).

In other words, STs have over time become not only a tool for promoting industrial development, but also a means through which to favour a re-balancing of provincial development, in an effort to increase the innovative potential of less developed areas.

The results of the process of ST recognition in terms of sectoral distribution are shown in Figure 6.6.

The situation in 2011 is noticeably different from the 2003 picture, only a few years after the beginning of the programme's implementation: the low-tech STs have gone from being 47 per cent of the total in 2003 to 27 per cent in

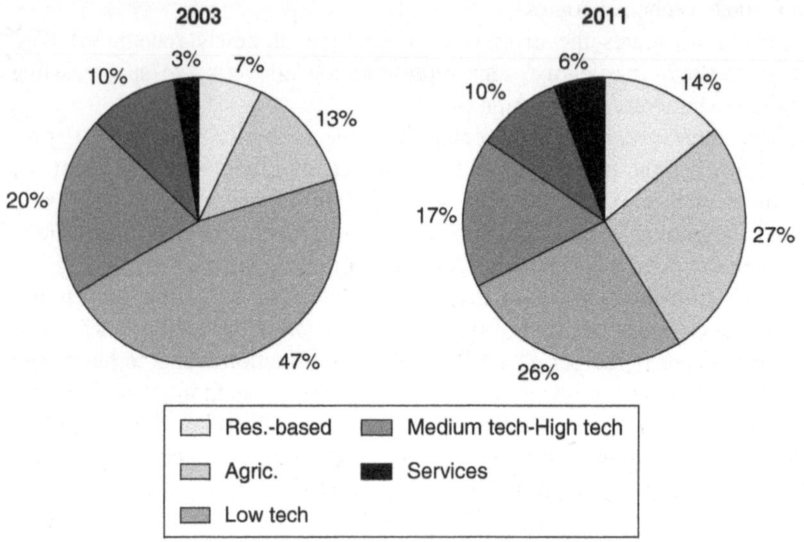

Figure 6.6 Distribution of total number of STs according to the sector, 2003 and 2011.

Source: Authors' elaboration.

2011, counterbalanced by a wide increase in rural STs (from 13 per cent in 2003 to 26 per cent in 2011) and in resource-based STs (from 7 to 14 per cent). The tertiary sector has increased from 3 per cent to 6 per cent. In particular, among the newly recognized STs operating in this field we find Fuxing in Meizhou, Jingxiyuan in Jieyang, Danxiazhen in Shaoguan or Lubao in Foshan for tourism, Dalang in Dongguan for business services and Shatian in Dongguan for logistics.

The emergence of the above-mentioned recent new trends does not mean that traditional sectors do not play a relevant role anymore. In fact, the so-called 'traditional' specializations are still at the core of the industrial development of the province, in coordination with the emerging ones. For example, there are recently acknowledged low-tech STs that continue to focus on textiles/clothing (Xintang in Guangzhou, Junbu and Huicheng in Jieyang, only to mention some), ceramics (e.g. Yujiaozhen in Jieyang and Rencun in Yunfu), furniture (Sanxiang in Zhongshan, recognized in 2008), metal products (e.g. Jindu in Zhaoqing) and handcraft productions (among others, Nipizhen and Anliuzhen in Meizhou). Furthermore, there are agriculture-related towns specializing in aquaculture and fishery, wine, the cultivation and processing of tea, fruits and vegetables (among the most recently recognized, we find Dongli in Zhanjiang, Mianyangzhen and Huanshi in Meizhou, Songbaizhen in Yangjiang and Tiaofeng in Zhanjiang, only to mention some).

Finally, as regards the medium-tech STs, there is an increase in machinery manufacturing and chemical production, while electronics is still the field accounting for the majority of high-tech STs. Nevertheless, also as a consequence of the recent attention of policy makers towards innovation and technology upgrading (for more details, see Chapter 7), some new specializations are also emerging within high-tech productions, such as pharmaceutical chemistry, solar photovoltaic panels or environmental-friendly materials.

According to official sources, several STs produce the vast majority of the national total in their sector of specialization. Among others, Shiling firms (in Guangzhou prefecture) account for one-third of the national production of leather articles, Xintang (Guangzhou) for 60 per cent of the Chinese production of jeans and Fucheng (Yunfu prefecture) for 30 per cent of the world's production of battery chargers (DSTC, 2010, 2011a).

6.3 The support to specialized towns: studying the framework of the 'one city, one product' programme

6.3.1 The overall policy framework and the main policy lines

The data presented in the previous sections show that Guangdong policy makers have used – and still use – the formal recognition of the ST as a tool which goes beyond a mere support of industrial development. In particular, by means of the formal recognition of specialized aggregations of firms, local authorities clearly recognize the importance of the so-called *meso-level*, that is, the territorial dimension of industrial development. Analyzing the policy choices made by governmental authorities in these last few years, it is clear that policy makers are well aware of all the benefits available to firms as a result of their agglomeration, their proximity and cooperation, and their joint action and collective support services. Chinese policy makers seem to have paid particular attention to the successful cases of industrial districts in the developed world, in Europe and in particular in Italy (Di Tommaso and Rubini, 2006; Bellandi and Di Tommaso, 2006; Becattini, 1989).

The formal acknowledgement of STs is, however, not sufficient per se to obtain the economies and advantages that the international literature traditionally assigns to the agglomeration of firms. It is also necessary to foster and consolidate the establishment of relationships among actors. This is particularly difficult if we consider that some STs, as observed by the Department of Science and Technology of Guangdong province, not only tend to overcome the administrative boundaries (city, prefecture and town) but also become inter-sectoral, increasingly involving actors operating in other fields, with growing linkages among agriculture, industry and services (DSTGG, 2003).

In these last few years, the provincial government authorities are concentrating most of their efforts in the attempt to increase innovative capacity and to facilitate the technology upgrading of STs (see Chapter 7 for more details on the innovation policies).

To summarize, the main policy lines recently followed by the DSTGG are (Barbieri *et al.*, 2009b; Di Tommaso and Rubini, 2005, 2006; OECD, 2010) as follows:

1 Support for the innovative capacity of traditional sectors: In this case, the aims are to facilitate the cooperation among firms, to improve workforce quality (the target sectors are mainly labour-intensive) and to support firms' technology upgrading.
2 Promotion of high-tech sectors: As data show (Figure 6.3), the number of high-tech STs is still relatively low, and in many cases there is still a prevalence of foreign-funded companies with control over technology. The government is particularly worried about this situation, especially in light of the already-mentioned attention recent policy measures give to the strengthening of the local productive system (as described in Chapter 4). Therefore, in the future the government will try to increase the foothold of STs in the location in order to better control their technological potential. This cannot be done overnight, but gradually by starting to encourage the collaboration among local and foreign firms and the promotion of capital-sharing initiatives.
3 Promotion of ST establishment in rural and mountainous territories: We have seen that recent efforts of the Guangdong government have been devoted to re-balancing the degree of industrial development among the various prefectures. The DSTGG has already started to pursue this objective by formally acknowledging new STs in rural areas, especially in resource-based and agriculture-related sectors. A second measure moving in the same direction is the promotion of the relocation of high-tech sectors and services to the central PRD area, while moving the low value-added industries towards the external area, in compliance with the double relocation policy presented in Chapter 4. This attempt to also re-balance the development of the province by means of STs is confirmed in the previously mentioned 'Coordinated plan for cluster development in the PRD, 2004–2020', launched by the Guangdong government to increase the competitiveness of the area by supporting the development of *ad hoc* clusters. In particular, as we can see from Table 6.4, the plan clearly identifies specific industrial priorities to be reached in the next few years in terms of ST promotion.

Some of the priorities summarized in Table 6.4 are already being pursued. For example, six agriculture-related STs have been acknowledged since 2004 in Huizhou and seven in Zhaoqing, in accordance with the goal of developing advanced technologies for farming and breeding.

6.3.2 Limitations in the development of specialized towns

The analysis carried out in this chapter shows the strong weight of the 'one city, one product' programme in terms of industrial development, territorial re-balancing and technological upgrading at the provincial level. However, as was reasonable to expect, a policy that was possible in only ten years to spur the recognition of more than 320 STs cannot be problem free. In fact, thanks to the

Table 6.4 Selected development priorities identified by the 'Coordinated plan for cluster development in the PRD, 2004–2020'

	Industrial clusters	*Location*
Agriculture	Special agriculture products	Aquatic plants and flower clusters in Foshan; vegetable clusters in Huizhou and Zhaoqing
	Agriculture modernization	Guangzhou, Shenzhen, Zhuhai, Foshan, Jiangmen, Dongguan, Zhongshan, Huizhou, Zhaoqing
Manufacturing	Central region: electric and building materials	Gaoxin area in Nanhai (Foshan), Sanshui, Gaoming; Zhaoqing
	Eastern region: electric appliances	Dongguan; Longgang and Baoan (Shenzhen); south-western Huizhou
	Western region: household electric appliances, metal products and textiles	Shunde (Foshan); north-western Zhongshan; road no. 325 in Jiangmen
Heavy industry	Steel and petrochemical industries	Industrial area in Shenzhen; Huizhou and Huiyang: petrochemical facilities in Daya Bay
	Steel, petrochemical and paper-making industries	Gaonan Port (Zhuhai); Yinzhouhu (Jiangmen); Doushan in Nanwan
Large-scale equipment manufacturing	Automobile and shipbuilding industries	Wandunsha in Nansha (Guangzhou)
	Auto, electronics and telecom equipment industries	Areas around Baiyun International Airport
High-tech industries	Central region: electronic information, software and biotech industries	Guangzhou Technology City; Guangzhou University City; Guangzhou Biological Island; Guangzhou New City New development districts in Foshan and Nanhai
	Eastern region: high-tech appliances	Songshanhu (Dongguan); Guangming (Shenzhen); Shenzhen University City; Shenzhen Technology Industry Development Zone
	Western region: IT and biotech	Zhongshan Huoju Development Area; Zhuhai University Area; Zhuhai Technology Industry Development Zone
International logistics hub	Strengthen regional and international logistics development	Nansha, Huadou, Baiyun, Huangpu (Guangzhou); Qianhai, Baoan, Pinghu, Yantian (Shenzhen); Western region, Sanzao, Hengqin (Zhuhai)

Source: Authors' elaboration on Li&Fung (2006).

meetings we held over the years with several local actors, to official documents and interviews reported by the local press and to previous studies on this matter (Li&Fung, 2006; Wang, 2009), it has been possible to identify the following problems:

1 Under-utilization of measures supporting innovation: The formal acknowledgement of a ST is usually followed by the establishment of innovation centres serving all firms that operate in the town. The mere creation of these centres, however, is not a guarantee of their success (see Chapters 7 and 8 for more details on this aspect). In many cases, in fact, these innovation platforms are under-utilized: on one side, large firms have their own internal Research and Development (R&D) resources, and on the other, often small firms do not believe in the utility and safety of external resources to promote innovation, fearing information leakages and a consequent loss of competitiveness. This fear is also fuelled by the absence of clear regulation on the protection of Intellectual Property Rights (IPRs), delivering insufficient defence both at the national and international level. Finally, in some cases the publicly funded innovation centres fail to serve as reference points for the promotion of innovation in STs because they are not properly connected to the local production system and the external world, they do not employ adequately prepared personnel and they are not able to properly sensitize potential users as to the benefits of their support measures (Barbieri *et al.*, 2010).

2 Insufficient coordination in ST promotion: The tumultuous growth of STs, coupled with a fierce antagonism among Guangdong municipalities, has caused the multiplication of 'overlapping' towns in the provincial area (Qian and Stiglitz, 1996). Many of them are directly competing with one another because they concentrate on similar productions. In some cases, the situation is even worse and STs operate not only in the same field, but also in the same specific phase of the productive process (Li&Fung, 2006). A strong boost to the whole ST production system would derive from an increased effort on the part of government authorities in developing vertical specializations. This implies driving each ST towards the gradual concentration in a specific stage of the production process, while at the same time facilitating the establishment of vertical relationships among STs (supplier–customer and not competitor–competitor relationships). The result of this action would possibly be a reinforced industrial system at the provincial level and the reduction of internal competition among Guangdong ST. Official sources report that some results are already being seen in this direction. For example, the production of furniture in Shunde (Foshan) is strictly tied to the woodworking machinery in Lunjiao (Foshan), to the paints of Ronggui (Foshan), to the metals of Junan (Dongguan) and so on. These relationships have resulted in the creation of a complex furniture production system that has increased its overall competitive capacity, capable of selling furniture items all over the world (DSTC, 2011a).

3 Problems related to the impact of fast industrial development: The use of the ST promotion tool has undoubtedly been among the factors allowing for rapid development in Guangdong province (and in particular in the PRD). The other side of the coin has been an equally astonishing increase in problems such as air, water and land pollution, resource scarcity, increased labour costs, decrease in the overall quality of life and so on. For this reason, many ST governments are now designing sets of policies specifically aimed at fostering a harmonious development in the area and at decreasing the 'collateral effects' of rapid industrial growth.

6.3.3 The role of local government in the promotion of specialized towns

After the launch of the 'one city, one product' policy, the Department of Science and Technology of Guangdong province strongly encouraged the local governments of STs to increase their role in local development.

This became possible following the 1994 fiscal reform of the tax-sharing system, allowing local governments to share part of the tax revenue with the central government. This change has strongly stimulated local governments to play an active role in the development of the local economic system (Wang and Yue, 2010).

In particular, the DSTGG has identified specific goals for local town government actions (DSTGG, 2003; Barbieri *et al.*, 2009b; Di Tommaso and Rubini, 2005; Bellandi and Di Tommaso, 2005; OECD, 2010):

- To facilitate the creation of support institutions providing services for all firms in the town.
- To promote R&D, coherently with the national focus on industrial technological enhancement (see Chapter 4).
- To favour the diffusion of knowledge within the town, facilitating the flow of specific and reliable information on market scenarios, new technologies, local and international competitors and so on, to single firms. This measure is strategic in STs where there is a prevalence of small and medium-sized firms, for which access to the aforementioned strategic information is more difficult and more expensive to reach.
- To design and implement sector-specific professional training programmes. Once again, this indication is coherent with the overall priority set by the national and provincial governments in improving the quality and skills of the People's Republic of China's (PRC's) workforce as a way to raise the innovative capacity and the competitiveness of Chinese enterprises.
- To favour the diffusion of technology by supporting the relationships between firms and universities/research centres. Many scholars consider technology transfer as an effective tool for the promotion of innovation (see, among others, Audretsch and Feldman, 1996; Bercovitz and Feldman, 2007; Bozeman, 2000; Cohen and Levinthal, 1989; Henderson *et al.* 1998;

Mowery *et al.*, 1996; Niosi, 1994; Powell and Owen-Smith, 1998; Roessner and Wise, 1994). In line with this belief, the Chinese government works at reinforcing the university–industry connection (Barbieri *et al.*, 2010).

- To increase the international visibility of towns by means of national and international events. In accordance with this, many towns have organized sectoral-specific trade fairs, attracting companies not only from China, but from all over the world. Examples of this include the 'International Famous Furniture Fair' in Houjie (Dongguan), the 'China International Lighting Fair' in Guzhen (Zhongshan) or the 'International Fashion Fair' in Humen (Dongguan).

Local governments seem to have followed the indications coming from the DSTGG and have strongly supported the growth of their STs, implementing a wide variety of support actions, ranging from vocational training courses to branding policies at the town level and from the construction of town-level exhibition centres to the organization of big events at the national and international levels.

A common feature of all these interventions is the intent of the local government to avoid supporting specific groups of firms, instead fostering the development of the town as a whole and, as was explicitly argued by one of the interviewed policy makers, maintaining a stable environment that can favour the social and economic development of the town.

In January 2011, a large meeting took place in Dongguan on the development and future evolution of STs, with the participation of policy makers operating at the local and provincial levels. There are two key foreseeable actions for the future of STs (DSTC, 2011a, 2011b).

The first is related to the recent increase in attention towards sustainable development. If, on one side, this can simply be considered a political slogan, several public parks and green areas have actually been established, in addition to industrial infrastructure.

Guangdong policy makers refer to the case of Nanzhuang, in Chancheng prefecture, as an example of excellence in the realignment of ST productions with green standards. The town is famous for the production of ceramics and tiles, accounting for 25 per cent of the national total and 12.5 per cent of the world total. This flourishing sector has increased the wealth of the local population, while at the same time worsening its living conditions because of pollution. The town has worked hard to solve this problem, establishing a research and engineering centre for the study of new clean production processes and pushing for a general requalification of the firms operating in the town. Local policy makers assert that the results are already visible, with a great improvement in air and water quality.

Shilong (Dongguan), a town specialized in the production of digital office equipment, is going in the same direction. In these last few years, the local government has been investing greatly in the diffusion of clean technologies, reduction of power consumption and re-utilization of industrial waste (reaching 100 per cent, according to official sources). For this reason, the town is now called the 'green town of Guangdong'.

In order to facilitate the first application and subsequent diffusion of best practices among STs, there is a plan to select one 'pilot ST' to test the implementation of a sustainable urbanization process, integrated with and supported by technology upgrading, and sustainable growth both at the regional and national levels (DSTC, 2011b, 2011c).

The second action identified by policy makers during the 2011 Dongguan meeting is to promote the evolution of the ST system in order to reach the so-called 'one city, one policy' objective (DSTC, 2011a, 2011c). This means that every town has to find its own development path, while simultaneously supporting the overall economic development of Guangdong province. This implies the following actions defined by five main keywords:

1 '*To free*': To simplify the political administration of STs by further decentralizing the town's economic management to local authorities.
2 '*To transfer*': To optimize and strengthen the industrial structure of STs and to manage urban development.
3 '*To invest*': To restore public accounts to good order in order to have the resources for the renewal of old infrastructures and the construction of new ones.
4 '*To transform*': To promote quality enhancement, especially in traditional industries.
5 '*To defend*': To help STs increase their GDP, their innovation potential and, more generally, their competitive capacity.

7 Innovation dynamics and innovation policies in Guangdong

For a long time, Chinese industrial growth seems to have been based on low-tech manufacturing exports and on the large availability of low-cost human resources, rather than on its capacity to promote innovation and technological upgrading. However, as we partly anticipated in previous chapters, things appear to be changing quickly in the Chinese scenario (see, among others, Zhou and Leydesdorff, 2006; Arvanitis and Jastrabsky, 2006; Kroll and Tagscherer, 2009; Lai *et al.* 2005; Xiang *et al.*, 2011). As China expresses its potential for innovation, Guangdong province is pushing to emerge as a crucial player and specialized towns (STs) seem to be a relevant unit of analysis, where policies for innovation are thought up, experimented with and applied.

This chapter presents some key figures on the innovation dynamics of Guangdong province and Guangdong cities in comparison to other Chinese areas. At the same time, we report the data and information we have collected on the specific policies for innovation that have been promoted in Guangdong in general, as well as within STs. The degree of effectiveness and the cost/benefit ratio of such policies are still an open issue in many respects. We will discuss this aspect more deeply in Chapter 8, by commenting on some recent findings from our research on the coherence of the governments' objectives and firms' innovative behaviour and on the concordance of policy interventions with industrial performance in Guangdong territories. However, before discussing the effectiveness of policies and the desirability of public incentives for innovation, it seems important to us to provide a detailed description of the most relevant measures Guangdong province is taking in this respect. In the second part of this chapter (Sections 7.2–7.4), we highlight the remaining innovation challenges of Guangdong and the policies that are being implemented to face them.

7.1 Key figures on innovation in Guangdong

Although measuring innovation is a controversial issue, there are a number of parameters that can be used as proxies of the innovative capacity of a province or an area: patents, R&D expenditures, investment in human capital, number of established public innovation centres, share of high-tech firms, growth of the high-tech

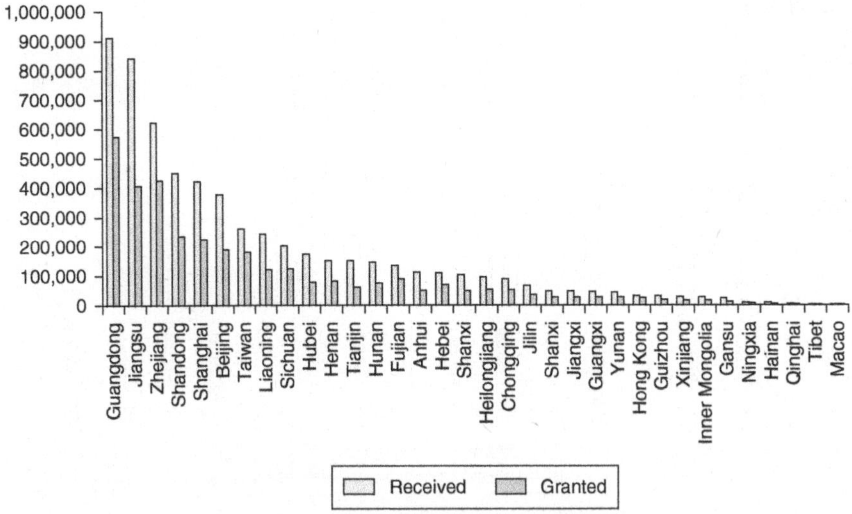

Figure 7.1 Number of accumulated patents in Chinese provinces (1985–2010).

Source: Authors' elaboration on data from State Intellectual Property Office (SIPO) of the PRC.

sector, sales of new products and so forth. As we will see, the comparative figures on Guangdong and other Chinese provinces show that the southern province, in coherence with the objectives set by the recent policies (see Chapter 4), is committed to moving away from a low-tech manufacturing base, displaying significant improvements in this respect and placing high priority on innovation. At the same time, however, figures also show some open issues that call for improvements.

7.1.1 Patents

Even though patenting covers only part of the innovation activities of a country, place or firm, it can reveal important aspects of the capacity to create original products and commercialize innovation. Starting from Figure 7.1, as it is shown, up to 2010, Guangdong was the Chinese province with the highest number of both received and granted patents. It was followed by Jiangsu with a similar number of received patents, but a significantly lower amount of granted ones. Third is Zhejiang, where the rate of patents granted over received is the highest. Among Chinese cities (Figure 7.2), Shenzhen's number of accumulated patents is outstanding. Shenzhen is followed by Guangzhou, Hangzhou, Chengdu and Ningbo, which have considerably lower amounts of accumulated patents. Guangdong has been the province with the highest number of granted patents for 15 years and in 2008, it became the province with the highest number of patents granted for new inventions (Intellectual Property Rights Office, Italian Institute for Foreign Commerce

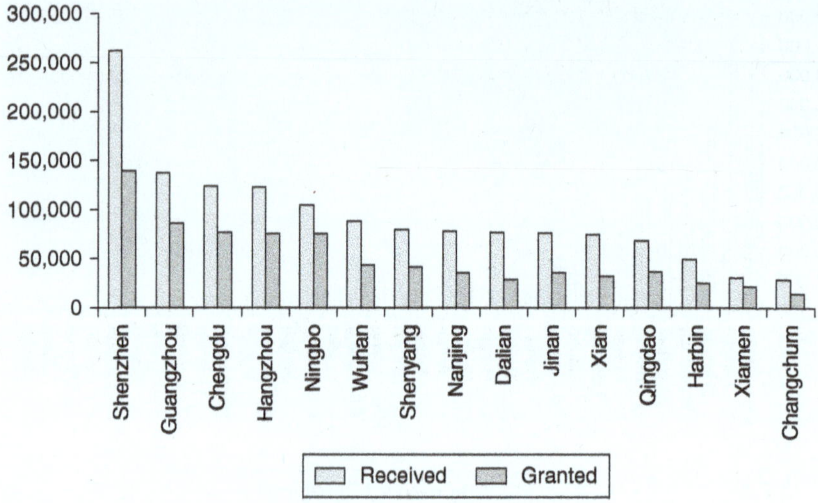

Figure 7.2 Number of accumulated patents in selected Chinese cities (1985–2010).

Source: Authors' elaboration on data from SIPO of the PRC.

(IPR-ICE), 2009). This is an important turn for a province that had a reputation of patenting mainly designs and utility models (Kroll and Tagscherer, 2009).

In the year 2010, Guangdong province was granted a total of 119,346 patents. Of these, 13,691 were patents for new inventions, making Guangdong the leader in this respect, followed by Beijing with 11,209 patents. About 70 per cent of new inventions came from Shenzhen (9,615 patents in 2010). Huawei Technologies Ltd, a leading world producer of telecommunication equipment, on its own was granted 2,776 patents, thus accounting for 23 per cent of the Shenzhen total. This confirms a trend in which patenting activity is concentrated in one single city and one single firm, as is also highlighted by other authors [Kroll and Tagscherer, 2009; Organization for Economic Co-operation and Development (OECD), 2010; IPR-ICE, 2009]. According to OECD (2010), Huawei Technologies Ltd, which has recently become the first applicant under the WIPO Patent Cooperation Treaty, today holds 70 per cent of all Shenzhen patents.

It is worth noting that according to the Department of Science and Technology China (DSTC, 2011c), the total number of patents granted to firms in Guangdong STs in 2010 is 27,000 (out of 41,000 applications). STs therefore produce nearly 23 per cent of the total Guangdong patents. This means that, despite being mainly an agglomeration of small and medium enterprises (SMEs), STs express a remarkable potential for innovation, especially if it is considered that Huawei Technologies Ltd, being located in Shenzhen, does not belong to a ST.

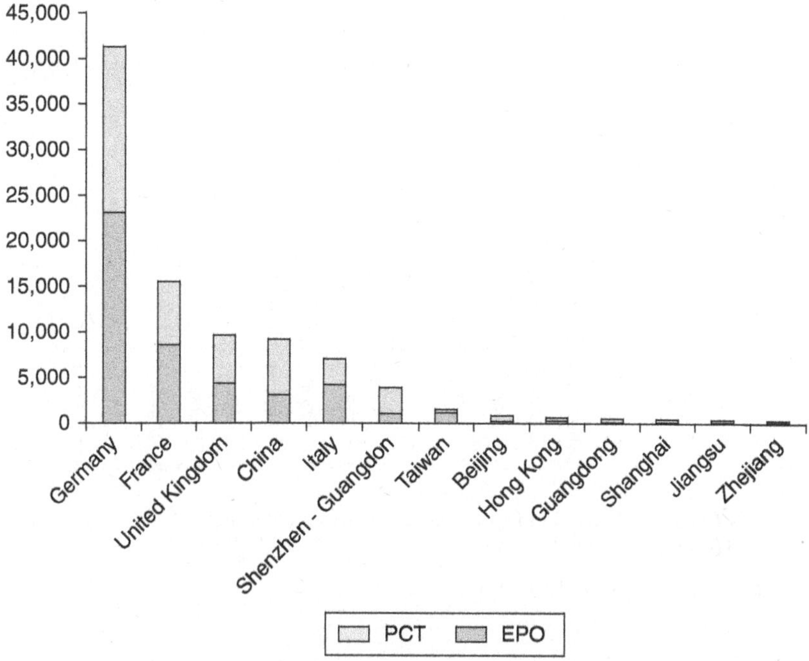

Figure 7.3 Number of patent applications (European Patent Office and Patent Cooperation Treaty) in selected countries and Chinese cities (2007).

Source: Authors' elaboration on OECD statistics.

Although the numbers on patents are constantly increasing, China as a whole still has little weight on the figures of international patent offices [see Figure 7.3 on European Patent Office (EPO) and Patent Cooperation Treaty (PCT)] when compared to other countries such as Germany and France. At the same time, Shenzhen on its own starts displaying figures that are comparable, for instance, to Italy's, and that are well above Taiwan's.

7.1.2 R&D and innovation activities

According to OECD (2010), Guangdong ranks second in China in terms of cumulative R&D spending (1998–2007), and R&D investment is increasing. However, in comparative terms, it appears that other regions are increasing their R&D expenditures at an even faster pace and with a higher intensity. Guangdong ranked sixth in 2008 in terms of R&D per capita and its ratio of R&D expenditures on gross domestic product (GDP) was 1.41 per cent in 2008, below that of other seven provinces (Beijing, Shanghai, Tianjin, Shaanxi, Jiangsu, Zhejiang and Liaoning). Moreover, R&D over GDP increased by only 0.3 per cent in the period 2000–2008, compared to the much higher figures of Zhejiang and Jiangsu (1.1 per cent), Shanghai (1 per

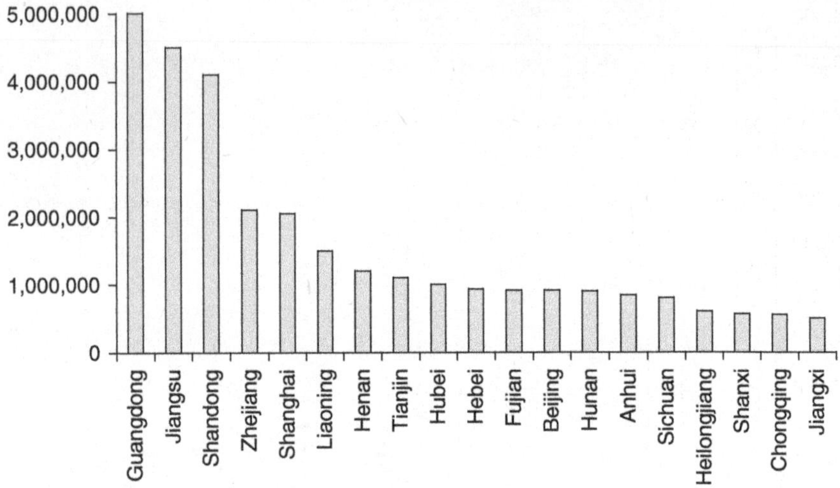

Figure 7.4 R&D expenditures in medium–large enterprises in selected Chinese provinces (10,000 RMB, 2009).

Source: Authors' elaboration on NBS (2010).

cent) and Tianjin (0.9) and several other provinces (OECD, 2010). Guangdong's total expenditure on R&D is remarkably enterprise-led. Around 90 per cent of the total R&D investment in 1998–2007 was made by a few large and medium-sized enterprises (OECD, 2010). We do not know from the Statistical Yearbook data how much of this investment comes from state-owned enterprises (SOEs) and how much from private ones. We know that SOEs in Guangdong account for 16 per cent of industrial output [of above designated size (ADS) firms] and that large and medium firms account for 66 per cent of the output, but no specific information is available on the distribution of R&D investment among firms. According to OECD (2010), the major proportion of R&D investment is private, 39 per cent of which is from multinationals. Figure 7.4 shows how Guangdong ranks first in China in terms of large and medium enterprises' investment in R&D. Figure 7.5 shows how it also ranks first in terms of new product development. This latest figure can be seen as a result of the relatively higher concentration of R&D within firms, whose research is directed more towards marketable results. Jiangsu, Shandong and Shanghai, which also rank high in terms of new products, have an R&D expenditure structure similar to Guangdong's, with firms' expenditures accounting for more than 70 per cent of total investment.

7.1.3 High-tech sectors

The National Bureau of Statistics of Guangdong province (Statistical Bureau of Guangdong Province (SBGP), 2010) identifies as high-tech products those

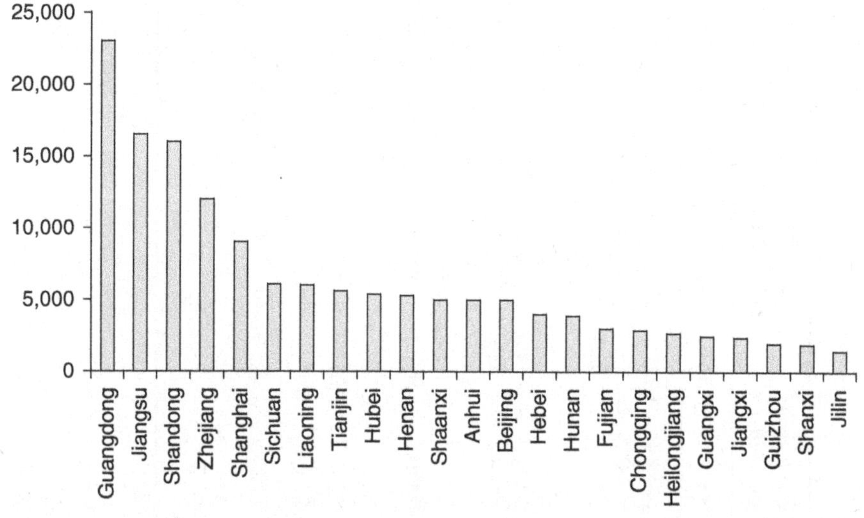

Figure 7.5 Number of new products in selected Chinese provinces (2009).

Source: Authors' elaboration on NBS (2010).

belonging to the following sectors: information, chemical products, medicines, aircraft and spacecraft, electronic and communication equipments, computers and office equipment, and finally medical equipment, instruments and devices. As a whole, Guangdong province produces high-tech items for an output value of 1,722.435 million RMB (242.09 million US$, in 2009), representing nearly 30 per cent of the total Chinese high-tech industrial output (Table 7.1). It accounts for 33 per cent of Chinese employment in high-tech sectors and 21 per cent of high-tech enterprises. The figures have been increasing since 2000, with a slight decrease in 2009. Both in terms of output and value added, sectors related to computers and office equipment seem to be the ones that suffered most from the economic crisis, as shown by the decreasing figures in 2009. As we have already underlined, this could be explained by the fact that in Guangdong these are the high-tech sectors that triggered the export-oriented growth of the last decades and were therefore more exposed to the shocks of external demand (see also Section 2.2.2). Other sectors, such as communication equipment, maintained a positive growth trend even in 2009, but it is the medicinal sector that registered the highest increases in the 2008–2009 period. Taking into account the whole period 2000–2009, the highest growth in terms of output is registered by the manufacturing of aircrafts and spacecraft, and also, as expected, by computers and office equipment, communication and electronic equipments and medical equipment, instruments and devices.

Indicators on high-tech exports and imports are available from the Guangdong Statistical Yearbook (GSY) (SBGP, 2010). However, the product classification

Table 7.1 Main economic indicators of high-tech sectors in Guangdong province

	Number of enterprises (unit)			*Average number of employees (10,000 persons)*			*Gross industrial output value (million RMB)*			*Value-added industry (million RMB)*		
	2000	*2008*	*2009*	*2000*	*2008*	*2009*	*2000*	*2008*	*2009*	*2000*	*2008*	*2009*
Total	1,738	5,789	5,661	81.65	316.55	313.91	274.3	1,687.1	1,722.4	68,831	366,362	385,274
% on China	18	22	21	21	33	33	26	30	29	n.a.	n.a.	n.a.
Information chemical products	45	52	58	1.47	1.45	1.45	26.1	57.1	62.4	6.71	16.96	20.96
Medicines	255	377	396	6.28	8.87	9.94	186.1	498.7	618.0	66.43	168.26	211.05
Manufacture of aircraft and spacecraft	1	6	7	0.22	0.80	0.49	4.7	45.2	44.0	2.26	15.00	13.19
Electronic and communication equipment	1,145	4,194	4,033	59.94	221.10	216.33	1,867.8	10,150.4	11,007.2	459.90	2,421.66	2,658.90
Computers and office equipment	187	693	681	11.50	71.82	73.51	606.6	5,630.4	5,067.0	135.53	883.73	816.22
Medical equipment, instruments and meters	105	467	486	2.24	12.52	12.20	52.1	489.9	425.7	17.48	158.01	132.43

Source: Authors' elaboration on NBS (2010) and SBGP (2010).

used for high-tech import and export is different from the one used for high-tech industrial output. Therefore, figures are not immediately comparable. As a whole, high-tech exports in 2009 amounted to 139.374 million US$, representing 55 per cent of the total high-tech output value. Exports of computers and communication technologies accounted for 84 per cent of the total exports. On the other hand, imports amounted to 115.084 million US$. Of this, 56 per cent was in electronic technology, followed by computer and communication technology (26.36 per cent) and photoelectric technology (12 per cent).

In SBGP (2006), the classification of high-tech sectors is the same for trade and industrial output. The number of high-tech firms in 2005 is consistent with that of Table 7.1. In 2005, there were 4,998 high-tech firms producing output for 1,195.971 million RMB (144.5 million US$).

High-tech exports in 2005 were 83.579 million US$. This means that, already in that year, 56 per cent of the total industrial output value in high-tech sectors was exported. Imports amounted to 70.472 million US$.

Table 7.2 represents the import and export values of high-tech industries by trade form and type of firm. Most high-tech import and export activities take place in enterprises 'solely funded' by foreign investors (91,031 million US$ in value, equal to 59 per cent of the total). However, a considerable amount of trade is also carried out by joint ventures (15.7 per cent of total) and SOEs (13.7 per cent of total). The majority of trade is processing trade with imported material (Kroll and Tagscherer, 2009). As regards exports, a relevant part of trade is also carried out with customer material,[1] while general trade and (to a lesser extent) storage of free trade zones account for a significant part of total imports. Data from SBGP (2006) also confirm a distinctive feature of Guangdong high-tech export development: it is highly concentrated in the cities of Shenzhen and Dongguan, which on their own accounted for 74 per cent of both exports and total trade of high-tech products in 2005.

7.1.4 Investment in human capital

A crucial aspect for the innovation potential of Guangdong is the investment in human capital. The investment in education, particularly in secondary and higher education, is a necessary step in building a wide base of people who can engage in R&D and innovation activities and who can contribute to increasing the knowledge content of Guangdong industrial productions.

As Table 7.3 shows, most educational funds are managed by local governments. In this context, Guangdong ranks first among Chinese provinces in terms of total funds for education (11.662 million RMB in 2008, equal to about 1.6 million US$). For all provinces, most educational funds come from budgetary appropriations from the central government. However, with respect to other top provinces, Guangdong shows a much higher component of funds coming from private schools and tuition fees. On the contrary, Jiangsu and Zhejiang (ranking second and third, respectively) display a lower contribution from private schools and tuition fees, but a higher contribution from donations, fundraising and other

Table 7.2 High-tech imports and exports in Guangdong province by the type of firm and trade form (2005)

Type of firm	*Total imports and exports (100 million US$)*	*Trade form (100 million US$)*	*Total exports (100 million US$)*	*Trade form (100 million US$)*	*Total imports (100 million US$)*
Total	*1,540.51*	*Total*	*835.79*	*Total*	*704.72*
State-owned	211.33	General trade	53.38	General trade	109.33
Cooperatives	46.05	Processing trade	762.82	Processing trade (with imported material)	478.56 (412.55)
Joint ventures	242.87	Processing with customer material	117.56	Equipment with customers' material	10.75
Solely funded	910.31	Processing with imported material	645.26	Leasing trade	11.17
Collective-owned	43.79	Import and export of bonded warehouse	4.05	Equipment with investment	25.79
Private	85.67	Storage of free trade zones	15.53	Import and export of bonded warehouse	5.64
Others	0.49	Others (including aid material)	0.01	Storage of free trade zones	63.22
				Others*	0.26

Source: SBGP (2007).

Note: * Including equipment of export processing zones.

Table 7.3 Main figures on educational funding: selection of top Chinese provinces (10,000 RMB, 2008)

	Total funds	*Government appropriation for education*	*Budgetary (%)*	*Funds from private schools*	*Donations and fund raising*	*Income from teaching and research*	*Tuition fees (%)*	*Other educational funds*
Central government's total	15,690,032	9,816,068	98.1		138,558	4,784,690	49.3	950,717
Local government's total	129,317,342	94,680,228	92.1	698,479	888,105	28,886,021	73.2	4,164,509
Guangdong	11,661,554	8,013,744	93.9	119,170	89,064	3,088,448	73.6	351,128
Jiangsu	9,964,272	6,484,818	87.9	31,551	147,410	2,650,610	64.2	649,883
Zhejiang	7,972,834	5,172,415	83.3	20,620	177,646	2,035,378	71.6	566,775
Shandong	7,749,148	5,747,058	88.8	23,057	24,128	1,801,350	72.7	153,555
Sichuan	6,578,338	4,894,707	94.0	61,106	75,537	1,437,698	57.3	109,290
Henan	6,561,523	4,976,900	95.2	39,889	3,850	1,424,592	78.4	116,292
Hebei	5,584,914	4,171,281	91.8	10,606	4,971	1,196,773	80.2	201,283
Hunan	5,066,050	3,436,066	94.5	35,152	20,764	1,376,082	75.4	197,987
Shanghai	4,823,026	3,674,055	87.1	4,816	12,762	835,427	82.4	295,967
Liaoning	4,792,311	3,674,925	91.7	25,737	2,544	1,011,819	81.3	77,287
Beijing	4,690,166	3,833,068	91.8	13,447	42,640	677,724	70.0	123,286

Source: Authors' elaboration on NBS (2010).

Table 7.4 Number of students per 100,000 persons: selection of Chinese provinces (2009)

Province	*Senior secondary*	*Ranking (secondary school)*	*Higher education*	*Ranking (higher education)*	*% of higher education on total population*	*Number of higher education institutions*
Shaanxi	4,901	1	3,045	4	0.030	89
Hubei	4,480	2	2,829	5	0.028	120
Shanxi	4,444	3	2,050	14	0.021	71
Ningxia	4,167	4	1,721	25	0.017	15
Henan	4,149	5	1,774	22	0.018	99
Chongqing	4,028	6	2,317	10	0.023	50
Gansu	3,969	7	1,806	20	0.018	39
Guangdong	3,950	8	1,952	18	0.020	125
Qinghai	3,763	9	1,080	30	0.011	9
Fujian	3,725	10	2,039	16	0.020	84
Jiangsu	3,677	13	2,786	6	0.028	148
Tianjin	3,040	24	4,432	2	0.044	55
Beijing	2,475	29	6,410	1	0.064	86
Shanghai	1,982	31	4,393	3	0.044	66

Source: Authors' elaboration on NBS (2010).

finance channels. As a whole, it seems that top investing regions are differentiating funding sources, although from different channels. One way is to fund the public education system with additional funds from donors (e.g. former students who are now wealthy) or with other sources (e.g. enterprise investments); the other way is to align public education with private institutions. While in both cases, there is a need to increase the total available resources, in the latter there is also a perception of the scarce capacity of the public system to provide for the population's educational needs. Although formally accepted by the central government, private education and the rules that should govern it are still at the centre of debate in China (Zhu and Ip, 2002; Yeung and Chu, 1998).

Despite the high investment in education, Guangdong ranks lower in terms of number of students than it does in other fields (Table 7.4). While the position in terms of students in secondary education over total population is good, Guangdong ranks particularly poorly in terms of number of students engaged in higher education over total population, especially if compared with other high-income provinces. This could be explained by two features of Guangdong. First, it is a place where rapid industrial growth has created many job opportunities in the last decades. These have attracted people from rural areas in search of new jobs. Thus, people choose to live in Guangdong mainly for working purposes (see Chapter 5). This could justify in part the lower proportion of students. Second, it might reflect the lack of top-ranked universities, which implies that students might prefer migrating to other provinces to obtain a third-level degree. In particular, if we compare Guangdong with other fast-growing provinces such as Shanghai and Beijing, it is clear that Guangdong has more higher education

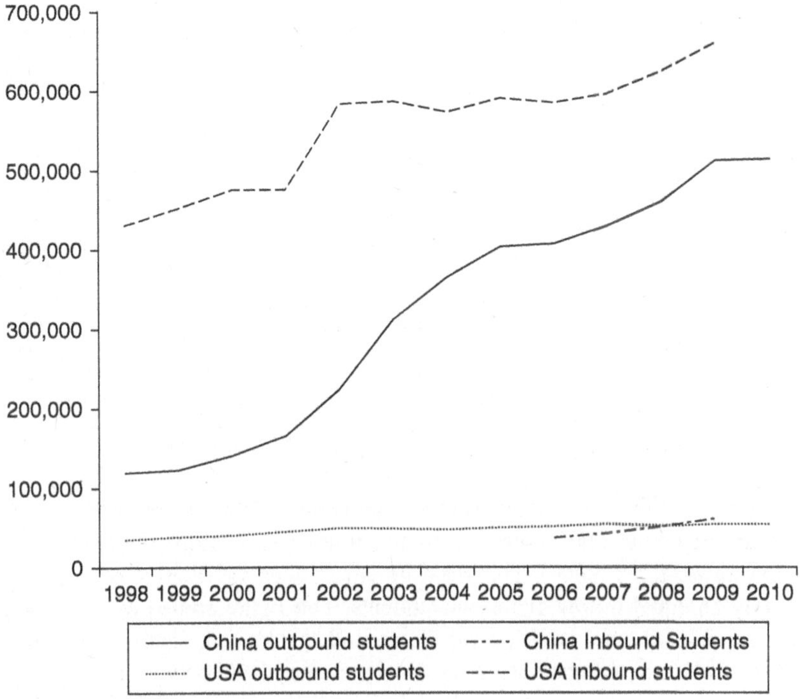

Figure 7.6 Outbound and inbound international students in China and the United States ISCED levels 5 and 6 (higher education and PhD).

Source: Authors' elaboration on data from the UNESCO Institute of Statistics (2010).

institutions, but a lower number of graduate students as well as a lower incidence of graduate students over total population.

7.1.5 Internationalization of the innovation system

While trying to describe the main features of Guangdong's innovation system, it is interesting to note its degree of internationalization. Given the lack of specific data on this, we are forced to offer a more general view of China as a whole. One can argue that a country's innovative capacity is enhanced through the confrontation with other places and the interaction with people from different cultures. We have seen in Chapter 4 that China has undergone decades of reform to gradually open up to foreign investment, foreign trade, foreign capital, but yet foreign academics find it difficult to understand many of the mechanisms guiding China's economic development. As academics, after many years of fieldwork, we still feel it is difficult to permeate Chinese internal debates, to exactly understand their research projects and to read what they write in Chinese. There has been some opening towards other education systems as witnessed by the

Table 7.5 Outbound and inbound international students (1,000 students): 2009 ranking and changes from 2007

	Outbound students				*Inbound students*		
	2009	*Ranks*	*2007*		*2009*	*Ranks*	*2007*
China	512	↔	283	United States	661	↔	596
India	195	↔	146	United Kingdom	369	↔	351
Korea	126	↔	103	Australia	258	1↑	247
Germany	92	↔	76	France	250	↔	212
Malaysia	54	3↑	42	Germany	198	↔	207
United States	54	1↑	46	Japan	132	↔	115
France	51	1↓	53	Russia	130	2↑	60
Turkey	47	4↑	37	Canada	93	↔	80
Russia	47	1↑	43	Italy	66	1↑	57
Canada	46	1↓	43	China	61	3↓	97

Source: Authors' elaboration on data from the UNESCO Institute of Statistics (2010).

increase in the number of students sent abroad (Figure 7.6). Many of these students return to China and contribute to the internal diffusion of knowledge[2] (Zhou and Leydesdorff, 2006). This flow, however, does not seem to be counterbalanced by an equal inflow of foreign students. The figure compares the trends in outbound and inbound students for China and the United States. Very little data are available for inbound students. However, the data show an unbalanced situation between Chinese students abroad and foreign students in China, with the latter being much less numerous, whereas the US experience is precisely the opposite.

In addition, the international rankings on inbound and outbound students call for attention (Table 7.5). China ranked first in terms of Chinese students abroad, both in 2007 and 2009. However, it ranked tenth in terms of inbound students in 2009, after losing three positions since 2007. Thus, while China maintains the leadership in terms of students abroad, the number of international students studying in China is actually decreasing.

This data give some first interesting insights into the human capital investment strategy of China. Up to now, China seems to have invested in a one-way flow of knowledge, that ensures a pool of young people formed abroad, who can then share their acquired knowledge of other cultures and systems with Mainland China. The opposite strategy of attracting foreign students, adopted, for example, by the United States, at the moment does not seem to apply to the Chinese scenario. This is probably also due to the rapidly changing internal demand for education, which is sufficiently high to match the available supply.

In addition to the data on human capital internationalization and in the absence of specific data on research projects with foreign universities or international R&D and innovation collaborations, some useful insights can come from the analysis of the percentage of patents held by foreigners in China, held by Chinese abroad and of co-invented patents. Figure 7.7 displays, for each of the selected

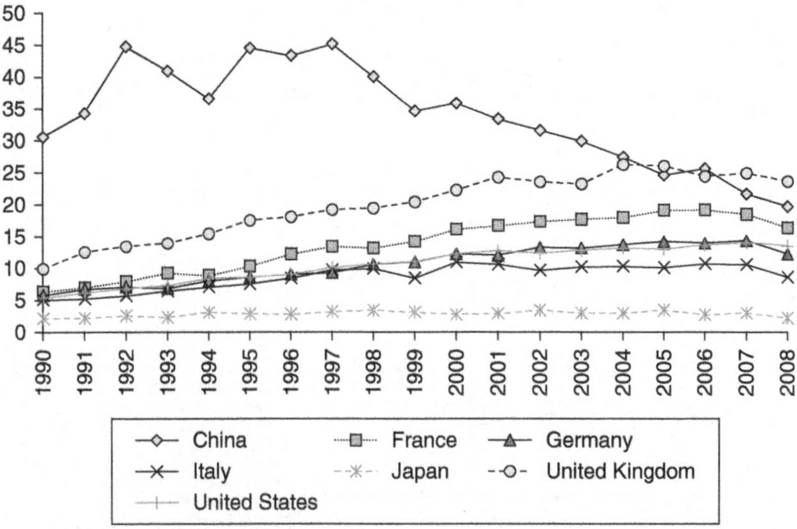

Figure 7.7 EPO patent applications: percentage of patents with foreign co-inventors by country of inventor's residence (1990–2008).

Source: Authors' elaboration on OECD statistics.

countries of inventor's residence, the percentage of patent applications to the EPO that are co-invented with other countries. Western economies have registered either stable or increasing trends up until 2005 and 2006, then there is a slight decrease in the years 2007–2008. When looking at China, on the contrary, it is clear that the decrease started long before and it has a much more evident trend.

Similar trends can be traced for applications under the Patent Cooperation Treaty (PCT), whereas there is a slight increase in patent grants of Chinese co-inventions under the US patent office (USPO). This percentage increased from 17 per cent to 35 per cent in the years 1990–1993 and has remained stable (at around 38 per cent) ever since.

Proceeding with the analysis of patents under EPO, Figures 7.8 and 7.9 show the percentage of patents owned by foreign residents and that of patents invented abroad but owned by domestic residents.

The trends for China are again decreasing, whereas those of other countries are stable. If we match these trends with an overall increase in absolute numbers of Chinese patents, we can highlight a scenario where basically EPO patents are owned increasingly more by Chinese residents in China.[3]

The picture on the exchange of students and on the collaboration in patenting activities would seem to imply a possible exclusionary attitude towards cooperation in knowledge-intensive activities, even though, as we will argue in this chapter, policy documents stress the importance of internationalizing the innovation system. There could be several reasons for such an attitude. At this stage, an 'infant industry argument' for collaboration in highly innovative activities might

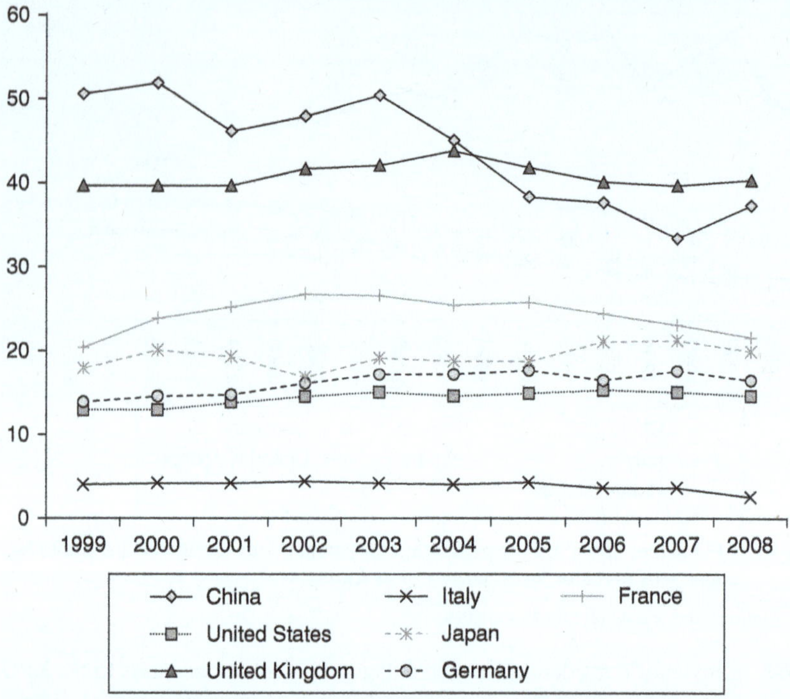

Figure 7.8 EPO patent applications: percentage of patents owned by foreign residents (1999–2008).

Source: Authors' elaboration on OECD statistics.

prevail. In other words, favouring inflows of information over outflows could give China a sort of comparative advantage on the accumulation of knowledge. At the same time, it allows for management and control of the agenda of an internal diffusion of cultural diversity that could pose threats to the government's reform schedule. A possible interpretation is that China intends to open up to collaborations in knowledge-intensive activities but, as in other reforms, governments want to set the timing, conditions and speed of such an opening. This implies slowing down certain changes even though they might be declared (and we will see this is the case) as desirable in the long run.

7.2 Challenges and limitations of the Guangdong innovation system

According to the data discussed above and to other contributors (see, among others, OECD, 2010), there appears to be a number of limitations to Guangdong province's innovation model:

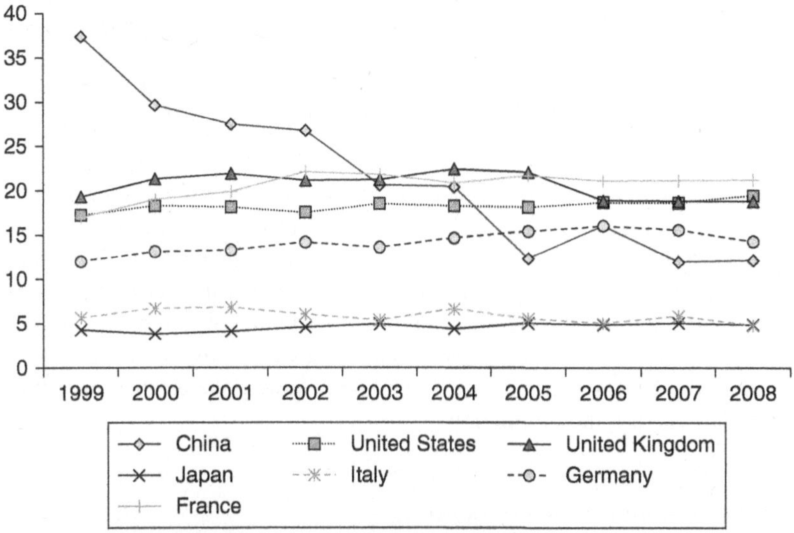

Figure 7.9 EPO patent applications: percentage of patents invented abroad (owned by domestic residents) (1999–2008).

Source: Authors' elaboration on OECD statistics.

1 Innovation mainly takes place within firms. This can be a positive feature since it can spur the competitiveness of manufacturing sectors, but at the same time it can indicate a lower R&D and innovative capacity of public research institutions. Besides, firms' research activities tend to focus on applied R&D, and in the absence of a strong commitment from public institutes, basic R&D could be neglected. This could favour incremental innovation to the detriment of new cutting-edge technologies and radical innovation.
2 Firms tend to innovate with a market-driven approach, meaning that they follow market demand, rather than anticipating it. This leaves firms more exposed to the competition with external actors on innovation. Furthermore, foreign investors to a large extent continue to see Guangdong as a place in which to invest in assembling activities, although this perception is gradually changing (Walsh, 2003; Li and Zhong, 2003).
3 Innovation in Guangdong still seems to be over-concentrated in a very few places and in an extremely small number of firms. Shenzhen and Guangzhou are basically the only places where new technologies are developed. And firms, such as Huawei Technologies, hold the vast majority of patents and are responsible for a great proportion of the province's R&D expenditures. This over-concentration makes it difficult to develop a widespread culture of research and innovation.

4 The accumulation of knowledge and the investment in human capital, which are basic elements for stimulating innovation, still seem to be characterized by a low degree of internationalization.

In other words, at the moment the Guangdong innovation model appears to be unbalanced favouring firms as the main actor of innovation, and moreover favouring very few firms. The collaboration among firms and with other institutions (such as universities, public research institutes, innovation and service centres, financial services, etc.) is still at the very initial stage and it is not the standard operating model. This makes it hard to identify a proper system of innovation in Guangdong. Given these limitations, it becomes important to understand the provincial and local governments' degree of awareness of these limitations. In the following paragraphs, we analyse the policies that are being implemented to address such limitations.

7.3 Innovation policies for Guangdong

Guangdong government policy documents clearly state that industrial upgrading and innovation are seen as key determinants of the capacity to increase competitiveness and to maintain a good export performance in the long run (Department of Science and Technology of Guangdong Government (DSTGG), 2006a; DSTC, 2011a, 2011b; Clark and Guy, 1997). This focus on innovation has emerged from the official documents of specific government departments (such as the DSTGG) and from more general planning documents such as the already mentioned 'Outline of the Plan for the Reform and Development of the Pearl River Delta (2008–2020)' (hereinafter, Outline for the PRD), issued by the National Development and Reform Commission in December 2008 (see Chapter 2).[4] According to this document, the PRD has to boost its innovative capacity in critical areas, such as, among others, electronics, biology and new medicine, new materials, energy conservation and so on. This will be done by building new university-based science and technology parks, incubators for research and pilot experiment bases. These policy interventions have to be directed towards the improvement of the capacity of firms to carry out independent innovation activities and to strengthen their connections with university and research centres.

Even if specifically targeting only the PRD area, this document is in line with the priorities identified by the Guangdong government that we have described in detail in Chapter 4. In particular, innovation has been a recurrent theme in many of the documents of the DSTGG in the last few years (among others, DSTGG, 2006a, 2006b; DSTC, 2011c, 2011d).

These indications apply both for high-tech sectors and for more traditional ones. In fact, on one hand, Chinese governments feel the need to increase the value added of their industrial productions favouring the development of high-tech sectors. On the other, they wish to improve the quality and value added of more traditional productions, such as textiles, footwear, metal product, furniture and so on (Xie, 2006; Simmie, 2004; Maskel and Malmberg, 1999; Barbieri *et al.*, 2010).

Among the specific policy tools to promote innovation, Guangdong has in the last decades invested mainly in two types of activities: (1) designing laws and regulations in order to create an innovation-friendly environment and (2) promoting specific active programmes to encourage innovation.

1 Laws and regulations to create an innovation-friendly environment: In this field, Guangdong, following a trend also encouraged by the central government, has invested in particular in developing an appropriate institutional framework to protect property rights. Patenting activity has increased in the last decade as shown in the previous sections. At first, specific incentives and financial support for firms that are able to patent their innovations have facilitated such trends (IPR-ICE, 2009). However, as a side effect, these incentives have contributed to speculation and low-quality patents. This has forced the government to intervene with revisions of the Patent Law to increase the quality standards required to file applications. Several international agreements were also been signed by China when it joined the World Trade Organization (WTO). In addition, since 2004, the National System for the Protection of Intellectual Property Rights (IPRs) is in charge of guiding and monitoring IPRs procedures. The system is composed of 12 bodies, among which are the State Intellectual Property Rights Office, the Supreme People's Court, the Ministry of Commerce, the National Administration for Copyright (IPR-ICE, 2009). As a whole, the increase in the patenting figures under international patent offices and agreements is a sign of China's improved patenting capacity.
2 Specific active programmes to encourage innovation: The issue of technological upgrading and innovation is not a new one in China and in Guangdong. Already in the 1980s, shortly following the open-door policies, several programmes were launched to increase the scientific content of Chinese manufacturing. Two phases can be highlighted with respect to innovation policy.

In the first phase (1980s and 1990s), the focus was on the creation of areas devoted to high-tech research and to highly innovative firms. Programmes such as '831' and 'Torch' were launched at the national level and adopted by provinces (Arvanitis and Jastrabsky, 2006). The main result of these policies has been the creation of high-tech development zones and high-tech districts (see Section 4.4.5). The main aim of these policies was to attract foreign firms and multinationals that could transfer knowledge to the local economy. Innovation was basically seen as the imitation of more advanced technologies (Arvanitis and Jastrabsky, 2006; Kroll and Tagscherer, 2009).

A second phase of innovation policies was launched in China in 1998 and was acknowledged in Guangdong, as demonstrated by the publication of report no. 16 (Guangdong Government, 1998). Then again in 2006 it was reinforced with the diffusion of the central government's 'Outline of National Medium and Long Term Programme for Science and Technology Development (2006–2020)' (China State Council, 2006). These official documents marked a shift to an 'indigenous' and 'independent' model of innovation (IPR-ICE, 2009). The aim was, and still is, to move away from a paradigm of innovation based on imitation. Imitation is clearly not perceived as a long-term self-sustaining growth engine and furthermore, it has started to be considered a threat to China's manufacturing reputation. One of the key targets of new policies is to shift from a 'Made in China' manufacturing to a 'designed in China' one (Economist Corporate Network (ECN), 2011). In terms of policy instruments this has meant:

- greater attention to incentives for the patenting activities of big and innovative Chinese firms (IPR-ICE, 2009);
- subsidies, tax reductions and exemptions on R&D expenditures and revenues from innovation activities, preferential value-added tax (VAT) policies on software and high-tech exports (Arvanitis and Jastrabsky, 2006);
- an increased role for innovation in SMEs and clusters of SMEs: In this context, the programme for STs was developed in Guangdong together with investment in public innovation centres and public innovation platforms (see Section 7.4.1). Thus, the reality of STs is inherently related to the attempt to stimulate independent innovation not only in high-tech firms, but also in traditional productions;
- official qualification of indigenous innovation products: These products must have trademarks owned by Chinese firms, be produced in China and be protected by intellectual property rights owned by the firm, which also guarantees high-quality standards through official certifications. The crucial aspect is that these products are preferred over foreign ones in government procurement procedures [US–China Business Council (USCBS), 2011].

7.3.1 Recent developments in innovation policies: twelfth five-year plan

Both in the recent national five-year development plan and in Guangdong official documents (Guangdong Government, 2008a, 2008b), the concept of 'indigenous innovation' or 'independent innovation' is reinforced as being the core of the innovation strategy (ECN, 2011; DSTC, 2011b, 2011c, 2011d).

In the national scenario, coastal regions have a pivotal role for the future of China's innovation. They have been developing at a faster pace, they are the richest ones and the ones that have attracted the highest amount of foreign capital, as well as general private initiatives. In this context, coastal regions are required to use (1) traditional industrial policy measures, such as support for 'national champions' that should increase higher value-added activities and R&D and (2) experimental projects, pilot schemes and the setting up of new R&D centres (ECN, 2011).

It is clear from the prescriptions of Guangdong's twelfth five-year plan[5] that the province has accepted the challenge that the national government has placed on coastal regions. Not only does Guangdong wish to upgrade its industries, but also to increase the value added of its products and shift from a low-tech manufacturing base to a high-tech one. The ambition, as stated in the plan, is different: 'to 2015, the development of science and technology will contribute more to economic growth. Guangdong will *lead* the country in innovation capacity and carve out a new development mode driven by innovation' (authors' translation).

This general statement is followed by a number of specific indications on targets and objectives, financing and sector priorities (see the following section).

7.3.2 Main innovation targets and objectives of the twelfth five-year plan

As has been the case with the previous five-year plans, a number of specific objectives and quantifiable targets have been set in the current plan at the national level, and then integrated in the provincial plans. Some of them are binding targets. This means that they become 'performance indicators' for officials who are in charge of accomplishing the goals. If a goal is not met, the responsible officials will see the consequences to their career prospects (ECN, 2011; Li and Zhou, 2005).

With specific reference to innovation and industrial upgrading, the plan foresees a general 'breakthrough' in emerging strategic industries. In addition, it foresees (see also Section 4.5):

- an increase in the service sector value added by 4 percentage points (with respect to the previous plan), in order to account for 47 per cent of the total GDP (figures pertaining to 2011 point to a current 46 per cent);
- R&D expenditures should account for 2.2 per cent of the GDP (at the moment, they account for 1.8 per cent);
- patents should number 3.3 for every 10,000 people.

These targets are 'expected' rather than 'binding', which means that their compliance rules are less severe (ECN, 2011).

The achievements of innovation targets, as well as the more general restructuring targets, are conditioned upon a number of specific measures that include direct financing in innovative projects, emerging industry priorities and indications on foreign direct investment (FDI) (particularly on FDI with a strong R&D component).

Specifically, the twelfth five-year plan of Guangdong dedicates Chapters 2 and 3 to innovation, with the general aim of strengthening independent innovation and promoting an innovation-driven economic and social development.

Following the general statement, the plan lists a number of specific guidelines, which recommend the following:

1 Improvement of the innovation mechanism, to be achieved in particular, through:

   a Strengthening of innovative enterprises, which means investment in innovative programmes for SMEs as well as encouraging large SOEs and private firms to increase their R&D component and investment in the creation of 50 national innovation-oriented 'champions'.
   b Improvement in resource allocation by increasing government investment in innovation and improving the departmental coordination mechanisms, the information sharing procedures and the performance evaluation system; encouraging multinational companies to set-up R&D centres in Guangdong and to experiment with new forms of international collaboration in science and technology.
   c Develop cooperation among institutions, particularly through national and provincial alliances on R&D and through research cooperation among firms, universities and institutions.
   d Improve the system of innovation incentives by further accelerating tax breaks, deductions and other incentives for investment in R&D and by exploring other mechanisms such as human capital property right incentives to stimulate creative talents.

2 Enhancement of innovation capability to be achieved with the following measures:

   a Improvement of the infrastructures for innovation, including existing and new technology platforms, technology centres, provincial laboratories, engineering and enterprise centres, quality laboratories and the like. Guangzhou and Shenzhen are in charge of becoming the first 'innovation-oriented cities' and the PRD will take the lead in promoting the country's innovative region.
   b Promotion of breakthrough technologies, cutting-edge research and original innovation; development of new products with independent property rights in order to enhance the province's self-sufficiency; promotion of innovation in traditional industries through common innovation platforms in traditional industrial clusters.

3 Stimulus to creative talents, in order to achieve widespread high-level personnel:

   a Push the recruitment of a high-level workforce, strengthen guidance for overseas personnel and establish channels for the introduction of overseas talents.
   b Build a multi-level training system: Universities should encourage and guide enterprises to establish joint training mechanisms; continue the implementation of existing programmes to promote outstanding talents,

'pearl' scholars and PhDs; aim at having 800,000 people engaged in S&T activities by 2015 (in 2009 they amounted to 531,900; SBGP, 2010).

c Improve human resource services and management systems: Ensure basic functioning of the market in the allocation of human resources to eliminate restrictions to the flow of talent coming from different urban and rural areas, sectors and departments.

d Create an optimal environment for innovation, through the promotion of public awareness around science and innovation; the definition of laws and regulations to spur innovation; the stimulation of improved technology policies and competitive merit-based systems.

4 Accelerate the construction of a world-leading modern industrial base, mainly by:

a Developing the services for production: finance, insurance, information services, exhibitions and so on. One main focus is on financial services, with the creation of several zones for the experimentation of financial reforms and areas in which to demonstrate them. A second focus is on logistics, with the development of bi-lateral and international partnerships and demonstrative projects.

b Enhancing the development of the modern service industry, in order to speed up the growth of advanced manufacturing, upgrade traditional industries, build complete industrial chains and improve the competitiveness of the manufacturing sector.

c Developing advanced manufacturing clusters, particularly in the following sectors: energy, manufacturing equipment, rail transportation equipment, advanced medical devices and modern farm machinery. Automotive industry is a major focus especially in Guangzhou, Shenzhen and Foshan, where the government aims at expanding the automobile industrial chain, with independent brands and with a production capacity of over 3.3 million vehicles. Heavy industries such as steel, iron and petrochemicals are to be promoted particularly in Zhanjiang, Huizhou, Maoming and Jieyang, while the production of high-tech, super-large ships is promoted in Guangzhou, Zhongshan and Zhuhai aiming at a shipbuilding capacity of more than 800 million tonnes. As a whole, the target for high-tech manufacturing during the plan is 26 per cent of the total industrial value added (above-designated size).

d Improving traditional manufacturing especially through investment in product development, design, marketing and other value-added activities and through the construction of common technology platforms for the traditional sectors such as home appliances, textiles, food, building materials, paper and non-ferrous materials.

5 Development of strategic new industries, through the promotion of key sectors such as electronic information, new energy vehicles, alternative energy

sources (solar, wind, nuclear), bio-pharmaceuticals, new materials and aerospace. By 2015, the share of strategic and emerging sectors should reach 10 per cent of the GDP.

6 Enhancement of industrial competitiveness, through various mechanisms including enhancing the leading role large firms play as a support mechanism for SMEs, strengthened cooperation with the world's top 500 enterprises, bigger and stronger SOEs to enhance the vitality of the state-owned economy, promotion of corporate and regional brand building as well as that of independent brands and promotion of industrial clustering.

7.3.3 Industrial policy instruments to implement the twelfth five-year plan

Following the twelfth plan objectives, three major policy tools can be tracked as to the achievement of the declared targets: (1) financing innovation; (2) identifying strategic and priority sectors and (3) regulating FDIs with respect to R&D.

These being the latest measures set by the government, little academic debate has developed on this matter. Most of the information circulates through official documents, press and websites. Yet, we believe that this information is valuable and crucial, both in terms of what we can expect governments will do in the near future and in terms of the signals Guangdong is sending to the rest of the world. They are as follows:

1 *Financing innovation*: As a direct investment in innovation, Guangdong provincial officials have set aside 1 trillion RMB (about 157.34 billion US$ at the November 2011 exchange rate) to finance approximately 500 innovation projects equally divided into rising industries, advanced manufacturing, traditional sectors, modern industry and modern agriculture. Among these, the provincial government has planned about 25 mega projects (with more than 10 billion RMB budget). Roughly 70 per cent of these 500 projects have started construction, with a total initial injection of about 100 billion RMB (15.7 billion US$ at the November 2011 exchange rate).[6] SOEs have been declared to be an important part of the process of industrial upgrading and innovation financing. The press reports investment agreements by Guangdong officials with over 70 SOEs on strategic projects, particularly in the areas of Guangzhou, Shenzhen and Jiangmen. It also highlights the fact that SOEs are strong in the fields of R&D, capital, technology, information and branding and they can thus contribute to industrial upgrading particularly through investment in the industry service sector and in the energy sectors.[7]

2 *Identifying sector priorities*: As stated in the plan, the service sector (in particular, services to industry) is number one priority for the Guangdong government, which aims to bring the tertiary sector's contribution to provincial GDP to 48 per cent. Besides the service sector, attention is placed on rising industries and giant enterprises, which will be aided by several measures starting in 2012. Rising industries include high-end electronics and

information, light-emitting diode (LED) lighting, electric autos, photovoltaic solar energy, wind energy, biopharmaceutical products, new materials, energy saving products and environmental protection, aerospace and the marine industry.[8] Some targets have been mentioned such as a production capacity of 200,000 electric vehicles in the next four years. In order to reach these targets, governments are encouraged to buy electric vehicles, which should account for 10 per cent of total purchasing in 2012. Moreover, charging stations for electric vehicles will be included in the infrastructure plans of big cities in the PRD over the course of the next few years, together with a proportion of parking lots for electric cars and special electric car parking spaces in business zones (Mo, 2011). Together with electronic vehicles, LED lighting is the other rising priority industry, given Guangdong's production capacity and its ambitions to move up in the value chain from middle and downstream activities where most enterprises still work. On this front, government efforts are mainly directed towards setting quality standards through new approved regulations, creation of business unions to coordinate government and private efforts and establishment of Guangdong investment funds to stimulate new companies (Wing, 2011).

3 *Encouraging foreign R&D investment*: This is mainly done by ensuring the protection of property rights and by further strengthening the regulation on patents.

7.4 Specific innovation policies for specialized towns in Guangdong

The formal document of the DSTGG titled 'Guangdong Province Government's Suggestion on the Promotion of the Development of Specialized Towns', published in 2006, sets the general framework for the province's innovation policy and defined the main steps to be taken in order to promote technological innovations, with particular reference to STs. These steps are briefly reviewed in the following paragraphs.

7.4.1 The 'Plan for the ST Technological Innovation: Pilot Test'

STs and innovation policies in Guangdong are inherently related. Back in 2000, two formal policy documents from the government of Guangdong province were issued to implement innovation policies through the promotion of professional specialized industrial clusters. The two documents – 'Plan for the ST Technological Innovation: Pilot Test' and 'Managerial methods for the ST Technological Innovation: Pilot Test' (DSTGG, 2008a) – identified two main tools for the implementation of the policy supporting innovation:

1 The formal acknowledgement of STs at the provincial level by means of specific identification criteria (see Section 6.2).

2 In each officially recognized ST, over time, the establishment of a 'technology innovation platform', whose aim is to provide services to firms (mainly SMEs) that could improve the quality standard and the innovation component of products realized by the specialized sector of the town (Barbieri *et al.*, 2010).

The innovation platform provides a wide range of different services and activities, among others, sharing of specific knowledge for the sector of specialization, R&D in industrial engineering, productivity enhancement, sector and market studies, services of business incubation, professional consultancy, qualified information gathering and diffusion, development of commercial websites for the promotion of the specialized sector and so on (Xie, 2003; Barbieri *et al.*, 2010).

According to surveys carried out by the DSTGG, up until 2008, innovation platforms had been established in 108 STs (DSTGG, 2008b). More recent documents report the establishment of a total of 196 innovation platforms in Guangdong STs (DSTC, 2011f). These platforms have common targets but they can differ from town to town according to the form of government intervention. In particular, it is possible to identify three main categories of innovation platforms (DSTGG, 2008c; Barbieri *et al.*, 2010):

1 *Information networks*: The information networks are mainly used to increase relations and knowledge-sharing opportunities for firms within the STs. They promote the circulation of commercial information and they encourage internet-based cooperation among actors. In fact, these networks mainly operate by means of *ad hoc* websites, allowing firms to access online information or to collaborate with dedicated information centres.
2 *Innovation centres*: Most of the local financial support given to officially recognized towns is invested in the establishment of innovation centres. These are physical structures, where firms can find expertise, assistance, advanced technological instruments and opportunities to develop innovative projects. The innovation centres are institutions directly created or supported by funding provided by the local and provincial government (Barbieri *et al.*, 2010; Arvanitis and Jastrabsky, 2006).
3 *R&D centres within leading firms*: The third type of innovation platform refers to the already existing technology R&D departments within some leading firms of the ST. Over the years, these firms have been able to establish R&D centres, thanks also to the favourable and innovation-friendly local environment created by the provincial government's implemented policies (Barbieri *et al.*, 2010). These firm-based centres contribute to the diffusion of knowledge and they are considered very important by local governments for the improvement of the innovation capacity of the whole town. For this reason, some of these centres are officially recognized by local governments as town-centres or are specifically mentioned by local governments as reference centres for the innovation activities of the town (Barbieri *et al.*, 2010). In doing so, the local

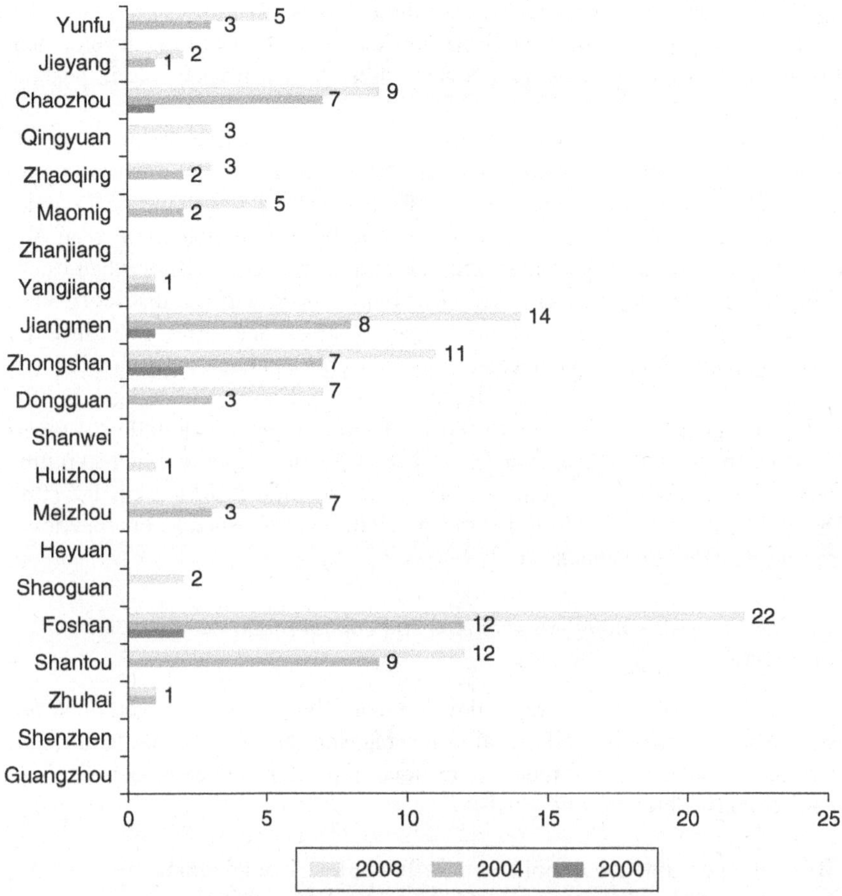

Figure 7.10 Trends in the development of innovation platforms in Guangdong.

Source: Authors' elaboration on original dataset CIRLP database, University of Ferrara.

government encourages the collaboration of these centres with other firms in the town. For instance, the very well-known case of the great technological development of Beijiao town (in Shunde, prefecture of Foshan) was greatly supported by the innovation activity of the firm 'Midea', a leading local producer of home appliances (Zhu, 2005).

Several prefectures, as shown in Figure 7.10, have over the years invested in the creation of innovation centres. The most active local governments in this field are Foshan, Shantou, Jiangmen and Zhongshan. It has to be said that this could reflect the fact that these prefectures are historically characterized as having systems of SMEs specialized in traditional manufacturing (mainly low or medium tech). These are sectors where, by nature and tradition, innovation is often perceived to be a marginal aspect and where the entrepreneurial attitude is seldom devoted to accumulating R&D or innovation skills.

The twelfth five-year plan confirms the centrality of STs in the development process of Guangdong and in particular it stresses their pivotal role in pushing indigenous innovation.

Some city examples are taken by the press and the media as reference points to encourage virtuous imitation processes. Among these are the e-business platforms widely used by Lechong furniture firms (Foshan), the single firm's innovation services established in Xiaolan (Zhongshan) involving more than 500 professionals and 6,284 service enterprises and four towns in Zhongshan establishing a hardware and household electrical appliance industrial district (DSTC, 2011a). Furthermore, the local governments stress and offer assistance on improving regulations on intellectual property rights and branding strategies.

There are a few innovation targets for STs specifically defined by the Guangdong government[9]: by 2015, 80 innovation-driven single-industry towns will be established; of these, over ten will each produce an output of 100 billion RMB per year (about 15.73 billion US$ at the November 2011 exchange rate). More public innovation and service systems will be established and competitiveness and R&D will be enhanced.

7.4.2 Coordination among governments and collaboration with universities

After the first years of STs' rapid development, the provincial government felt the need to improve the collaboration mechanisms of STs in order to increase their innovation capacity. It therefore decided to push the development of STs in two directions (Barbieri *et al.*, 2010):

1 a better coordination of policies at different levels of government;
2 an increased collaboration with universities in order to encourage technology-transfer processes.

With respect to the first point, a first document was launched in 2005, giving directions for the coordination of cities' policy actions at the provincial and prefecture levels (Lin, 2006). The plan confirmed the general policy setting already in place in previous years, but it also envisioned an increased involvement of the city-level government in the promotion and implementation of innovation policies.

A particularly challenging objective for STs regards collaboration with universities since only a few universities are located in the towns, especially if we consider rural areas. In order to facilitate such a connection, in 2006 the Guangdong government designed a specific pilot programme in selected STs in which cases demonstrating collaboration with local universities were promoted (DSTGG, 2007; Lin, 2007; Barbieri *et al.*, 2010). Up until the end of 2006, cases offering collaboration demonstrations took place in three STs (located in the prefectures of Foshan, Maoming and Meizhou) and six successful collaboration alliances were established between an ST and a university (Barbieri *et al.*, 2010).

More recent policy documents confirm that collaborations among governments and between STs and universities are still an important feature of the strategy for the development of innovation within STs. In 2007 alone, 13 provincial research projects, 23 city-level research collaborations, 11 new collaborations between STs and universities and 131 collaboration projects between education institutions and firms were signed (Zhang, 2011).

8 Policy effectiveness

When looking at the current post-crisis debate on the desirability of government intervention, we feel there is a tendency to refer back to well-analysed and consolidated arguments on market failure on the one hand, and government failure on the other (see Chapter 1). Even Chinese economic performance is often measured, explained and judged in terms of convergence (or divergence) from 'Western models'. As already explained, the risk of analysing the Chinese case with only 'Western' lenses is to ground the debate on policy intervention on ideological rather than factual arguments. In this context, policy evaluation exercises and policy analysis, as part of the policy-making process, become fundamental. Research agendas focusing on rigorous and thorough policy analyses and evaluations can be a powerful tool in offering solutions to government failures, instead of merely offering evidence that failures exist.

8.1 Policy evaluation and China

The international debate on policy evaluation (see, among others, Dunn, 1994; Haveman, 1987; Katz, 1988; Rossi and Freeman, 1989; Shadish *et al.* 1991; Martini, 2008; Stame and Rist, 2011; Sanderson, 2003; Campbell, 1969) shows that the term 'evaluation' is often used with different meanings, depending on the specific information needs expressed by the policy maker or stakeholders. The practice of policy evaluation itself can be employed for different purposes and using different methods. In a broad view, we can identify three main reasons to undertake evaluation research: (1) government accountability to higher level institutions and regulations; (2) improvement of public sector management; and (3) creation of political consensus on government action, thus legitimizing government intervention.

Countries around the world show very diverse experiences in this respect. In the United States, for instance, evaluation has its roots in social experiments and counterfactual methods. Evaluation in Europe, on the other hand, grew mainly thanks to the European Union's (EU's) pressure on member states' compliance and accountability regarding EU structural funds spending [European Commission (EC), 1999]. In this scenario, the 'new public management' movement has also had great influence in pushing evaluation mechanisms (Barbieri, 2010).

The few contributions to the international literature on evaluation in China suggest that in the country some forms of evaluation are used (see, for instance, Furubo *et al.*, 2002; Edin, 2003; Tsui and Wang, 2008; Schubert and Ahlers, 2011). So far it appears that evaluation is (a) mainly devoted to improve public sector management, particularly in terms of capacity of upper-level governments to control policy implementation at lower levels and to hold local governments accountable to central policy priorities; (b) mainly based on a wide range of target indicators that are constantly monitored; and (c) mainly carried out internally, by party departments, even though some forms of 'democratic evaluation' and public opinion hearings are included in the evaluation process. Several authors point out that in parallel with the economic reforms, China has undertaken a reform in the cadre management system, based on rigid performance evaluation mechanisms (Whithing, 2001; Qian and Xu, 1993; Li and Zhou, 2005). In practice, on the one hand, the central government was handing over some control of selected provinces, such as Guangdong, in order to let them experiment a market economy (see Chapter 4). On the other hand, the central government was making public officials in these provinces more and more responsible for the economic successes of the areas they governed. Thanks to these reforms, the degree of economic success of a county, a town or a prefecture became strictly linked to the career success of the governor of that county, town or prefecture. This link was, and still is, established through a formal contract (Edin, 2003) between the mayor of the town and upper-level governments, where priority targets are fixed together with specific incentives for meeting them (or consequences, including losing one's job, if the most important targets are not met). In this way, monitoring and performance evaluation are extensively used to give public officials directions and targets.

Some suggest that what really has made the difference in the Chinese transition process is the capacity of governments (the party first, but also the bureaucratic structures) to adapt to the changing scenario (Edin, 2003; Qian and Xu, 1993; Li and Zhou, 2005; Wu and Ma, 2009). These authors remind us that the Chinese government organization (from central state to local authorities) resembles the M-form organizational structure of a big enterprise, with an incentive system for managers (local policy makers) based on economic results (and more recently on the provision of public services).

When looking at policy evaluation from this perspective, it is hard to argue that the government did not have a prominent role in promoting China's economic growth. However, the extent to which policies were implemented in order to be effective or rather to ensure political survival and stability is still debatable. Some of the above-mentioned authors highlight that the cadre's incentive system forced policy makers to do all they could to achieve growth-related results. The targets, of course, were mainly linked to industrial growth. According to most observers this had some side effects that now challenge future development and well-being in some areas (pollution, congestion, poor quality of life). New changes are needed, and the modification of the long-term objectives that we have highlighted in the first chapter seems to be confirmed by the evolution of the cadre evaluation systems where priority targets are more and more linked to people's well-being (Wu and Ma, 2009).

Despite the evidence of an effective management system of state cadres, the 'what-if' question remains. How effective are programmes such as the specialized towns (STs) programme extensively studied in Chapter 6? Do relocation policies and their instruments really make a difference in determining the relocation of firms in marginal areas? Or would these changes have occurred eventually, anyway, thanks to market mechanisms that make land and labour more costly in congested areas? Our understanding is that the impact is not to be studied in terms of things 'that would/would not have happened anyway'. It is rather a matter of looking at the velocity of such a change, a matter of choosing and governing the pace of desired changes. However, even this perspective is challenged by the 'what if' question. As suggested by Sachs and Woo (1997), two different viewpoints can be identified in the research on China's economic performance. According to the first viewpoint, 'gradualism in economic reforms has been key to China's rapid growth' (p. 6) and according to the second viewpoint, 'China's rapid growth has come despite gradualism, in areas of the economy characterized by radical rather than gradual reforms' (p. 6). In this second viewpoint, in particular, gradualism is not the result of a deliberate choice, but rather stems from a lack of consensus over the proper course of action (Sachs and Woo, 1997). In this scenario, there are two possible ways forward: (1) to better understand the extent to which gradualism was planned (and a great deal of this book has dealt with this issue) and (2) to stimulate the need for research lines on *ex post* policy evaluation in China, which is the aim of this chapter.

At present, *ex post* impact evaluation remains a mostly unexplored area in the Chinese context. The application of counterfactual methods to analyze the effects of policies that have been widely debated in 'the West' (we think for instance about the extensive literature on the evaluation of policies for innovation, such as Research and Development (R&D) subsidies, technology transfer policies or innovation centres) has not been found to be significantly used in China. The scarce permeability of the internal Chinese debate on these issues probably acts as a deterrent for Western scholars and so does the lack of both micro-level data and easily accessible information on how the selection procedures function, for instance regarding firms' subsidies. Furthermore, in the aforementioned evaluation literature itself, there are arguments for being sceptical of counterfactual methods in general and arguments stating their usefulness as a tool for policy decisions.

However, what we would like to stress in this chapter is the perspective from which we see policy evaluation. As mentioned, we suggest viewing policy evaluation as a tool to better inform governments, to make them more accountable, thus helping them overcome some of the well-known government failures. In this context, stimulating an international debate over policy analysis and policy evaluation in China, with different tools, including *ex post* impact evaluation, can help us understand the role of the Chinese governments and can inform the 'Western' debate about the role of governments in fostering development processes.

8.1.1 Evaluation of industrial policies in Chinese regions

As explained in previous chapters, the opening-up process of the Chinese economy started in Guangdong, in particular through the establishment of special economic zones (SEZs), where the national and the local governments could 'test' the functioning of a market economy (see Chapter 4). In such scenario, the widespread presence of government control and intervention in the transition process is generally acknowledged. However, while some authors believe that government intervention and the specific policy instruments adopted explain how the economy was able to boom, others believe that growth occurred despite such interventions (Nee and Opper 2007; Nee and Cao, 1999; Parish and Michelson, 1996). As a first methodological step in overcoming the ideological dispute, we have stressed the need to go beyond the general 'Chinese' case, to study in depth China's very different territories, to analyse and understand the specific programmes adopted in the local economies and to place them in the peculiar socio-economic context in which they were implemented.

Some very detailed case studies at the level of single industrial clusters or single firms in different parts of China argue that, when looking at the micro-level, government policies appear to have played a role and, at least from the perspective of several actors (firms, entrepreneurs, scholars, experts), that it was an effective role (Barbieri *et al.*, 2011; Arvanitis and Qiu, 2009; Unger and Chan, 1999; Krug, 2004). A few contributors study the effectiveness of policies in China from an economic geography perspective (see Démurger *et al.*, 2002). In this case, the investigation is carried out in the whole country, comparing provinces. The general conclusion is that policies have a positive effect. However, the authors concentrate on SEZs as the main policy tool, which is described as a form of deregulation. As a consequence of defining SEZs as a tool for deregulation, the derived policy implications mainly insist on deregulation as the major reform to be promoted.

We have shown in this book (see Chapter 4) that SEZs are only a part of a wider set of policy instruments (Barbieri *et al.*, 2009a, 2009b; Arvanitis and Jastrabsky, 2006; Di Tommaso and Rubini, 2006) and were designed as a tool for investment attraction. From this perspective, we can say that it was indeed a very regulated tool. It was implemented with other policy tools and with strict controls pertaining to other aspects of the economy (ex. credit and financing systems). In a sense, the importance of SEZs does not lie in the SEZ itself, but also in the fact that areas surrounding them were kept regulated. Labelling SEZs as a 'deregulation' is but one way to characterize them.

In this book, and in this chapter in particular, we would like to promote future research lines that investigate the issue of policy effectiveness from an empirical perspective and focus on the *meso*-level, meaning on the specific sub-province experiences, taking unexplored units of analysis: the town, the county, the prefecture, the province. Fan (1995) highlighted the need to shift from provincial-level studies to the county scale to capture the complexities of policy intervention. The author's contribution, however, which referred to 1990s data, did not translate into systematic research lines for other international scholars.

8.2 Investigating firms' response to policy instruments

As explained in Chapter 7, the creation of innovation platforms and innovation centres is a crucial part of the innovation policy of Guangdong province, and it is realized, in particular, in the framework of the STs programme. As shown by the increase in the number of innovation platforms, it is clear that the efforts of Guangdong province to promote innovation are concrete (Figure 7.10). However, the international debate on the effectiveness of such policies and on their capacity to have a real influence on firms' technology innovation strategies is still at a very initial stage. At the moment, there are basically two sources to collect information on policy effectiveness: the Guangdong government reports and the Chinese academic papers. Therefore, while we perceive that some evaluation exercises are done, either by the government itself or by Chinese academics, the results of these exercises are not fully debated in the international literature nor by international observers. We believe that an open debate on these issues could (1) help clarify the role of Chinese governments in promoting innovation and industrial growth and (2) help shift the debate away from the ideological perspective and provide empirical evidence to corroborate or reject theory-based arguments.

According to the Department of Science and Technology of Guangdong Government (DSTGG) (see, among others, DSTGG, 2006a; Barbieri *et al.*, 2010), the innovation policy has had a positive impact especially where physical innovation centres have been established. In particular, according to DSTGG, innovation centres have promoted an innovation-friendly atmosphere for firms operating in STs, sped up the process of industrial upgrading in rural areas, developed information and networking services within STs, helped create regional brands and sped up the urbanization process.

In addition to DSTGG reports, some academic contributions have undertaken research and fieldwork in Guangdong STs (Qiu and Xu, 2007; Huang and Qiu, 2003; Chen and Hou, 2006; Li, 2002; Zhang *et al.*, 2007; Wang and Yue, 2010; Wang, 2002). These studies have mainly focused on interviews to selected firms within a number of case study STs. They have tried to establish a link between the innovation performance of firms and the presence of innovation centres or between the innovation policy and more general economic indicators of the STs. Most of these studies conclude that there has been some positive effect of the government policy on the overall innovation performance of firms and towns. For some authors (Wang, 2002; Wang and Yue, 2010) the main role of governments in this field is to introduce an external innovation source. Such external source is important for firms, particularly in traditional sectors and in the first stages of technological upgrading, when firms need to build innovation capabilities. Furthermore, the innovation centre can help firms build their own R&D centres. After these first steps, the function of the innovation centre arguably changes and it is limited to training, maintenance and information services (Wang, 2002; Barbieri *et al.*, 2010).

Based on the available literature on the effectiveness of innovation centres in Guangdong, so far, academic contributions have mainly focused on case studies. On the one hand, researchers concentrate on the industrial policies promoted by the different levels of government to favour innovation, and on the other hand, they focus on firms' choices in terms of innovation strategies. There seems to be space for further investigation on the general contribution of innovation centres.

First, there seems to be space to bridge business and management approaches with those of industrial policy and to try to quantify at the whole provincial-level firms' response to the innovation platforms. Second, to understand the contribution of innovation centres, it is important to view them as part of a multifaceted policy framework. These two research perspectives will be discussed in the next section.

8.2.1 Firms' response to innovation centres

One of the research questions we have addressed in our previous studies (Barbieri *et al.*, 2009a, 2009b, 2010, 2011) is as follows: given that government industrial policy exists, to what extent are firms' strategies influenced by government policy? A starting point to address this issue is the search for proxies that can help measure the degree of collaboration between firms and innovation platforms. In a recent exercise (Barbieri *et al.*, 2010), we searched for evidence of a relationship between firms' choices and the degree of strength of government action. As a first step, we focused on the leading firms of STs, assuming that they could act as an example for the strategies of other firms in the same town.[1] We tested the hypothesis that the firms' response to the innovation policy depends on the strength of the policy, that is, the degree of government investment and commitment, as well as on the channels through which the government can influence firms' choices. We attempt to explain the probability of having increasing firms' responses to the policy in terms of degree of policy strength (where the innovation centre is stronger as a policy than a generic innovation platform), government control (measured as the firm's ownership type) and entrepreneurial background (to capture previous or current public appointments that could influence the propensity of a firm to collaborate with public innovation centres). In addition, a number of control variables are used (see Table 8.1 for details).

The analysis was carried out for all the towns that had an innovation platform or centre. In a few cases, it was not possible to identify the leading firm and we excluded them from the analysis. The final sample for analysis was composed of

Table 8.1 List of variables

Variable	*Type*	*Categories*
Government policy	Ordinal	0: The town has an innovation platform (weaker government policy) 1: The town has an innovation platform and an innovation centre (stronger government policy)
Firm's strategic response to government policy	Ordinal	1: No evidence of response 2: The firm is recommended by the innovation platform/innovation centre as a model for innovation, but there is no clear cooperation between them 3: The firm's internal R&D centre is registered by the Guangdong province 4: The firm is a member of the innovation platform/ innovation centre 5: The firm has a real cooperation project with the innovation platform/innovation centre 6: The firm accepted training by the innovation platform/innovation centre 7: The firm's internal R&D centre is recognized as the innovation centre of the town or was jointly built with the government
Ownership	Ordinal	1: Foreign-owned 2: Private Chinese-owned 3: SOE
Entrepreneur's linkage with government	Dummy	0: No linkages between the entrepreneur and the government 1: The entrepreneur is the deputy of different levels of the legislature (NPC), or a deputy of the local committee of the Chinese People's Political Consultative Conference (CPPCC), or he/she is a government official
Age of the ST	Count	Number of years since the town has been officially recognized by the Guangdong government
Age of the innovation platform	Count	Number of years since the innovation platform (or centre) was established
Urbanization rate	Scale	Percentage of urban population to total population
Sector (non-manufacturing/ manufacturing)	Dummy	1: The firm is specialized in a non-manufacturing sector, such as agriculture and services 0: the firm is specialized in a manufacturing sector

Source: Selection from Barbieri et al. (2010).

95 firms in 95 towns. The descriptive statistics of the aforementioned variables show that most leading firms are Chinese (77), private (61) or foreign (16), with no entrepreneurs being official government appointments. Of these, 39 firms displayed no evidence of collaboration with the innovation centre, while the

remaining ones were mainly distributed between categories 2, 3 and 7 of the policy response. In brief, the overall degree of involvement of leading firms in the innovation centre activities is low. An ordered logit regression was performed to capture the relative importance of the variables in explaining such distribution. We regressed the variable measuring firms' response over policy strength, ownership of the firm, entrepreneurs' linkages with government and the remaining control variables. The most significant results of the analysis are reported in Table 8.2. For further details on the different regression models and on the diagnostic tests, see Barbieri *et al.* (2010).

These results suggest that the likelihood of having a higher response degree to government policy is 68 per cent lower for firms whose entrepreneurs do not have linkages with the government, all other things being equal. At the same time, a standard deviation increase in the ownership variable [meaning an ownership structure closer to the state-owned enterprises (SOE)] raises the likelihood of having a positive response to the policy by a factor of 0.53. The policy variable itself sends out ambiguous signals. It is significant in four models and it always appears with a positive sign. This suggests that having an innovation centre creates more appeal for firms' collaboration than having the innovation platform without an innovation centre. At the same time, given that the policy variable is not always significant, it could be that the innovation centre and the platform have basically very similar purposes and it might be difficult to capture differences in terms of firms' behaviour. Starting from this preliminary exercise, future refinements of the analysis are of course possible. Building control groups to compare innovation performances of supported firms with other similar unsupported enterprises is but one possibility.

8.3 Analyzing Guangdong's multiple policy tools

Innovation centres are a particular policy tool that characterize the specific industrial policy experience of Guangdong province in the field of innovation and technological upgrading. However, as shown in the previous chapters of this book, the industrial policy framework adopted by Guangdong province is more complex. The STs programme itself is a specific policy tool used to manage industrial development and to promote a more balanced industrialization within the province. The very first instruments of the SEZs were proper industrial policy tools used to attract foreign investment and to control the speed of the opening-up process. In addition, public investment in infrastructures and in R&D and innovation are always part of the activities of the Guangdong government. The issue of policy analysis can also be addressed with reference to the different policy instruments in order to gain additional insights into the utility of policy interventions and on their effects, overall, on the industrial, economic and development performance of Guangdong territories. Measuring the magnitude of the different interventions and capturing the additional effects they had on economic and social variables can be a very

Table 8.2 Ordered logit regression results

	Model 1	*Model 2*	*Model 3*	*Model 4*	*Model 5*	*Model 6*	*Model 7*	*Model 8*
Policy strength	0.7454**	0.6685*	0.6291	0.6147	0.6160	0.6495*	0.7344*	0.111
	(0.3774)	(0.3828)	(0.3851)	(0.3886)	(0.3889)	(0.3923)	(0.3978)	(0.5484)
Ownership of the firm		1.1982***	1.1439***	1.1519***	1.1538***	1.1439***	1.255***	0.004***
		(0.4012)	(0.4032)	(0.4036)	(0.4040)	(0.4054)	(0.4277)	(0.4215)
Entrepreneur's linkage with the government			1.1212**	1.132**	1.1454**	1.1461**	1.1119*	0.044**
			(0.5484)	(0.5512)	(0.5715)	(0.5753)	(0.5686)	(0.5607)
Length of policy programme				0.0337	0.0385	0.0544	0.0906	
				(0.1235)	(0.1343)	(0.1359)	(0.1393)	
Age of platform/ centre					−0.0094	−0.0075	−0.0189	0.9600
					(0.1025)	(0.1027)	(0.1037)	(0.947)
Urbanization rate						−0.0059	−0.0103	
						(0.0081)	(0.0088)	
Sector (non-manufacturing/ manufacturing)							−1.3086	0.483
							(0.9100)	(0.5886)
Log-likelihood	−150.217	−145.489	−143.384	−143.347	−143.343	−143.078	−142.024	−143.135
Pseudo-R^2	0.0130	0.0441	0.0579	0.0581	0.0582	0.0599	0.0668	0.0595
Logit regression χ^2	3.95**	13.41***	17.62***	17.69**	17.70***	18.23***	19.00***	18.12***

Source: Barbieri *et al.* (2010).

Notes: The standard errors are in parentheses. *, **, ***Correlation is significant at 10%, 5% and 1%, respectively.

difficult, if not an impossible, task, especially if data availability is limited. However, we believe that more and more research lines should be promoted in this field and that the results should inform both the Chinese and the international debates on industrial policy effects. Below are the results of an initial exercise we have carried out (see also Barbieri *et al.*, 2011). The aim was to build synthetic policy and performance indexes that could help in reading the trends of policy efforts and economic performances, within a specific territorial unit of analysis: the province (and then the county and the township). This unit of analysis can provide a different perspective, than that of the general Chinese case, to understand industrial development policies in China and elsewhere.

8.3.1 Measuring Guangdong's policy efforts and industrial performances

A synthetic policy effort index can help in understanding which prefectures within Guangdong have invested more to promote innovation, industrial specialization and industrial growth. The index we propose [Index of Policy Intensity (IPI)] is composed of five variables, three of which represent the specific policy programmes for STs, innovation centres and SEZs and the remaining two provide a more general indication on government investments in the economy. Therefore, the variables that compose the IPI are (see also Barbieri *et al.*, 2011) as follows:

1 *Specialized towns*: For each prefecture and for each year, the variable captures the number of towns officially recognized by the Department of Science and Technology of Guangdong province. It seems reasonable to hypothesize that towns that received an earlier official recognition might be systematically different from others in terms of industrial performance (as emphasized in Chapter 6, earlier recognitions were mainly directed to fast-growing towns, in urban areas, in the Pearl River Delta (PRD), while more recent recognitions refer to more marginal areas). Therefore, the value of the variable, for each town, is weighted for the number of years since the town's recognition.
2 *Development zones (other than SEZs)*: For each prefecture, the variable indicates the number of development zones weighted for the number of years since each was established by the national, provincial or local government.
3 *Innovation centres*: The variable identifies the number of innovation platforms, productivity promotion centres and similar, built by the provincial or the local government, weighted for the number of years since the establishment of each centre.
4 *Expenditure/revenues ratio*: The variable measures the ratio between the prefecture government expenditures and revenues.
5 *R&D expenditures*: The variable summarizes the expenditures for research and development generated by public research institutions. They include

both the expenditures for basic and applied research, and the management and administration expenditures related to the research activity.

After normalizing each variable, the index is calculated for each prefecture and for each year in the period 2001–2008 according to Fisher's combining formula:

$$IPI = \sum_{I=1}^{k} w_i \ln(1 - \lambda_i)$$

with k equal to 5 and where λ_i indicates the normalized value of the ith variable X_i (i = 1, 2,..., k). The term w_i represents the degree of importance of X_i (at present, we assign equal weight to the five variables). Fisher's formula tends to rank those prefectures higher that have high values in all the variables that are taken into account rather than prefectures that perform particularly well in only one area. The index varies from zero to one. As the index gets closer to one, the higher the policy effort. Figure 8.1 shows the relative strength in policy effort of Guangdong prefectures, comparing the year 2001 with 2008.

Figure 8.1 confirms the trend we have observed in previous chapters when analyzing the single policy instruments (see in particular Chapter 6). The official acknowledgement of new STs and innovation platforms in specific areas of the province pushed the relocation of some of the industries of the PRD towards the outer prefectures, in order to stimulate a more balanced industrialization of the province (Barbieri *et al.*, 2009a, 2009b, 2010, 2011). In 2001, the prefectures that displayed a higher policy effort were those of the central PRD area together with those of the eastern zones of Heyuan and Chaozhou. In other words, in 2001 the policy efforts were visibly linked to the early interventions of the SEZs in the PRD and in the eastern part of the province. In 2008, we observe some differences in the distribution of the policy effort, in particular, in favour of the areas surrounding the PRD. The policy effort appears to literally shift from the PRD to the areas outside it. Apart from Jiangmen (i.e. part of the PRD), all the prefectures that display an improvement in their policy index from 2001 to 2008 are located outside the PRD. Altogether in 2008, the greater policy efforts in terms of attraction of investment, increased specialization, clustering and investment in innovation are observed outside the PRD. Again, these data appear to confirm the stated long-term objectives, presented in the official documents diffused by the national and provincial government (and illustrated in Chapters 4 and 6).

Following a similar procedure as for the IPI, and applying the same Fisher's formula, we computed a synthetic index of industrial performance (PERF). In this case, the variables used to capture industrial performance are (see also Barbieri *et al.*, 2011) as follows:

1 *Density*: It counts the number of industrial firms per square kilometre. This component is taken into account since some of the policy instruments (e.g.

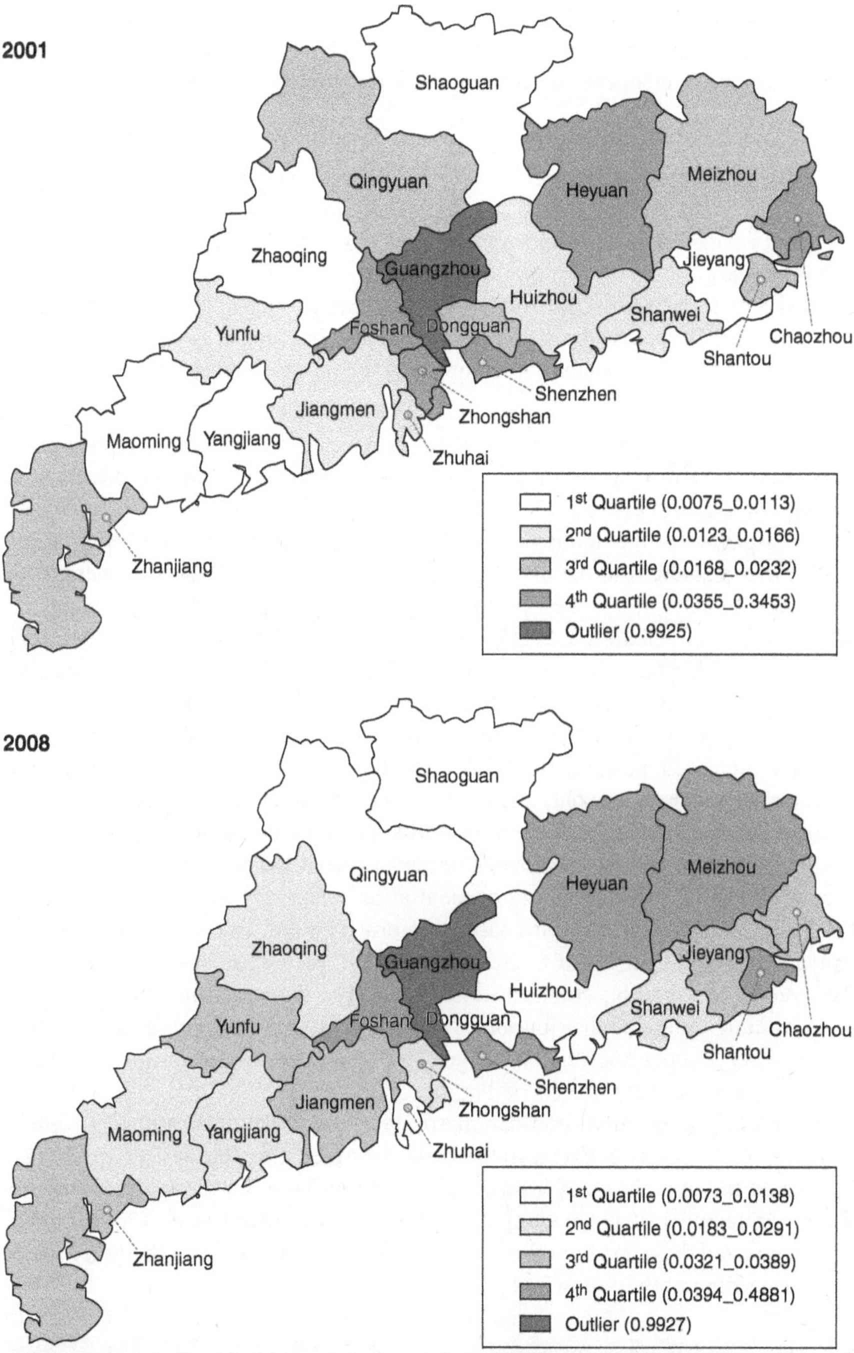

Figure 8.1 Index of policy intensity in Guangdong, 2001 and 2008.

Source: Authors' elaboration on data from DSTGG and Statistical Bureau of Guangdong Province (SBGP) (various years).

STs or development zones) aim specifically at increasing firms' density by creating industrial clusters.

2 *Value added*: It measures the industrial value added produced by industrial firms in the different prefectures. It is employed as a proxy for industrial growth.
3 *Output of new products*: It captures the value of new products produced by industrial above designated size (ADS) firms. New products refer to both goods produced with new technologies and to products that display a better performance; thanks to changes in their structure, materials and production processes.
4 *Export*: It measures the total value of exports generated by Guangdong industrial firms and directed outside Chinese borders. It is taken as a proxy for a prefecture's capacity to compete in the international markets.

Figure 8.2 shows the changes in the relative rankings of Guangdong prefectures from 2001 to 2008 for the performance index (for further details, see Barbieri *et al.*, 2011).

The figures on the industrial performance of Guangdong territories show some limited changes in the distribution of industrial growth among Guangdong territories. In 2001, the highest performances are registered in the PRD, in particular in Shenzhen, Guangzhou, Dongguan, Foshan, Zhongshan and in the eastern prefecture of Jieyang. In general, all PRD prefectures display above median (0.0104) index values. In 2008, only a few changes can be observed. All PRD prefectures remain above the median value (0.0053) and half of the prefectures with an increased performance index in the period are located in the PRD (Foshan, Zhongshan, Zhuhai). Altogether, the observed trend of industrial performance does not seem to show a clear change in the distribution of high industrial performances in the province. Contrary to what we observe for the IPI, the core of industrial production and concentration seems to basically remain in the PRD and partly in the eastern coastal regions (Barbieri *et al.*, 2011). This evidence alone is not sufficient to conclude that the policy has been ineffective. In the absence of a credible counterfactual, it could be that we would have observed an even more polarized distribution of industrial growth in the absence of policy intervention. Deeper analysis on the correlation and on the causal links between the two indexes needs to be carried out.

We report on an initial non-parametric test of correlation [National People's Congress (NPC) test] between the two indexes (see also Barbieri *et al.*, 2011). We tested the hypothesis of a positive correlation between the two indexes for the 21 prefectures of Guangdong for the seven considered years (2001–2008). We then tested the same hypothesis for sub-groups of prefectures that were identified according to the following:

1 The overall trend in the policy index (always increasing, always decreasing or mixed).

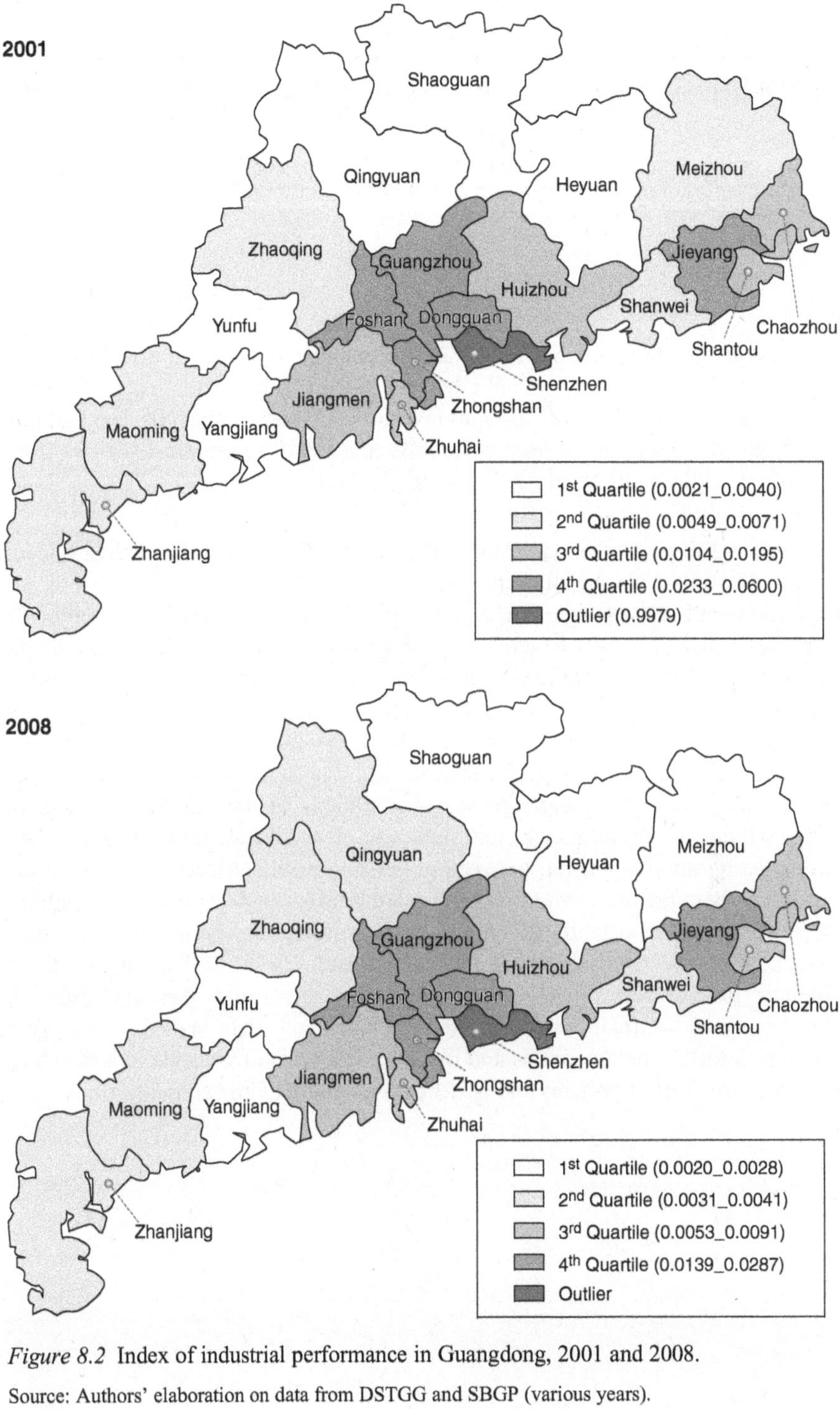

Figure 8.2 Index of industrial performance in Guangdong, 2001 and 2008.

Source: Authors' elaboration on data from DSTGG and SBGP (various years).

Table 8.3 NPC partial correlation between IPI and PERF

Policy index trend (2001–2008)	*p-value*	*PRD*	*p-value*	*SEZ*	*p-value*	*Coast*	*p-value*
Increasing	0.9300	Yes	0.005**	Yes	0.008**	Yes	0.009**
Decreasing	0.002***	No	0.017*	No	0.964	No	0.961
Mixed	0.001*						
Total	0.002***	Total	0.005**	Total	0.005**	Total	0.014*

Source: Barbieri et al. (2011).

Notes: *, **, ***Correlation is significant at 10%, 5% and 1%, respectively.

2 The geographic location, in terms of proximity to a SEZ, the PRD and the coast. These three factors have had a historical role in creating preferential access, particularly for foreign investors, to some areas of Guangdong. Therefore, they can be used to identify areas that systematically differ from others in their industrial performance.

Table 8.3 displays the synthesis of the results of the NPC test carried out for the period 2001–2008 for all prefectures.

The overall test of significance (the 'total' value) allows us to accept the hypothesis that there is a general positive correlation between the policy intensity index and the performance index, once the confounding factors are taken into account. Furthermore, these confounding factors (SEZs, the coast, the trend in policy index and the PRD) turn out to be determinant dimensions of the relation between policies and performances. We can suggest that a coastal geographic location and the early policy interventions of the SEZs still matter in today's industrial performances and represent clear discriminating factors when investigating the relationship between policy and results. Moreover, at the present stage, these factors seem to be even more relevant in describing this relationship than are the constantly increasing policy efforts that, on the contrary, take place to a great extent outside the PRD and outside the SEZs. Building on these findings, future research needs to be promoted to investigate the nature and the direction of causal relationships between policies and performance. We suggest moving towards single counties and townships as units of analysis to better capture the variations of policies and performances among Guangdong territories.

9 Final remarks

9.1 Guangdong's experience of industrial development

Our analysis of the Guangdong province industrial growth and industrial development policy has highlighted three main issues.

First, the rates of growth that have characterized this province in the last three decades, even with respect to the more general and often cited Chinese experience, are unique. This outward-oriented growth, mainly driven by an external demand for Chinese exports, has been based on a process of industrialization and gradual structural change that has been undoubtedly successful.

Second, these exceptional performances have been accompanied by an impressive battery of industrial policies rooted in a complex set of long-run national and local government plans, with the explicit aim of promoting growth, industrialization and gradual and continuous structural change. The impressive changes of these decades have been based on gradualism as a distinctive feature of the reform process. The aim was initially to experiment with the opening of the economy both to the market and to foreign countries. However, planning has guided the promotion of industrialization and structural adjustment in the long run. In this scenario, industrial policy has been interpreted as a tool to achieve long-term strategic goals.

Third, focussing on industrialization policy and planning, the promotion of technological upgrading has been considered one of the main goals. In this framework, we have analyzed what we consider the three main pillars of this strategy: migration policy, local development policy and innovation policy. Migration policy was designed, at the beginning of the reform era, with the goal of guaranteeing an increasing labour supply, thus maintaining a low labour cost. This was done in order to maintain the attraction of foreign investment that was considered necessary to acquire foreign technology. Local development policy was implemented with the goal of encouraging economies of agglomeration and clusters of specialized knowledge. Innovation policy was promoted with the goal of building new knowledge-based competitive advantages in a growing number of goods and services productions.

9.2 Challenges for Guangdong

Looking at what Guangdong has become in the last decades, we may underline some of the limitations and challenges connected to this unique experience of change.

Our detailed analysis of the evolution of policy targets and aims suggests that limitations and challenges are mainly connected to the relationship between growth, development and social stability.

Particularly, in the context of the current economic crisis several challenges and critical points have to be highlighted.

First, we may say that the growth rate cannot decelerate. Today, this is the first great challenge of a trajectory of change that has been socially sustainable because an increasing number of people have progressively gained access to the benefits associated with this industrial growth. Consensus and social stability have been based on this capacity to grow while involving an increasing number of people and territories.

Second, the growth rates so far recorded have been strongly connected to foreign demand. Today, this dependency also has to be interpreted as a limitation of the system's economic and social sustainability. In this context, *ad hoc industrial policy* interventions capable of encouraging entry into the Chinese domestic market may offer an important contribution in making the model of growth less rigid.

Third, there must be concern related to the 'quality' of growth. This is true from an industrial development point of view, because industries no longer need to grow, but need to place themselves in other, more innovative, segments of production. However, the issue of the quality of growth is also crucial for another reason: the demands of an increasing portion of society are changing and are today also directed towards goods and services connected to people's quality of life (i.e. welfare, housing, education, health, environment). The sustainability of the whole economic, social and political system is probably based on the capacity to satisfy these demands. In this context, *ad hoc* industrial policy interventions encouraging the development of these "new industries" should be considered a priority.

Fourth, the effectiveness of policy interventions and the efficiency of government continue to be a priority for Guangdong's economy and society. Fighting rent-seeking practices, promoting policy transparency and accountability and enhancing (ex-ante and ex-post) policy evaluation are just some of the areas in which problems and solutions should be identified.

9.3 Beyond the Guangdong case: more general implications

9.3.1 Methodology

At the beginning of this book we posed a question: do we know what the optimal role of industrial policy in contemporary capitalism would be? At the end of our book we may rephrase the question as: does Guangdong province's story reinforce the arguments in favour of, or against, industrial policy?

To provide a contribution to this complex and ambitious question, there is first of all a methodological issue to be considered that is related to the way in which Western scholars read the Chinese experience of industrialization, growth and development.

As we argued in the first chapter, China can no longer be considered a marginal case, rather it is one of the most relevant components of contemporary manufacturing and industry. Moreover, as we showed with reference to the Guangdong case, there is no doubt that in this experience governments have been strongly present in these last decades of impressive change and development. Thus, to improve our understanding of the role of governments in contemporary industry, we should deepen our studies on contemporary China. This is necessary in order to make the study on contemporary China something more than 'a special case' in the wider context of established economics and business studies. Rigorous and detailed studies of the Chinese experience can offer provocative insights capable of providing fresh new contributions to contemporary economic disciplines. However, in Western literature, this perspective of study is still only beginning to develop for several reasons. First, we observe an excessive generalization of the 'China case', which means: many generic analyses on China, limited studies on the regional diversity within China, few and fragmented empirically based analyses. Moreover, the emerging economic literature seems to underestimate the diversity of Chinese capitalism even in the main categories like public and private, firms, governments and markets. Furthermore, there is an issue related to the quality of official data diffused in China that differ in the way they are collected, made accessible and presented. Finally, there are still problems for 'Western scholars' in actively taking part in the domestic economic debate in Chinese. For all these reasons, there is a high risk of utilizing theoretical models – based on Western countries' realities – and empirical databases that are unsuitable for both positive and normative purposes.

It was our wish in writing this book to suggest an alternative perspective and methodology. We started with fieldwork in China in order to adopt an inductive perspective. We jointly collected data with our Chinese counterparts in order to offer a detailed picture of the status quo. We have built our databases. We have meticulously analyzed government documents (reports, studies, datasets, websites). We have limited the object of our analysis to a specific region and topic: industrial development policy in Guangdong.

From a methodological point of view this analysis calls for further similar studies on other Chinese territories. These studies are needed in order to have a more complete picture of the industrial development policies adopted in China. They are also needed to have a more precise understanding of the role of governments in the industrial development of Chinese provinces.

9.3.2 Implications for contemporary industrial development policies

Coming back again to our question about the role of industrial policy in contemporary industry, we now have to discuss how our studies in China, in particularly those in the southern Guangdong province, may have some useful normative implications.

The first intuitive consideration is on the effects that the existence of industrial policy and planning in China might have on government practices throughout the world.

Given the weight that China has acquired in the globalized market and given its model of production in which governments play an active role, this may probably be enough to push other countries to rethink their industrial strategies and to seriously reopen their debates on industrial policy.

In this context, there are two main contributions that the Guangdong experience can offer:

1 Industrial policy can no longer be viewed as 'money to firms'. In contemporary industry, the role of industrial policy is not just a matter of selecting and supporting some firms and not others. Industrial policy should be viewed as a set of coherent programmes and investments (in people, infrastructure, universities, governments, associations, clusters) characterized by a long-term view and an aim to promote a structural change in industrial dynamics. One of the main findings in our study on the Guangdong experience is that most of these investments have been targeted, directed and coordinated with the main aim of increasing industrial and economic growth. And now that other objectives are putting pressure on the stability of Guangdong's (and China's) economy, new challenges related to the quality and inclusive nature of growth are setting the reform agenda's next steps.
2 An increased focus on the sub-national level of governments is needed. Regions like Guangdong province – which has become one of the main platforms for contemporary globalized manufacturing and industry – have actively promoted their industrial development strategy through industrial policy interventions. This approach has an impact on other Chinese and local foreign governments reinforcing the local dimension of contemporary industrial policy (Bellandi and Di Tommaso, 2006). Contemporary competition has a 'territorial face' that goes beyond the mere sum of individual companies that compete with each other. The capacity of firms and industries to compete in the global market is strictly connected to the way local economies are organized.

The second consideration refers to the desirable degree of government intervention in industry development.

Is the evidence from Guangdong sufficient to say that other contemporary governments should play the same role government has in China? The answer is absolutely not. We are not searching for another 'miracle' to confirm predetermined policy prescriptions. And above all, we believe that there is no such thing as *the optimal* rate of government intervention.

Quite the contrary, even if governments in the international global arena continue to be called upon to respond to market failures and strategic needs, the truth is that they continue to show different degrees of involvement, success and failure.

In particular, we note that the reactions to government failure appear quite different. What we understand from Guangdong is that there is a clear perception of how severe government failures are in some cases. However, this recognition has not meant the reduction of government interventionism. The issue of government inefficiencies and lack of effectiveness has been part of the political agenda. The 'laboratory' approach to policy intervention, the reforms of the cadre system and the several forms of monitoring and evaluation attest to the awareness of some level of risk of government failure.

Thus, when discussing the existence of government failures, it is important to accept exactly how different government performances can be across countries and regions. Different managerial practices, different civic traditions, different individual and collective incentive mechanisms, different models for the selection of policy makers (from elections to recruiting and carrier rules), different political systems and political functioning are just some examples of the factors that affect how governments *work* or *do not work.*

This said, different solutions to government failures are perfectly legitimate. What we suggest here is that the different territories of China are relevant case studies through which international scholars can study different practices and approaches to the government failure issue.

9.3.3 Implications for studies on contemporary industry

A final consideration refers to the capacity of contemporary international industry studies to suggest different and appropriate solutions to government failures.

With very few exceptions, along a continuum of possible reactions to the recognition of government failures, the debate seems to have focussed mainly on two extremes:

1 The minimalist approach: very reduced interventions to minimize costs of government failure. In this scenario, what are the priorities for the future research agenda? First, as it has been traditionally argued we should be ready to accept *market failure costs* (including the ones in very crucial fields like health, education, knowledge, environment) and also *market functioning costs*, as others have argued (Chang, 1996).

  However, we should probably go even further in considering other types of costs: basically the ones related to not having a strategy in that international arena in which some of the actors (beginning with China) do have a strategy. In other words, the minimalist reaction to government failure leaves some important questions unanswered: who will be in charge of defining development strategies that represent present and future collective interests? In particular, who will be in charge of the long-term industrial strategy? Who will be in charge of designing approaches to include and represent all social segments characterized by different 'voice' capacities? If governments are not the designated actors, then there is a serious need for economic and industrial policy studies to open a debate on and rethink the mechanisms of accountability for the other influential actors that seem to guide the destiny of economies and societies [i.e. financial institutions; business associations; unions; European Central Bank (ECB), International Monetary Fund (IMF), World Bank (WB); 'the markets'].

2 The interventionist approach: government intervention is called for, despite the government failure arguments. We see space for further research in the industrial policy debate even in this scenario. In this case, the justification for government intervention comes from the assumption that the costs of non-intervention are too high. This seems to be the main reason why we accept a resurgence of industrial policy in these times of crisis. Little has changed in terms of how governments function and fail, but government intervention is invoked, because the consequences (social, political, economic, etc.) of leaving the solution up to the market are considered unacceptable.

If the minimalist approach suffers by underestimating several sources of cost associated with this perspective, the sudden resurgence of government industrial policy also carries some risks and concerns. Given that governments can fail and policy may be largely inefficient and ineffective, the priority should be placed on studying and adopting sophisticated and rigorous remedies for these failures. Independent policy evaluation, reduction of information asymmetries, reforms to the career system and so on are but some of the possible research lines.

Thus, we suggest putting governments' functioning at the core of the research agenda of industrial development studies, concentrating on possible corrections to existing traditional government failures. We need economic studies, and industrial policy studies even more so, that include governments in their analyses, because their functioning is strictly connected to industrial, economic and development performances. This of course reopens the sphere of analysis of economic studies to also include the internal managerial dimension of governments and governments' relation with society, politics and the mechanism of representation of public interest. It is in this particular context and in this difficult historical moment that we have to discuss how to promote *better governments for better societies*.

Appendix 1

Guangdong administrative division at county level

Prefecture	*Area (km²)*	*County level*	
		Name	*Typology*
PRD			
Guangzhou (capital)	7,434	Guangzhou UA	Core municipality
		Conghua	County-level city
		Zengcheng	County-level city
		Yuexiu	Urban district
		Haizhu	Urban district
		Liwan	Urban district
		Tianhe	Urban district
		Baiyun	Suburban district
		Huangpu	Suburban district
		Luogang	Suburban district
		Huadu	Suburban district
		Nansha	Suburban district
		Panyu	Suburban district
Shenzhen	2,016	Shenzhen UA (SEZ)	Core municipality
		Futian (SEZ)	Urban district
		Luohu (SEZ)	Urban district
		Nanshan (SEZ)	Urban district
		Yantian (SEZ)	Urban district
		Bao'an	Suburban district
		Longgang	Suburban district
Foshan	3,883	Foshan UA	Core municipality
		Chancheng	Urban district
		Shunde	Suburban district
		Nanhai	Suburban district
		Sanshui	Suburban district
		Gaoming	Suburban district
Dongguan	2,520	Dongguan UA	Core municipality
Zhongshan	1,800	Zhongshan UA	Core municipality
Zhuhai	1,560	Zhuhai UA (SEZ)	Core municipality
		Xiangzhou (SEZ)	Urban district

(*continued*)

Appendix 1 (continued)

Prefecture	*Area (km²)*	*County level*	
		Name	*Typology*
		Doumen	Urban district
		Jinwan	Urban district
Huizhou	10,792	Huizhou UA	Core municipality
		Huicheng	Urban district
		Huiyang	Urban district
		Boluo	County
		Huidong	County
		Longmen	County
Zhaoqing	14,978	Zhaoqing UA	Core municipality
		Duanzhou	Urban district
		Dinghu	Urban district
		Gaoyao	County-level city
		Sihui	County-level city
		Guangning	County
		Deqing	County
		Fengkai	County
		Huaiji	County
Jiangmen	9,259	Jiangmen UA	Core municipality
		Pengjiang	Urban district
		Jianghai	Urban district
		Xinhui	Suburban district
		Taishan	County-level city
		Kaiping	County-level city
		Enping	County-level city
		Heshan	County-level city
Eastern region			
Shantou	2,131	Shantou UA	Core municipality
		Nan'ao	County
		Jinping	Urban district
		Longhu	Urban district
		Haojiang	Urban district
		Chaoyang	Urban district
		Chaonan	Suburban district
		Chenghai	Suburban district
Shanwei	4,728	Shanwei UA	Core municipality
		Chengqu	Urban district
		Lufeng	County-level city
		Haifeng	County
		Luhe	County
Chaozhou	3,090	Chaozhou UA	Core municipality
		Xiangqiao	Urban district
		Chao'an	County
		Raoping	County
Jieyang	5,057	Jieyang UA	Core municipality
		Rongcheng	Urban district

(*continued*)

Appendix 1 (continued)

Prefecture	*Area (km²)*	*County level*	
		Name	*Typology*
		Jiedong	County
		Huilai	County
		Jiexi	County
		Puning	County-level city
Western region			
Yangjiang	7,748	Yangjiang UA	Core municipality
		Jiangcheng	Urban district
		Yangdong	County
		Yangxi	County
		Yangchun	County-level city
Maoming	11,493	Maoming UA	Core municipality
		Maonan	Urban district
		Maogang	Urban district
		Dianbai	County
		Gaozhou	County-level city
		Huazhou	County-level city
		Xinyi	County-level city
Zhanjiang	11,517	Zhanjiang UA	Core municipality
		Chikan	Urban district
		Xiashan	Urban district
		Potou	Urban district
		Mazhang	Suburban district
		Xuwen	County
		Suixi	County
		Leizhou	County-level city
		Lianjiang	County-level city
		Wuchuan	County-level city
Northern region			
Shaoguan	18,900	Shaoguan UA	Core municipality
		Zhenjiang	Urban district
		Wujiang	Urban district
		Qujiang	Urban district
		Lechang	County-level city
		Nanxiong	County-level city
		RuyuanYao	County
		Renhua	County
		Shixing	County
		Wengyuan	County
		Xinfeng	County
Heyuan	15,440	Heyuan UA	Core municipality
		Yuancheng	Urban district
		Dongyuan	County
		Heping	County
		Longchuan	County
		Zijin	County

(*continued*)

Appendix 1 (continued)

Prefecture	*Area (km²)*	*County level*	
		Name	*Typology*
		Lianping	County
Meizhou	16,003	Meizhou UA	Core municipality
		Meijiang	Urban district
		Meixian	County
		Dapu	County
		Fengshun	County
		Wuhua	County
		Pingyuan	County
		Jiaoling	County
		Xingning	County-level city
Qingyuan	18,932	Qingyuan UA	Core municipality
		Qingcheng	Urban district
		Qingxin	County
		Fogang	County
		Yangshan	County
		Lianshan	County
		Liannan Yao	County
		Yingde	County-level city
		Lianzhou	County-level city
Yunfu	7,564	Yunfu UA	Core municipality
		Yuncheng	Urban district
		Xinxing	County
		Yu'nan	County
		Yun'an	County
		Luoding	County-level city

Source: Authors' elaboration on SBGP (2010) and OECD (2010).

Appendix 2

The township and village enterprises

The category 'Township and Village Enterprises' (TVEs) includes non-state-owned enterprises located in rural areas. They can be collectively owned or private and operate both in the secondary and tertiary sectors (with prevalence in the secondary one). They include a wide variety of different realities and it is very difficult to provide a detailed definition of such a heterogeneous world. Several authors (see, among others, Bolognini, 2000; Zou, 2003; Weitzman and Chenggang, 1994; Taube, 2002; Field *et al.*, 2006; Qian and Stiglitz, 1996) have contributed to draw a clearer picture. A simple definition suggested by Bolognini (2000) is the following: 'firms localised in rural areas as defined by the Chinese administrative classification system'. However, within the category of TVEs we may find the following:

- *Firm at village level*: multi-product unit operating in a wide variety of activities; workers are part-time employees in agriculture and this firm invests a part of its profits to mechanize agriculture.
- *'Still' rural firm*: specialized in a labour-intensive sector. After serving a period as subcontractor for a state-owned enterprise, it has been able to access the international market and can now be the main contractor for other firms, controlling the whole technological cycle. The firm is managed by someone from the local administration. It is called rural if the labour force is not available during the harvest season.
- *Advanced rural firm*: specialized in the production of consumer goods, such as household appliances. Initially, it was a private initiative that has gradually been able to gather funds and know-how from Hong Kong and other localities of the Chinese Diaspora in South East Asia. In a second phase, it is then controlled by the local administration that contributes to its development with ad hoc funding. An independent third party is in charge of the management of this firm, while the local administration limits its actions to a general supervision. At this level, there are no more linkages with agricultural activity.

- *Pseudo-rural firm*: large plant with thousands of workers localized in the suburbs of a city or of a special economic zone (SEZ). Its activity is often linked to a branch located in the centre of the city or of the SEZ. The local administration only supervises the activity of the firm, which is strongly connected to international markets. Sometimes the firm is so well developed that it is itself an investor in other countries such as Hong Kong or Taiwan. However, it is still considered a rural firm (i.e. a TVE) because it is located in a rural area.

Notes

2 The southern China engine: Guangdong province

1 Hainan is a province located in the south of China made up of several islands (the main one is the Hainan island). In 1944, it became an SAR (with more autonomy, a separated political system and an economy more oriented towards the capitalistic system), then becoming an independent province in 1988 (Vogel, 1989).

2 The NBS specifies that 'Total Population refers to the total number of people alive within a given area at a certain point of time. It can be divided into the permanent population and the population with residence registration according to different statistical coverage' (NBS, 2008).

3 To convert Chinese RMB to US$, we have used the following yearly average exchange rates, according to the year of competence:

2005: 1 RMB = 0.12082 US$
2006: 1 RMB = 0.12047 US$
2007: 1 RMB = 0.12623 US$
2008: 1 RMB = 0.13810 US$
2009: 1 RMB = 0.14055 US$
2010: 1 RMB = 0.14184 US$

4 Yuan is another way to indicate the Chinese currency other than RMB.

5 According to some authors, a better definition in terms of homogeneity should include Shanghai and only the parts of Zhejiang and Jiangsu provinces that are closer to Shanghai and the Delta (Hook, 1998; CBM, 2004).

6 The rules defining the system of minimum wage are included in the Law on Labour enacted in 1994 and revised in 2004 (www.ilho.org).

7 See, for example, the following: Asian Business (25 October 2004), The Straits Time (17 August 2004), La Repubblica (18 August 2004), China Daily (21 September 2004), The New York Times (3 April 2005), The Economist (April 2005) and Chan (2010a).

8 In this case, we have applied the monthly average RMB/US$ exchange rate for March 2011 (1 RMB = 0.15233 US$).

9 In this case, we have applied the monthly average RMB/US$ exchange rate for November 2011 (1 RMB = 0.15734 US$).

10 For further information on the Coordinated Plan for Cluster Development in the Pearl River Delta 2004–2020, see Greater Pearl River Delta Business Council (2006a, 2006b).

3 The geography of industry in Guangdong

1 In the text, we will use the terms *prefecture* and *prefecture-level city* as synonymous.
2 Once again the analysis is limited to ADS firms because of the availability of data.

4 Industrial development policy in Guangdong

1 Equity joint ventures (EJVs) are joint investments by Chinese and foreign partners in limited liability enterprises with shared profit/losses (Lemoine, 2000).
2 Wholly foreign-owned enterprises (WFOEs) are 100 per cent foreign-owned firms located in China using Chinese resources, with all profits/losses accruing to the foreign investor (Chen *et al*., 1995).
3 Special economic zones (SEZs) are defined as 'contained geographic regions within countries – a demarcated area of land used to encourage industry, manufacturing, and services for export, and are typically characterized by more liberal laws and economic policies than a country's general economic laws' (Wang, 2010).
4 A fifth SEZ was established in 1988 in Hainan isle, which also became a province (ICE, 2011).
5 Even if physically more distant from Hong Kong and Macao than the other two Guangdong's SEZs, Shantou benefited from a close ethnical proximity to Hong Kong, and to the southeast Asia in general, thanks to the presence in such areas of many overseas Chinese coming from Shantou (Sit, 1985).
6 Source: Guangzhou Development Districts, www.getdd.gov.cn (accessed 2 September 2011).
7 2008 Yearly average exchange rate.

5 Migration policies and the role of migrant workers in Guangdong industrial development

1 For a detailed history of the origin and background of the *hukou* system, see Cheng and Selden (1994).
2 Often, this procedure has been used for local governments to collect money. For this reason, in many areas the only criteria required to obtain the blue-stamp *hukou* is the ownership of a valid temporary residence permit (www.chinalaborwatch.org; accessed July 2011).
3 According to Woon (1999), this category also includes those who have not been able to buy a blue-stamp *hukou*.
4 See, for example, the 16 suicide attempts of migrant workers employed in Foxconn in Shenzhen in May 2010, or the multiple strikes for higher wages at Honda assembly plants in Foshan and Zhongshan in June of the same year [Chan, 2010a; China Labor Watch (CLW), 2010]. Ngai *et al*. (2009) report that the number of demonstrations of workers in China passed from 8,700 in 1993 to 87,000 in 2005 and that there is at least one strike with more than 1,000 workers involved every day in the PRD.

6 Local development policy in Guangdong: the 'specialized town programme'

1 November 2011 monthly average exchange rate.

7 Innovation dynamics and innovation policies in Guangdong

1 In this case, the processing enterprise does not need to pay for the imported components. These are supplied by the seller of the final product, who also pays to the processing enterprise a processing fee.
2 According to the National Bureau of Statistics (NBS, 2010), a peak of students abroad was registered in 2002 (125,179 students). After that year there was a slight decrease, presumably due to repatriations, soon recovered by new outbound students. In 2009, the number of returned students amounted to 108,000.
3 A similar conclusion can be drawn when considering PCT and USPO patent data.
4 Full report available at http://www.newsgd.com/specials/PRD/default.htm (accessed 15 September 2011).
5 English version available at http://www.newsgd.com/specials/12thFive-Year/default.htm. Chinese version available at http://zwgk.gd.gov.cn/006939748/201105/t20110513_86534.html (accessed 15 September 2011).
6 Official press releases available at http://www.newsgd.com/specials/12thFive-Year/news/content/2011-05/26/content_24654283.htm (accessed 15 September 2011).
7 Official press releases available at http://www.newsgd.com/news/weeklynews/content/2011-04/06/content_22346917.htm (accessed 15 September 2011).
8 Press releases available at http://www.newsgd.com/specials/12thFive-Year/news/content/2011-06/02/content_24960950.htm (accessed 15 September 2011).
9 Press releases available at http://www.newsgd.com/specials/12thFive-Year/news/content/2011-05/30/content_24791481.htm (accessed 1 September 2011).

8 Policy effectiveness

1 For details on the selection of the ‘leading firms’, see Barbieri *et al.* (2010).

References

Abrami, R. and Zheng, Y. (2008) *The New Face of Chinese Industrial Policy: Making Sense of Anti-Dumping Cases in the Petrochemical and Steel Industries*, Harvard Business School Working Paper, 11-042. Online. Available at: http://www.hbs.edu/research/pdf/11-042.pdf (accessed 5 September 2011).

Aghion, P., Dewatripont, M., Du, L., Harrison, A. and Legros, P. (2011) *Industrial Policy and Competition*, GRASP Working Paper, June 2011. Online. Available at: http://www.economics.harvard.edu/faculty/aghion/files/Industrial%20Policy.pdf (accessed 13 November 2011).

Amann, R., Cooper, J. and Davies, R.W. (eds) (1977) *The Technological Level of Soviet Industry*, New Haven, CT: Yale University Press.

Amsden, A.H. (1989) *Asia's Next Giant: South Korea and Late Industrialization*, New York: Oxford University Press.

Arvanitis, R. and Qiu, H. (2004) *R&D in Universities and Different Institutional Settings in South China: Research for Policy*, Final Research Report for IDRC (International Development Research Centre).

Arvanitis, R. and Jastrabsky, E. (2006) 'A regional innovation system in gestation: Guangdong', *China Perspectives*, 63: 1–17.

Arvanitis, R. and Qiu, H. (2009) 'Research for policy development: industrial clusters in South China', in M. Graham and J. Woo (eds) *Fuelling Economic Growth: The Role of Public–Private Research in Development*, Ottawa, ON: CRDI/IDRC.

Audretsch, D.B. and Feldman, M. (1996) 'R&D spillovers and the geography of innovation and production', *American Economic Review*, 86(3): 630–40.

Barbieri, E. (2010) 'The evaluation of policies for knowledge transfer: some emerging issues', *Journal of Healthcare Technology and Management*, 11(4): 263–82.

Barbieri, E., Di Tommaso, M.R. and Rubini, L. (2009a) 'Industrial development policies in southern China: the specialized towns programme', *Economia e Politica Industriale*, 36(3): 179–98.

Barbieri, E., Di Tommaso, M.R. and Rubini, L. (2009b) *Industria Contemporanea: Governi, Imprese e Territori nella Cina Meridionale*, Rome: Carocci Editore.

Barbieri, E., Di Tommaso, M.R. and Huang, M. (2010) 'Industrial policy and firm strategy in southern China: government targets and firms' behaviour', *European Planning Studies*, 18(1): 83–105.

Barbieri, E., Di Tommaso, M.R. and Bonnini, S. (2011) 'Industrial development policies and performances in Southern China: beyond the specialised industrial cluster program', *China Economic Review*, (in press).

Becattini, G. (1989) 'Sectors and/or districts: some remark on the conceptual foundation of industrial economics', in E. Goodman, J. Bamford and P. Saynor (eds) *Small Firms and Industrial Districts in Italy*, London: Routledge.

Bellandi, M. and Di Tommaso, M.R. (2005) 'The case of specialized towns in Guangdong, China', *European Planning Studies*, 13(5): 707–29.

Bellandi, M. and Di Tommaso, M.R. (2006) 'The local dimensions of industrial policy', in P. Bianchi and S. Labory (eds) *International Handbook on Industrial Policy*, Cheltenham: Edward Elgar.

Bercovitz, J. and Feldman, M. (2007) 'Fishing upstream: firm innovation strategy and university research alliances', *Research Policy*, 36: 930–48.

Bianchi, P. and Labory, S. (2006) *International Handbook on Industrial Policy*, Cheltenham: Edward Elgar.

Bianchi, P. and Labory, S. (2011) *Europe and the Financial Crisis*, Hampshire: Palgrave MacMillan.

Bianchi, P., Cowling, K. and Sugden, R. (eds) (1994) *Europe's Economic Challenge: Analyses of Industrial Strategy and Agenda for the 1990s*, London: Routledge.

Bingham, R.D. (1998) *Industrial Policy American Style: From Hamilton to HDTV*, Armonk, NY: M.E. Sharpe Inc.

Birdsall, N. and Fukuyama, F. (2011) 'The Post-Washington consensus: Development after the crisis', *Foreign Affairs*, 90(2): 45–53.

Boisot, M. and Meyer, M.W. (2008) 'Which way through the open door? Reflections on the internationalization of Chinese firms', *Management and Organization Review*, 4(3): 349–65.

Bolognini, A. (2000) 'Piccole imprese nella grande Cina', in P. Bianchi, M.R. Di Tommaso and L. Rubini (eds) *Le api audaci: piccole imprese e dinamiche industriali in estremo oriente*, Milano: Franco Angeli.

Bozeman, B. (2000) 'Technology transfer and public policy: a review of research and theory', *Research Policy*, 29: 627–55.

Campbell, D.T. (1969) 'Reforms as experiments', *American Psychologist*, 24(4): 409–29.

Carter, C. (2011) 'A tale of two Chinese SEZs: from exogenous to sustainable endogenous growth?' in C. Carter and A. Harding (eds) *Special Economic Zones in Asian Market Economies*, Abingdon, VA: Routledge.

CB (China Briefing) (2011) 'Guangdong to Lift Minimum Wage Standards Once Again', *China Briefing*, 21 January. Online. Available at: http://www.china-briefing.com/news/2011/01/21/guangdong-to-lift-minimum-wage-standards-once-again.html (accessed 4 November 2011).

CBM (China Business Monthly) (2004) *Business Guide to the Greater Pearl River Delta*, China Briefing Media Ltd. in association with Dezan Shira & Associates.

Chan, K.W. (2010a) 'A China paradox: migrant labor shortage amidst rural labor supply abundance', *Eurasian Geography and Economics*, 51(4): 513–30.

Chan, K.W. (2010b) 'The global financial crisis and migrant workers in China: "there is no future as a labourer; returning to the village has no meaning"', *International Journal of Urban and Regional Research*, 34(3): 659–77.

Chan, K.W. and Buckingham, W. (2008) 'Is China abolishing the hukou system?' *The China Quarterly*, 195: 582–606.

Chan, M. (2004) 'Pan-Pearl-River-Delta (PPRD). A new common market emerges in the booming southern China', *GC. Comm.*, 8: 15–17.

Chandra, N.K. (1999) 'FDI and domestic economy – Neoliberalism in China', *Economic and Political Weekly*, 34(45): 3195–212.

Chang, H.J. (1996) *The Political Economy of Industrial Policy*, London: Macmillan Press.

Chang, H.J (ed.) (2001) *The Rebel Within: Joseph Stiglitz and the World Bank*, London: Anthem Press.

Chang, H.J. (2002) *Kicking Away the Ladder: Development Strategy in Historical Perspective*, London: Anthem Press.

Chang, H.J. (2006) *The East Asian Development Experience: The Miracle, the Crisis, and the Future*, London: Zed Press.

Chang, H.J. (2007) *Bad Samaritans: Rich Nations, Poor Policies, and the Threat to the Developing World*, London: Random House.

Chen, C., Chang, L. and Zhang, Y. (1995) 'The role of foreign direct investment in China's post-1978 economic development', *World Development*, 23(4): 691–703.

Chen, C.F. and Hou, X.R. (2006) 'Comparative institution analysis of the innovation dissemination in Guangdong clusters', *Special Zone Economy*, 11: 61–2 (in Chinese).

Chen, X. (2007) 'A tale of two regions in China: rapid economic development and slow industrial upgrading in the Pearl River and the Yangtze River Delta', *International Journal of Comparative Sociology*, 48(2–3): 167–201.

Chen, X.M. and Cheng, P.Y. (2005) 'The formation development and upgrading of the clusters in Guangdong', *Shangdong Economic Studies*, 1: 68–71 (in Chinese).

Cheng, T. and Selden, M. (1994) 'The origins and social consequences of China's hukou system', *The China Quarterly*, 139: 644–68.

China State Council (2006) *Outline of National Medium and Long Term Program for Science and Technology Development (2006–2020)*, Publication of People's Republic of China Government, Bejing: China State Council.

Chu, D.K.Y. (1998) 'Synthesis of economic reforms and open policy', in Y.M. Yeung and D.K.Y. Chu (eds) *Guangdong: Survey of a Province Undergoing Rapid Change*, Hong Kong: The Chinese University Press.

Chung, C.J., Inaba, J., Koolhaas, R., and Leong, S.T. (2001) *Pearl River Delta: Great Leap Forward, Growth of Modern China Urban Landscape*, Cambridge, MA: Harvard Design School.

Chung, P.T.Y. (1998) 'Changing relations between the central government and Guangdong', in Y.M. Yeung and D.K.Y. Chu (eds) *Guangdong: Survey of a Province Undergoing Rapid Change*, Hong Kong: The Chinese University Press.

Clark, J. and Guy, K. (1997) *Innovation and Competitiveness*, Brighton: Technopolis.

CLW (China Labor Watch) (2010) *2010 Annual Report*, New York: CLW.

Cohen, W.M. and Levinthal, D.A. (1989) 'Innovation and learning: the two faces of R&D', *The Economic Journal*, 99: 569–96.

Colman, D. and Nixon, F.I. (1994) *Economics of Change in Less Developed Countries*, London: Harvester Wheatsheaf.

Dai, Y. (2005) 'A roundabout development road of private economy red-cap enterprises', *Southern China Journal of Economics*, 7.

Démurger, S. (2000) *Economic Opening and Growth in China*, Paris: OECD Development Centre Studies.

Démurger, S., Sachs, J.D., Woo, W.T., Bao, S., Chang, G. and Mellinger, A. (2002) *Geography, Economic Policy, and Regional Development in China*, Asian Paper Series, Cambridge, MA: Center for International Development and the Massachusetts Institute of Technology.

Department of Finance of Guangdong Government (2005) *Thoughts and Strategies for the Development of Clusters in Guangdong and for Brands Creation*, Zhongshan: Yang Chen Wan Bao (in Chinese).

Di Tommaso, M.R. and Rubini, L. (2005) 'La geografia della produzione nel Guangdong: agglomerazioni di imprese e città specializzate', in M. Bellandi and M. Biggeri M. (eds) *La Sfida Industriale Cinese Vista dalla Toscana Distrettuale*, Urbania: Stibu.

Di Tommaso, M.R. and Rubini, L. (2006) 'Cluster industriali e specialized towns nel Guangdong: la centralità del Delta del Fiume delle Perle', in M.R. Di Tommaso and M. Bellandi (eds) *Il Fiume delle Perle: La Dimensione Locale dello Sviluppo Industriale Cinese e il Confronto con l'Italia*, Turin: Rosenberg & Sellier.

Di Tommaso, M.R. and Schweitzer, S.O. (2012) *Breaking the Taboo: Industrial Policy in America*, Cheltenham: Edward Elgar.

DSTC (Department of Science and Technology China). (2010) 'Specialized towns: an important engine for the economic development of Guangdong', *Science and Technology Daily*, 23 December (in Chinese).

DSTC (Department of Science and Technology China). (2011a) 'The economy of specialized towns in Guangdong: "a third of the world"', *Science and Technology Daily*, 10 January 2011 (in Chinese).

DSTC (Department of Science and Technology China). (2011b) 'The role of innovation in promoting industrial change within specialized towns', *Science and Technology Daily*, 7 January 2011 (in Chinese).

DSTC (Department of Science and Technology China). (2011c) 'Specialized towns: the importance of sustaining wealth in Guangdong. Report on the innovation capacity building in Guangdong specialized towns', *Science and Technology Daily*, 6 March 2011 (in Chinese).

DSTC (Department of Science and Technology China). (2011d) 'Report on the innovation capacity building in Guangdong specialized towns', *Science and Technology Daily*, 9 March 2011 (in Chinese).

DSTC (Department of Science and Technology China). (2011e) 'Twenty-four new policies for the development and upgrading of specialised towns', *Science and Technology Daily*, 17 January 2011 (in Chinese).

DSTC (Department of Science and Technology China). (2011f) 'Guangdong specialized towns' economy: one third of the world', *Science and Technology Daily*, 10 January 2011 (in Chinese).

DSTGG (Department of Science and Technology of Guangdong Government). (2003) *The Innovation of Industrial Clusters in Guangdong Province*, Publication of the Guangdong Provincial Department of Science and Technology (in Chinese).

DSTGG (Department of Science and Technology of Guangdong Government). (2006a) 'Report on the summary of the five-year implementation of the plan of ST technology innovation pilot test and an overview of the development of the STs', *DST Magazine on Specialized Towns Technology Innovation Dynamics*, 15(6): 1–6 (in Chinese).

DSTGG (Department of Science and Technology of Guangdong Government). (2006b) *Guangdong Province Government's Suggestion on the Promotion of the Development of Specialized Towns*, Official Website of DST. Online. Available at: http://www.zhyz.gov.cn (accessed 15 November 2006) (in Chinese).

DSTGG (Department of Science and Technology of Guangdong Government) (2007) *Note on the 2006 Successful Collaboration Alliance between Specialized Towns in Guangdong and Universities*, Department of Science and Technology of Guangdong Province. Online. Available at: http://cxy.gdstc.gov.cn (accessed 23 April 2007) (in Chinese).

DSTGG (Department of Science and Technology of Guangdong Government). (2008a) *Policy and Instruments on Specialized Town Technology Innovation in Guangdong*, Department of Science and Technology of Guangdong Province. Online. Available at: http://www.zhyz.gov.cn (accessed 18 March 2009) (in Chinese).

DSTGG (Department of Science and Technology of Guangdong Government). (2008b) *List of the Technology Innovation Platforms in Specialized Towns in Guangdong*, Department of Science and Technology of Guangdong Province. Online. Available at: http://www.zhyz.gov.cn (accessed 25 November 2008) (in Chinese).

DSTGG (Department of Science and Technology of Guangdong Government). (2008c) *Patterns of Technology Innovation Platform in Specialized Town*, Department of Science and Technology of Guangdong Province. Online. Available at: http://www.zhyz.gov.cn (accessed 17 February 2009) (in Chinese).

Dunn, W.N. (1994) *Public Policy Analysis: An Introduction, Englewood Cliffs*, NJ: Prentice-Hall.

EC (European Commission) (1999) *The Means Collection: Evaluation Design and Management*, Luxembourg: Office for Official Publications of the European Communities.

ECN (Economist Corporate Network) (2011) *The 12th Five Year Plan: China's Economic Transition, The Economist: Project for Tekes*. Online. Available at: http://www.fin-node.fi/files/39/The_12th_Five-Year_Plan_China_s_Economic_Transition.pdf (accessed 5 October 2011).

Edin, M. (2003) 'State capacity and local agent control in China: CCP cadre management from a township perspective', *The China Quarterly*, 173: 35–52.

Eng, I. (1997) 'The rise of manufacturing towns: externally driven industrialisation and urban development in the Pearl River Delta of China', *International Journal of Urban and Regional Research*, 21(4): 554–68.

Enright, M.J., Scott, E.E. and Chang, K.-M. (2005) *Regional Powerhouse: The Greater PRD and the Rise of China*, Singapore: John Wiley & Sons.

Fan, C.C. (1995) 'Of belts and ladders: state policy and uneven regional development in post-Mao China', *Annals of the Association of American Geographers*, 85(3): 421–49.

Fan, C.C. (2004) 'The state, the migrant labour regime, and maiden workers in China', *Political Geography*, 23: 283–305.

Fan, C.C. (2008) 'Migration, hukou and the city', in S. Yusuf and T. Saich (eds) *China Urbanizes: Consequences, Strategies and Policies*, Washington, DC: The World Bank.

Fang, M.K.Y., Wai-Ming, H. and Zhu, L. (1999) 'Effects of government policy changes on the private sector development in a transitional economy: a long-run analysis', *Journal of Economic Development*, 24(2): 19–41.

Field, J., Garris, M., Guntupalli, M., Rana, V. and Reyes, G. (2006) 'Chinese township and village Enterprises: A model for other developing countries', paper prepared for the *International Economic Development Program, Ford School of Public Policy*, University of Michigan.

Fleisher, B.M. and Yang, D.T. (2003) 'Labour laws and regulations in China', *China Economic Review*, 14(25): 426–33.

Florence, E. (2007) 'Migrant workers in the Pearl River Delta. Discourse and narratives about work as sites of struggle', *Critical Asian Studies*, 39(1): 121–50.

Fu, J. (2000) *Institutions and Investments: Foreign Direct Investment in China during an Era of Reforms*, Ann Arbor, MI: The University of Michigan Press.

Furubo, J., Rist, R., and Sandahl, R. (2002) *International Atlas of Evaluation*, New Brunswick, NJ: Transaction Publishers.

Garcia Carrillo, B. (2004) 'Rural-urban migration in China: temporary migrants in search of permanent settlement', *Journal of Multidisciplinary International Studies*, 1(2): 1–26.

Garnaut, R. and Song, L. (2004) *China's Third Economic Transformation: The Rise of the Private Economy*, London: Routledge.

GDICC (Guangdong International Consultative Conference Preparatory Office). (2007) *GDICC Update*, A newsletter for the International Consultative Conference on the Future Economic Development of Guangdong Province, no. 14, November.

Ge, W. (1999) 'Special economic zones and the opening of the Chinese economy: some lessons for economic liberalization', *World Development*, 27(7): 1267–86.

Geroski, P.A. (1989) 'European industrial policy and industrial policy in Europe', *Oxford Review of Economic Policy*, 5(2): 20–36.

GPLTB (Guangdong Provincial Local Taxation Bureau) (2009) Guangdong Local Taxation Bureau Initiatively Provides Tax Policy Services to 'Going Abroad' Enterprises. Online. Available at: http://www.gdltax.gov.cn (accessed 14 September 2011).

Greater Pearl River Delta Business Council. (2006a) *Report on Guangdong Industrial Restructuring: Opportunities and Challenges for Hong Kong*, The Greater Pearl River

Delta Business Council. Online. Available at: http://www.cmab.gov.hk/doc/study_report_on_guangdong_industrial_restructuring_eng.pdf (accessed 3 March 2007).

Greater Pearl River Delta Business Council. (2006b) *The Development of Western Pearl River Delta Region and Its Prospects for Collaborations with Hong Kong*, The Greater Pearl River Delta Business Council. Online. Available at: http://www.cmab.gov.hk/doc/study_report_on_the_deveoopment_of_western_prd_eng.pdf (accessed 15 April 2010).

Guangdong Government. (1998) *On the Decision to rely on Scientific and Technological Progress to attain a Higher Level of Production in Guangdong*, Report of People's Government of Guangdong Province, no. 16.

Guangdong Government. (2008a) *The Announcement of the Practical Outline of Building an Innovative Guangdong Province*, Report of People's Government of Guangdong Province, no. 72.

Guangdong Government. (2008b) *The Outline of Guangdong's Plan for Indigenous Innovation*, Report of People's Government of Guangdong Province, no. 74.

Guo, W. and Feng, Y (2007) *Special Economic Zones and Competitiveness: A Case Study of Shenzhen, the People's Republic of China*, Islamabad: Asian Development Bank.

Haddad, M. and Shepherd, B. (2011) *Managing Openness: Trade and Outward-oriented Growth After the Crisis*, Washington, DC: World Bank Trade and Development Series.

Hassard, J., Morris, J., Sheehan, J. and Yuxin, X. (2010) 'China's state-owned enterprises: economic reform and organizational restructuring', *Journal of Organizational Change Management*, 23(5): 500–16.

Haveman, R.H. (1987) *Poverty Policy and Poverty Research: The Great Society and the Social Sciences*, Madison: University of Wisconsin Press.

Henderson, R., Jaffe, A. and Trajtenberg, M. (1998) 'Universities as a source of commercial technology: a detailed analysis of university patenting', *Review of Economics and Statistics*, 80(1): 119–27.

Hirsch, G. and Rubini, L. (2006) 'Il Guangdong e il delta del fiume delle perle: una delle locomotive della nuova industria cinese', in M. Bellandi and M.R. Di Tommaso (eds) *Il Fiume delle Perle – La Dimensione Locale dello Sviluppo Industriale Cinese e il Confronto con l'Italia*, Turin: Rosenberg & Sellier.

HKTDC (Hong Kong Trade Development Council). (2011) 'Guangdong boosts construction of industry relocation projects', *Business Alert China*, 1 January. Online. Available at: http://www.hktdc.com/info/vp/a/pprd/en/1/3/1/1X079Q8M/Guangdong-Boosts-Construction-Of-Industry-Relocation-Projects.htm (accessed 23 October 2011).

Hook, B. (1998) *Shanghai and the Yangtze River Delta, a City Reborn*, vol. 3, New York: Oxford University Press.

Huang, X. and Hu, C.W. (2007) 'Industry gathering style from the angle of origin and its characteristics: take Guangdong province specialized town as example', *Special Zone Economy*, 5: 39 (in Chinese).

Huang, Y., Yang, Z.B. and Meng, F.C. (2006) 'The empirical research and policy suggestion of the development of industrial clusters in Guangdong province', *Science and Technology Management Research*, 12: 15–17 (in Chinese).

Huang, Z.R. and Qiu, J.S. (2003) 'China's status in manufacture and Guangdong's industrial clustering', *Academic Research*, 28(3): 13–15 (in Chinese).

Huikang, J. (2002) *Aspects of Guangdong Province*, Guangzhou: Cartographic Publishing House of Guangdong Province.

ICE (Istituto per il Commercio Estero). (2002) *Profilo del Guangdong*, Guangzhou: ICE. Online. Available at: http://www.ice.gov.it/estero2/canton/default.htm (accessed 5 March 2007).

ICE (Istituto per il Commercio Estero). (2011) *Profilo Economico della Provincia del Guangdong*, Guangzhou: ICE. Online. Available at: http://www.ice.it/paesi/asia/cina/profguangdong.pdf (accessed 2 July 2011).

IPR-ICE (Intellectual Property Rights Office, Italian Institute for Foreign Commerce). (2009) *La Proprietà Intellettuale in Cina: Linee Generali e Focus sulle Province Meridionali e sui Marchi e Brevetti del Made in Italy*, Guangzhou: Publication of the Intellectual Property Right Desk of ICE.

Jin, H. (2007) *Aspects of Guangdong Province*, Guangzhou: Cartographic Publishing House of Guangdong Province.

Johnson, C. (1982) *MITI and the Japanese Miracle*, Stanford, CA: Stanford University Press.

Kamath, S.J. (1990) 'Foreign direct investment in a centrally planned developing economy: the Chinese case', *Economic Development and Cultural Change*, 39(1): 107–30.

Kassim, H. and Menon, A. (1996) *The European Union and National Industrial Policy*, London: Routledge.

Katz, B.M. (1988) 'Review: the war on poverty and the transformation of American social science', *Reviews in American History*, 16(1): 137–43.

Ketels, C.H.M. (2007) 'Industrial policy in the United States', *Journal of Industrial Competition and Trade*, 7(3–4): 147–67.

Kirkpatrick, C.H., Lee, N. and Nixon, F.I. (1984) *Industrial Structure and Policy in Less Developed Countries*, London: George Allen & Unwin.

Koehler, K. (2011) 'Profit repatriation strategies and tax optimization in China', *Chinainvest.biz*, 2(11): 3–5.

Kroll, H. and Tagscherer, U. (2009) 'Chinese regional innovation systems in times of crisis: the case of Guangdong', *Asian Journal of Technology Innovation*, 17(2): 101–28.

Krueger, A.O. (1990) 'Government failures in development', *Journal of Economic Perspectives*, 4(3): 9–23.

Krug, B. (ed.) (2004) *China's rational entrepreneurs*, London: Routledge.

Krugman, P.R. and Obstfeld, M. (1991) *International Economics*, New York: Addison Wesley.

Lachang, L. and Yehua, D.W. (2007) 'Domesticating globalization, new economic spaces and regional polarization in Guangdong province, China', *Tijdschrift voor Economische en Sociale Geografie*, 98(2): 225–44.

Lai, H. (2006) 'SEZs and foreign investment in China: experience and lessons for North Korean development', *Asian Perspective*, 30(3): 69–97.

Lai, H., Chiu, Y. and Leu, H. (2005) 'Innovation capacity comparison of China's information technology industrial clusters: the case of Shanghai, Kunshan, Shenzhen and Dongguan', *Technology Analysis and Strategic Management*, 17(3): 293–315.

Lan, H. (2008) 'Building Chinese "world-class enterprises": the advantages, paths and strategy choices', *Chinese Journal of Management*, 1: 213–224.

Lardy, N. (1992) *Foreign Trade and Economic Reform in China, 1978–1990*, Cambridge: Cambridge University Press.

Lavigne, M. (1974) *The Socialist Economies of the Soviet Union and Europe*, London: Martin Robertson & Co. Ltd.

Lemoine, F. (2000) *FDI and Opening Up of China's Economy, CEPII (Centre d'Etudes Prospectives et d'Informations Internationales) WP*, n. 2000-11, June.

Li, H. and Zhou, L. (2005) 'Political turnover and economic performance: the incentive role of personnel control in China', *Journal of Public Economics*, 89: 1743–62.

Li, J. (1989) 'Incentives for foreign investment in the People's Republic of China', *Review of International Business Law*, 4: 99–113.

Li, J. and Zhong, J. (2003) 'Explaining the growth of international R&D alliances in China', *Managerial and Decision Economics*, 24: 101–15.

Li, X.C. (2002) 'The acquisition and creation of capabilities and resources in the growth process of clusters in Guangdong', *Academic Research*, 7: 10–12 (in Chinese).

Li, Y.P. (2006) 'The pattern and experience of the development of SME clusters in Guangdong', *Enterprise Research*, 311(7): 58–61 (in Chinese).

Li&Fung. (2006) 'Industrial clusters in Pearl River Delta', Industrial Cluster Series, no. 2: 1–19.

Li&Fung. (2008) 'China's industry relocation and upgrading trends: implications for sourcing business', *China Distribution & Trading*, 56: 1–16.

Liang, G., You, A. and Kae, G. (2008) 'Guangdong', in Y.M. Yeung and S. Jianfa (eds) *The Pan-Pearl River Delta – An Emerging Regional Economy in a Globalizing China*, Hong Kong: The Chinese University of Hong Kong.

Liang, Z. and Ma, Z. (2004) 'China's floating population: new evidence from the 2000 census', *Population and Development Review*, 30(3): 37–51.

Lin, J.Y. (2012) *New Structural Economic: A Framework for Rethinking Development*, Washington DC: The World Bank.

Lin, P. (2006) 'What is "coordinated promotion plan between province and (prefecture) city"'? *Journal of Guangdong Science and Technology*, 14(8): 5–6 (in Chinese).

Lin, P. (2007) *The Development of Specialized Towns and the Implementation of the Specialized Town Technology Innovation Plan in Guangdong, Report presented at the opening of the China–Italy School of Policy*, Italian Ministry of Foreign Affairs, 17 September, 2007 (in Chinese).

Liu, L. (2005) *China's Industrial Policies and the Global Business Revolution*. The Case of the Domestic Appliance Industry, London: Routledge.

Liu, X., Buck, T. and Shu, C. (2005) 'Chinese economic development, the next stage: outward FDI?' *International Business Review*, 14(1): 97–115.

Lu, P. (2006) 'Specialized town is the strong engine to drive the economy of Guangdong: the five-year development of specialized town technology innovation pilot test', *Journal of Guangdong Science and Technology*, 8: 1–4 (in Chinese).

Luo, Y., Xue, Q. and Han, B. (2010) 'How emerging market governments promote outward FDI: experience from China', *Journal of World Business*, 45(1): 68–79.

Ma, J. (1999) *The Chinese Economy in the 1990s*, Basingstoke: Palgrave Publishers.

Martini, A. (2008) 'How Counterfactuals Got Lost on the Way to Brussels'. Online. Available at: http://egov.formez.it/files/Counterfactuals.pdf (accessed 15 September 2011).

Maruya, T. (1998) 'The economy', in Y.M. Yeung and D.K.Y. Chu (eds) *Guangdong. Survey of a Province Undergoing Rapid Change*, Hong Kong: The Chinese University Press.

Maskel, P. and Malmberg, A. (1999) 'The competitiveness of firms and regions', *European Urban and Regional Studies*, 6(1): 9–25.

Matthews, A. and Baum, J. (2011) *China's Rising Labour Movement*. Online. Available at: http://pulitzercenter.org/projects/china-migrant-workers-labor-movement-pearl-river-delta (accessed 29 August 2011).

Mo, Q. (2011) 'Guangdong Builds World-Class Electric Auto Base', *News Guangdong*. Online. Available at: http://www.newsgd.com/specials/12thFive-Year/news/content/2011-06/02/content_24961073.htm (accessed 15 September 2011).

MOLSS (Ministry of Labour and Social Security of China) (2004) 'Report on the Migrant Labour Shortage', *Asian Labour News*, September.

Mowery, D.C., Oxley, J.E. and Silverman, B.S. (1996) 'Strategic alliances and interfirm knowledge transfer', *Strategic Management Journal*, 17: 77–91.

Mueller, C. (2010) *Migrant Workers in Guangdong Allowed to Obtain Urban Residence Permits*. Online. Available at: http://www.xing.com/net/china/%E5%A4%A7%E4%B8%AD%E5%8D%8E-law-and-legislation-in-greater-china-recht-und-gesetz-in-greater-china-4020/migrant-workers-in-guangdong-allowed-to-obtain-urban-residence-permits-30620001 (accessed 29 August 2011).

Myerson, R., Hou, Y., Tang, H., Cheng, Y., Wang, Y. and Ye, Z. (2010) 'Home and away: Chinese migrant workers between two worlds', *The Sociological Review*, 58(1): 26–44.

Napoleoni, L. (2011) *Maonomics: Why Chinese Communists Make Better Capitalists than We Do*, New York: Seven Stories Press.

Naughton, B. (2007) *The Chinese Economy: Transitions and Growth*, Cambridge, MA: MIT University Press.
NBS (National Bureau of Statistics of China). (2003) *China Statistical Yearbook*, Beijing: China Statistics Press.
NBS (National Bureau of Statistics of China). (2008) *China Statistical Yearbook*, Beijing: China Statistics Press.
NBS (National Bureau of Statistics of China). (2009) *China Statistical Yearbook*, Beijing: China Statistics Press.
NBS (National Bureau of Statistics of China). (2010) *China Statistical Yearbook*, Beijing: China Statistics Press.
Nee, V. (2000) 'The role of the state in making a market economy', *Journal of Institutional and Theoretical Economics*, 156(1): 64–88.
Nee, V. and Cao, Y. (1999) 'Path dependent societal transformation: stratification in hybrid mixed economies', *Theory and Society*, 28(6): 799–834.
Nee, V. and Opper, S. (2007) 'On politicized capitalism', in V. Nee and R. Swedberg (eds) *On Capitalism*, Stanford, CA: Stanford University Press.
Ng, L.F.Y. and Tuan, C. (2001) 'FDI promotion policy in China: governance and effectiveness', *The World Economy*, 24(8): 1051–74.
Ng, Y.-T. and Chu, D.K.Y. (1985) The geographical endowment of China's special economic zones, in K.-Y. Wong and D.K.Y. Chu (eds) *Modernization in China: The Case of Shenzhen Special Economic Zone*, Hong Kong: Oxford University Press.
Ngai, P., Chan, C.K.C. and Chan, J. (2009) 'The role of the state, labour policy and migrant workers' struggles in globalized China', *Global Labour Journal*, 1(1): 132–51.
Niosi, J. (1994) *New Technology Policy and Technical Innovations in the Firm*, London: Pinter Press.
Nolan, P. (2001) *China and the Global Economy: National Champions, Industrial Policy, and the Big Business Revolution*, New York and Basingstoke: Palgrave.
Norton, R.D. (1986) 'Industrial policy and American renewal', *Journal of Economic Literature*, 24: 1–40.
Nove, A. (1992) *An Economic History of the USSR 1917–1991*, New York: Penguin Group.
NPC (National People's Congress of the People's Republic of China). (2004) Constitution of the People's Republic of China. Full Text after Amendment on March 14, 2004, Beijing. Available at: http://www.npc.gov.cn.
OECD (Organization for Economic Co-operation and Development). (2010) *OECD Territorial Reviews: Guangdong, China 2010*, Paris: OECD Publishing.
OECD (Organization for Economic Co-operation and Development). (2011) *China – Economic Forecast Summary*, November. Online. Available at: http://www.oecd.org/document/31/0,3746,en_2649_34573_45274719_1_1_1_1,00.html (accessed 20 December 2011).
Okimoto, D. (1990) *Between MITI and the Market: Japanese Industrial Policy for High Technology*, Stanford, CA: Stanford University Press.
Ota, T. (2003) 'The role of Special Economic Zones in China's economic development as compared with Asian export processing zones: 1979–1995', *Asia in Extenso*, March: 1–28.
Parish, W.L. and Michelson, E. (1996) 'Politics and markets: dual transformations', *The American Journal of Sociology*, 101(4) 1042–59.
Pearson, M.M. (1991) *Joint Ventures in the People's Republic of China*, Princeton, NJ: Princeton University Press.
Pieke, F.N. and Malee, H. (1999) *Internal and International Migration: Chinese Perspectives*, London: Curzon.
Piore, M.J. and Sabel, J.F. (1984) *The Second Industrial Divide: Possibilities for Prosperity*, New York: Basic Books.

Powell, W.W. and Owen-Smith, J. (1998) 'Universities and the market for intellectual property in the life-sciences', *Journal of Policy Analysis and Management*, 17(2): 253–77.

Qi, Z. (2009) 'Guangdong Set to Reform the Hukou System', *China Daily*, 8 January. Online. Available at: http://www.chinadaily.com.cn/business/2009-01/08/content_7379021.htm (accessed 28 July 2011).

Qian, Y. and Xu, C. (1993) 'Why China's economic reforms differ: the M-form hierarchy and entry/expansion of the non-state sector', *Economics Of Transition*, 1(2):135–70.

Qian, Y. and Stiglitz, J. (1996) 'Institutional innovations and the role of local government in transition economies: the case of Guangdong province of China', in J. McMillan and B. Naughton (eds) *The Growth of Market Institutions*, Ann Arbor, MI: The University of Michigan Press.

Qiu, H. and Xu, J. (2007) 'The actions of local governments in technological innovation in industrial clusters', in H. Qiu (ed.) *Regional Innovation and Development of Enterprises*, Beijing: Economic Science Publishing House (in Chinese).

Reich, R.B. (1982) 'Why the US needs an industrial policy', *Harvard Business Review*, 60(1): 74–81.

Roberts, D. (2008) 'China's Factory Blues', *BusinessWeek*, 27 March. Online. Available at: http://www.businessweek.com/magazine/content/08_14/b4078078846220.htm (accessed 8 October 2011).

Roberts, K.D. (1997) 'China's tidal wave of migrant labour', *International Migration Review*, 31(2): 249–93.

Rodrik, D. (2004) Industrial Policy in the Twenty-first Century, *paper prepared for UNIDO*, Boston: John F. Kennedy School of Government, September. Online. Available at: http://www.hks.harvard.edu/fs/drodrik/Research%20papers/UNIDOSep.pdf (accessed 18 November 2011).

Roessner, J.D. and Wise, A. (1994) 'Public-policy and emerging sources of technology and technical-information available to industry', *Policy Studies Journal*, 22(2): 349–58.

Rossi, P.H. and Freeman, H.E. (1989) *Evaluation: A Systematic Approach*, Newbury Park, CA: Sage Publications.

Rossi, V. and Burghart, N. (2009) 'As China's economy matures, its companies are looking for opportunities to expand around the world', *The China Business Review Online*, September-October. Online. Available HTTP: https://www.chinabusinessreview.com/public/0909/intro.html (accessed 17 November 2011).

Sachs, J.D. and Woo, W.T. (1997) *Understanding China's Economic Performance*, NBER Working Paper Series, WP 5935, Cambridge, MA: National Bureau of Economic Research.

Sakoh, K. (1984) 'Japanese Economic Success: Industrial Policy or Free Market?' *Cato Journal*, 4(2): 521–48.

Sanderson, I. (2003) 'Is it "what works" that matters? Evaluation and evidence-based policy-making', *Research Papers in Education*, 18(4): 331–45.

SBGP (Statistical Bureau of Guangdong Province). (2001) *Guangdong Statistical Yearbook*, Beijing: China Statistics Press.

SBGP (Statistical Bureau of Guangdong Province). (2003) *Guangdong Statistical Yearbook*, Beijing: China Statistics Press.

SBGP (Statistical Bureau of Guangdong Province). (2005) *Guangdong Statistical Yearbook*, Beijing: China Statistics Press.

SBGP (Statistical Bureau of Guangdong Province). (2006) *Guangdong Sciencial Statistical Yearbook*, Beijing: China Statistics Press.

SBGP (Statistical Bureau of Guangdong Province). (2007) *Guangdong Statistical Yearbook*, Beijing: China Statistics Press.

SBGP (Statistical Bureau of Guangdong Province). (2008) *Guangdong Statistical Yearbook*, Beijing: China Statistics Press.

SBGP (Statistical Bureau of Guangdong Province). (2009) *Guangdong Statistical Yearbook*, Beijing: China Statistics Press.

SBGP (Statistical Bureau of Guangdong Province). (2010) *Guangdong Statistical Yearbook*, Beijing: China Statistics Press.

SBGP (Statistical Bureau of Guangdong Province). (2011) *Guangdong Statistical Yearbook*, Beijing: China Statistics Press.

Schubert, G. and Ahlers, A.L. (2011) '"Constructing a new socialist countryside and beyond": an analytical framework for studying policy implementation and political stability in contemporary China', *Journal of Chinese Political Science*, 16: 19–46.

Shadish, W.R., Cook T.D. and Leviton, L.C. (1991) *Foundations of Program Evaluation: Theories of Practice*, Newbury Park, CA: Sage Publications.

Shari, N. and Huang, C. (2008) *Cross-border Investment and Economic Integration: The Case of Guangdong Province and Hong Kong SAR*, Working Paper no. 2008-035, Maastricht: United Nations University.

Shen, J. (2011) 'Migrant labour under the shadow of the hukou system', in T.-C. Wong and J. Rigg (eds) *Asian Cities, Migrant Labour and Contested Spaces*, New York: Routledge.

Shen, J., Wong, K., Chu, K. and Feng, Z. (2000) 'The spatial dynamics of foreign investment in the Pearl River Delta, South China', *Geographical Journal*, 166(4): 312–22.

Shenzhen Government. (2006) *Statistical Indicators*. Online. Available at: http://english.sz.gov.cn/ (accessed 15 June 2007).

Si-ming, L. and Yat-ming, S. (1998) 'Population mobility', in Y.M. Yeung and D.K.Y Chu (eds) *Guangdong: Survey of a Province Undergoing Rapid Change*, Hong Kong: The Chinese University Press.

Simmie, J. (2004) 'Innovation and clustering in the globalised international economy', *Urban Studies*, 41: 1095–112.

Sit, V.F.S. (1985) 'The special economic zones of China: a new type of export processing zone?' *The Developing Economies*, 23(1): 69–87.

Siu-Wai, W. and Bo-Sin, T. (2005) 'Challenges to the sustainability of 'development zones': a case study of Guangzhou Development District, China', *Cities*, 22(4): 303–16.

Soete, L. (2007) 'From industrial to innovation policy', *Journal of Industry, Competition and Trade*, 7(3–4): 273–84.

Stame, N. and Rist, R.C. (2011) *From Studies to Streams: Managing Evaluation Systems*, New Brunswick, NJ: Transaction Publishers.

Stiglitz, J.E. (2002) *Globalization and Its Discontents*, New York: WW. Norton and Co. Ltd.

Stoltenberg, C.D. (1984) 'China's special economic zones: their development and prospects', *Asian Survey*, 24(6): 637–54.

Tang, Q.Y., Xie, H.M. and Lan, H.L. (2005) 'Guangdong industry gathering's present situation, development trend and countermeasure: research based on Geordie coefficient', *Special Zone Economy*, 11: 22–24 (in Chinese).

Tassinari, A. and Tomba, L. (1996) 'Zhejiang-Pechino, Zhejiang-Firenze. Due esperienze migratorie a confronto', *La critica sociologica*, 117-118: 15–38.

Taube, M. (2002) 'Stability in Instability. China's TVEs and the Evolution of Property Rights', *ASIEN*, 84: 59–66.

Tsai, K.S. (2007) *Capitalism Without Democracy: The Private Sector in Contemporary China*, New York: Cornell University Press.

Tsui, K. and Wang, Y. (2008) 'Decentralization with political trump: vertical control, local accountability and regional disparities in China', *China Economic Review*, 19: 18–31.

ul Haque, I. (2007) *Rethinking Industrial Policy*, UNDP Discussion Paper, No. 183, April. Online. Available at: http://www.unctad.org/en/docs/osgdp20072_en.pdf (accessed 15 November 2011).

UNESCO Institute for Statistics. (2010) *Global Education Digest*. Comparing Education Statistics across the World, Montreal: UNESCO.

Unger, J. and Chan, A. (1999) 'Inheritors of the boom: private enterprise and the role of local government in a rural South China township', *The China Journal*, 42: 45–74.

UNIDO (United Nations Industrial Development Organization). (2002) *Industrial Development Report*, Geneva: UNIDO Publications.

USCBS (US–China Business Council). (2011) 'China's domestic innovation and government procurement policies', *Issues Brief of USBS*, March.

US–China Economic and Security Review Commission. (2009) *China's Industrial Policy and its Impact on U.S. Companies, Workers and the American Economy*, Federal Publications, Paper 642.

Vogel, E.F. (1989) *One Step Ahead in China – Guangdong under Reform*, Cambridge, MA: Harvard University Press.

VV.AA (2006) *Guangdongsheng Dituce (Atlas of Guangdong Province)*, Guangzhou: Cartographic Publishing House of Guangdong Province.

Wade, R. (1990) *Governing the Market: Economic Theory and the Role of Government in East Asian Industrialization*, Princeton, NJ: Princeton University Press.

Wade, R. (2012) 'Return of industrial policy?', *International Review of Applied Economics*, 26(2): 223–39.

Walsh, K. (2003) *Foreign High-Tech R&D in China*, Washington, DC: The Henry L. Stimson Center.

Wang, D. and Pei, H. (2010) 'Transfer of Shenzhen's hi-tech industries: an empirical study', *Chinese Management Studies*, 4(4): 401–18.

Wang, F.-L. (2004) 'Reformed migration control and new targeted people: China's hukou system in the 2000s', *The China Quarterly*, 177: 115–32.

Wang, J. (2002) 'Innovation process of enterprise cluster', *Management World*, 10: 102–10 (in Chinese).

Wang, J. (2004) 'Developing innovation-based industrial clusters: policy recommendation', *Economic Geography*, 7: 433–6 (in Chinese).

Wang, J. (2009) 'Interaction and innovation in cluster development: some experiences from Guangdong province, China', in B. Ganne and Y. Lecler (eds) *Asian Industrial Clusters, Global Competitiveness and New Policy Initiatives*, Singapore: World Scientific Publishing Co.

Wang, J. (2010) *The Economic Impact of Special Economic Zones: Evidence from Chinese Municipalities*, Mimeo. Online. Available at: http://www.wcu-snuecon.co.kr/upload/catalogue_file/d25b6a6cb26a453fabd96982a1a87f66.pdf (accessed 24 April 2011).

Wang, J. and Yue, F. (2010) 'Cluster development and the role of government: the case of Xiqiao textile cluster in Guangdong', in D.Z. Zeng (ed.) *Building Engines for Growth and Competitiveness in China: Experiences with Special Economic Zones and Industrial Clusters*, Washington, DC: The World Bank.

Wang, M.Y. (2002) 'The motivations behind China's government-initiated industrial investments overseas', *Pacific Affairs*, 75(2): 187–206.

Wang, M.Y. and Meng, X. (2004) 'Global-local initiatives in FDI: the experience of Shenzhen, China', *Asia Pacific Viewpoint*, 45(2): 181–96.

Wang, S. and Hu, A. (1999) *The Political Economy of Uneven Development: The Case of China*, Armonk, NY: M.E. Sharpe.

Wei, S.J. (1995) 'The open door policy and China rapid economic growth: evidence from city level data', in T. Ito and A.O. Krueger (eds) *Growth Theories in Light of Asian Experiences*, Chicago, IL: University of Chicago Press.

Weitzman, M. and Chenggang, X. (1994) 'Chinese township village enterprises as vaguely defined cooperatives', *Journal of Comparative Economics*, 18: 121–45.

Whithing, S.H. (2001) *Power and Wealth in Rural China*, Cambridge, MA: Cambridge University Press.

Wing (2011) 'Guangdong LED Industry Set for Bigger Boost', *News Guangdong*. Online. Available at: http://www.newsgd.com/specials/12thFive-Year/news/content/2011-06/02/content_24961342.htm (accessed 15 September 2011).

Woon, Y.-F. (1999) 'Labor migration in the 1990s: homeward orientation of migrants in the Pearl River Delta region and its implications for interior China', *Modern China*, 25(4): 475–512.

World Bank (1993) *The East Asian Miracle: Economic Growth and Public Policy*, New York: Oxford University Press.

Wu, J. and Ma, L. (2009) 'Does Government Performance Really Matter? An Event History Analysis of the Promotion of Provincial Leaders in China', *SSRN Working Paper Series*. Online. Available at: http://papers.ssrn.com/sol3/papers.cfm?abstract_id=1509806&;http://papers.ssrn.com/sol3/papers.cfm?abstract_id=1509806 (accessed 15 September 2011).

Xiang, Y., Hong, J. and Zuo, K. (2011) 'Evaluation on scientific and technological development of electronic information industry in Guangxi, *International Journal of Business and Management*, 6(2): 154–9.

Xiao, Q. (2010) 'Shenzhen 5th Most Crowded City in the World', *China Daily*, 25 February. Online. Available at: http://www.chinadaily.com.cn/china/2010-02/25/content_9504088.htm (accessed 2 July 2011).

Xie, M.Q. (2003) '*Disseminating the Experience of Specialized Town Technology Innovation and Accelerating the Development of Town Economy*', paper presented at *Working Conference on Guangdong Specialized Town Technology Innovation*, Department of Science and Technology of Guangdong Province, October (in Chinese), Guangzhou: Xie.

Xie, M.Q. (2006) 'Accelerating the development of ST, and improving GD industrial competitiveness. Director Xie Mingquan's speech on the conference of GD promotion of ST', *Guangdong Ke Ji* [Journal of Guangdong Science and Technology], 9: 1–3 (in Chinese).

Xinhua (2010) *China Expands Shenzhen Special Economic Zone, in China Daily*, 2 June. Online. Available at: http://www.chinadaily.com.cn/business/2010-06/02/content_9925392.htm (accessed 2 July 2011).

Yan, O. (2011) 'Guangdong Emphasizes People's Wellbeing in New Five-Year Plan', *Guangdong News*, 26 May. Online. Available at: http://www.newsgd.com (accessed 18 July 2011).

Yang, D.L. (1997) *Beyond Beijing: Liberalization and the Regions in China*, London: Routledge.

Yang, L. (2009) 'China's ambitions for Pearl River Delta region by 2020', *China View*. Online. Available at: http://news.xinhuanet.com/english/2009-01/08/content_10624936.htm (accessed 11 September 2011).

Yeung, Y.M. (2005) 'Emergence of the Pan-Pearl River Delta', *Geografiska Annaler: Series B, Human Geography*, 87(1): 75–9.

Yeung, Y.M. (2010) 'The further integration of the Pearl River Delta. A new beginning of reform', *Environment and Urbanization Asia*, 1(1): 13–26.

Yeung, Y.M. and Chu, D.K.Y. (eds) (1998) *Guangdong: Survey of a Province Undergoing Rapid Change*, Hong Kong: The Chinese University Press.

Yeung, Y.M. and Jianfa, S. (2008) *The Pan-Pearl River Delta: An Emerging Regional Economy in a Globalizing China*, Hong Kong: The Chinese University of Hong Kong Press.

Yeung, Y.M., Lee, J. and Kee, G. (2009) 'China's special economic zones at 30', *Eurasian Geography and Economics*, 50(2): 222–40.

Yuan, Y., Guo, H., Xu, J., Li, W., Luo, S., Lin, H. and Yuan, Y. (2010) 'China's first special economic zone: the case of Shenzhen', in D.Z. Zeng (ed.) *Building Engines for Growth and Competitiveness in China: Experiences with Special Economic Zones and Industrial Clusters*, Washington, DC: The World Bank.

Yue, W. and Haoyuan, H. (2010) '"Hukou" Scoring System Quickens China's Pace Towards Urbanization', *People's Daily Online*. Online. Available at: http://english.people.com.cn/90001/90776/90882/7197898.html (accessed 19 September 2011).

Zeng, D.Z. (2011) *How Do Special Economic Zones and Industrial Clusters Drive China's Rapid Development?* Policy Research Working Paper no. 5583, Washington, DC: The World Bank.

Zhang, A. (2002) *Going Abroad – China's Corporations Go Global*. Online. Available at: http://userwww.sfsu.edu/~yywong/Zhang.pdf (accessed 23 June 2004).

Zhang, H. (2010) 'The hukou system's constraints on migrant workers job mobility in Chinese cities', *China Economic Review*, 21: 51–64.

Zhang, H., Chen, J.R., Ye, F. and Huang, B.T. (2007) 'Comparative research on innovation dissemination in Guangdong clusters', *Science and Technology Management Research*, 27(7): 190–92 (in Chinese).

Zhang, M. and Ling, H. (2003) 'Building specialized town technology innovation platform with rich content: A interview to Mr. Ma Xianmin, Vice Director of Department of Science and Technology of Guangdong', *Journal of Guangdong Science and Technology*, 2: 15–18 (in Chinese).

Zhang, W. (2011) 'Technological Innovation in Guangdong Specialized Towns: A Ten-Year Ongoing Project', *Science and Technology Daily*, 6 March 2011 (in Chinese).

Zhang, X.G. (1999) 'Foreign investment policy, contribution and performance', in Y.R. Wu (ed.) *Foreign Direct Investment and Economic Growth in China*, Cheltenham: Edward Elgar.

Zhang, Y. (2002) 'Hope for China's migrant women workers', *The China Business Review*, 3: 30–6.

Zhang, Y. (2011) '10 Billion RMB to fund rising industries', *News Guangdong*. Online. Available at: http://www.newsgd.com/specials/12thFive-Year/news/content/2011-06/02/content_24960950.htm (accessed 15 September 2011).

Zhao, J. (2009) 'China's Outbound Investment Rules', *The China Business Review Online*. Online. Available at: https://www.chinabusinessreview.com/public/0909/intro.html#investmentrules (accessed 17 November 2011).

Zhao, X.X. (2007) 'Empirical research of the development stage of Guangdong enterprise clusters', *Journal of Tianjin Manager College*, 9(1): 33–4 (in Chinese).

Zhao, Z. (2003) *Migration, Labor Market Flexibility and Wage Determination in China. A Review, CCER (China Center for Economic Research)*, Beijing University, no. E1003007. Online. Available at: http://info.worldbank.org/etools/docs/library/152363/%286%29%20Labor_WB_Revised.pdf (accessed 18 September 2011).

Zheng, H. and Yang, Y. (2009) *Chinese Private Sector Development in the Past 30 years*, Discussion Paper no. 45, The China Policy Institute, The University of Nottingham.

Zhou, P. and Leydersdorff, L. (2006) 'The emergence of China as a leading nation in science', *Research Policy*, 35(1): 83–104.

Zhu, Y. (2005) *Chinese Foreign Investment Abroad and Global Business Strategy, Fujitsu Research Institute*. Online. Available at: http://jp.fujitsu.com/group/fri/en/economic/publications/report/2005/report-232.html (accessed 17 November 2011).

Zhu, Y. and Ip, K. (2002) 'The diversified development of private schooling in basic education in China: a comparison between Shanghai, Guangdong, Wenzhou and Tianjin', *Hong Kong Teacher's Centre Journal*, 1: 74–88.

Zhu, Y., Warner, M. and Zhao, W. (2011) 'Economic reform, ownership change, and human resource management in formerly state-owned enterprises in the People's Republic of China: a case study approach', *Human Systems Management*, 30(1–2): 11–22.

Zou, W. (2003) 'The changing face of rural enterprises', *China Perspectives*, 50: 2–17.

Index

Note: Numbers in **bold** indicate a figure or table.